Conflict in Personal Relationships

LEA'S COMMUNICATION SERIES
Jennings Bryant/Dolf Zillmann, General Editors

Selected titles include:

Biocca/Levy • Communication in the Age of Virtual Reality

Christ • Assessing Communication Education: A Handbook for Media, Speech, and Theatre Educators

Clifford/Gunter/McAleer • Television and Children: Program Evaluation, Comprehension, and Impact

Kaufer/Carley • Communication at a Distance: The Influence of Print on Sociocultural Organization and Change

McMahan/Rogers • Interactive Oral History Interviewing

For a complete listing of other titles in LEA's Communication Series, please contact Lawrence Erlbaum Associates, Publishers.

Conflict in Personal Relationships

Edited by

Dudley D. Cahn
State University of New York
The College at New Paltz

LEA   LAWRENCE ERLBAUM ASSOCIATES, PUBLISHERS
1994   Hillsdale, New Jersey   Hove, UK

R0106921573 4

BF
637
.I48
C64
1994

Lawrence Erlbaum Associates, Inc., Publishers
365 Broadway
Hillsdale, New Jersey 07642

Cover design by Cheryl Minden

Library of Congress Cataloging-in-Publication Data

Conflict in personal relationships / edited by Dudley D. Cahn.
    p. cm.
    Includes bibliographical references and index.
    ISBN 0-8058-1277-6. — ISBN 0-8058-1278-4 (pbk.)
    1. Interpersonal conflict. 2. Conflict management. 3. Conflict
(Psychology) I. Cahn, Dudley D.
BF637.I48C64 1994
303.6′9 — dc20
                                              93-48762
                                                 CIP

Printed in the United States of America
10 9 8 7 6 5 4 3 2 1

Contents

Part II   Approaches to Interpersonal Conflicts

Contributors

William L. Benoit is associate professor in the Department of Communication, University of Missouri, Columbia.

Nancy A. Burrell is assistant professor in the Department of Communication, University of Wisconsin, Milwaukee.

Dudley D. Cahn is professor in the Department of Communication, State University of New York, the College at New Paltz.

Daniel J. Canary is associate professor in the School of Interpersonal Communication, Ohio University, Athens.

William R. Cupach is professor in the Department of Communication, Illinois State University, Normal.

Clare Danielsson is executive director of Ulster Sullivan (Counties) Mediation, Inc., Highland, NY.

Crystal Dehle is a graduate student in the Department of Psychology, University of Oregon, Eugene.

Beth C. Emery is associate professor in the Department of Human Sciences, Middle Tennessee State University, Murfreesborough.

Frank D. Fincham is professor in the Department of Psychology, University of Illinois, Champaign.

James Halpern is professor in the Department of Psychology, State University of New York, the College at New Paltz.

Sally A. Lloyd is professor, School of Education and Allied Professions, Miami University, Oxford, OH.

Lori N. Osborne is a graduate student in the Department of Psychology, University of Illinois, Champaign.

Davis G. Patterson is a graduate student in the Department of Sociology, University of Washington, Seattle.

Pepper Schwartz is professor in the Department of Sociology, University of Washington, Seattle.

Brian H. Spitzberg is professor in the Department of Speech Communication, San Diego State University, San Diego, CA.

Stella Ting-Toomey is professor, Department of Speech Communication, California State University, Fullerton.

Robert L. Weiss is professor in the Department of Psychology, University of Oregon, Eugene.

Preface

This volume focuses on a particular aspect of personal relationships that is becoming increasingly important — interpersonal conflict. Although numerous studies on interpersonal conflict appear in several related disciplines (e.g., psychology, sociology, communication, and family studies), the research literature is extensive, varied, and confusing because it reflects different orientations to doing research, uses different types of measures, and is often written in a jargon unique to a particular discipline. In an attempt to organize and explain the research literature such that researchers in one discipline may benefit from the work in other disciplines, I previously edited *Intimates in Conflict: A Communication Perspective* (Cahn, 1990) and explained how the research literature could be organized according to the type of conflict communication studied. Later, in *Conflict in Intimate Relationships* (Cahn, 1992), I included more on theory and research methods and organized the theoretical research according to relevant research approaches, each with its own theories, definition of conflict, and research methods.

In this volume, I include different types of personal relationships as yet another way to look at research on interpersonal conflict. Although all three of my books deal with the subject of interpersonal conflict, they are different from one another and describe ways of organizing the research that are useful in their own way, but, if taken together, the books are complementary and offer a more comprehensive understanding of multidisciplinary research on the subject.

Essentially, this is a book in which scholars reflect on the research in their area of expertise and practitioners take time from their busy schedules to pass on knowledge they have acquired on the subject. In part I, this book attempts to supply much needed material on conflicts in specific types of relationships such as intimate same-sex couples, dating only violent partners, intimate intercultural couples, student peers, married spouses, parents and their young children, and adult children and their aging parents. As the authors of these chapters show, some of these types of relationships have been rather thoroughly studied in the past, whereas other types are wide open to investigation.

In part II, the book draws on research that does not focus on a particular type of personal relationship and describes a communication approach to everyday argument, a competence-based approach to the study of interpersonal conflict, and a holistic approach to dispute resolution at a community mediation center. These latter chapters demonstrate that some aspects of interpersonal conflict appear in a wide variety of different types of personal relationships, although the competence-based and holistic approaches are sensitive to the need to adapt research and training programs to different contexts and types of relationships.

This book is truly unique. No other edited volume discusses conflict in homosexual relationships, dating only violent partners, intimate intercultural couples, student peers, parents and their young children, and adult children and their aging parents, as well as married spouses. Moreover, in contrast to previous works that concentrate on more mainstream research, several of the contributing authors call attention to relevant research literature that has been overlooked or difficult to find. Thus, both the types of interpersonal relationships examined and the unique research literatures reviewed make this book an unusual treatment of interpersonal conflict.

Meanwhile, a great deal of the commonly cited research on interpersonal conflict is included in this book. Past research is either used to shed insight in new areas or extended beyond boundaries useful in the past. Thus, readers will see that past and familiar research continues to play a useful but different role as scholars define new frontiers for the study of conflict in personal relationships.

Finally, the book pulls together a variety of disciplines as sociologists, psychologists, social psychologists, and family studies and communication scholars examine interpersonal conflict. Authors offer ideas characteristic of different cultural orientations ranging from Western perspectives to Eastern views. They apply their findings to therapy, classroom teaching, and research. Thus, this book makes a number of contributions to both the theoretical and practical study of interpersonal conflict.

ACKNOWLEDGMENTS

I would like to take this opportunity to express my appreciation to the contributing authors for agreeing to take on this task, to share what they know with others, and to attend to editorial matters. In addition, I would like to thank our families and/or partners for their support and understanding.

Dudley D. Cahn

REFERENCES

Cahn, D. D. (1990). Intimates in conflict: A research review. In D. D. Cahn (Ed.), *Intimates in conflict: A communication perspective* (pp. 1–22). Hillsdale, NJ: Lawrence Erlbaum Associates.

Cahn, D. D. (1992). *Conflict in intimate relationships.* New York: Guilford.

Conflict Management/ Resolution in Specific Relationships

1 The Social Construction of Conflict in Intimate Same-Sex Couples

Davis G. Patterson
Pepper Schwartz
University of Washington

Modern couples, whether heterosexual or homosexual, married or cohabiting, seek love, intimacy, and long-term companionship. Homosexual couples are no exception: They often describe a successful relationship in ways similar to heterosexual couples (Dailey, 1979). But the challenges of establishing interdependence and "corporate" goals while maintaining individual happiness are substantially different for same-sex couples. The unique social forces that impinge on gay and lesbian intimate relationships create special issues that make conflicts a more difficult challenge. Without the institution of marriage, same-sex romantic partners also lack norms about how to be a couple. At the same time, these couples must often build their relationships in either nonsupportive isolation or gay and lesbian communities where local institutions and norms present new conflict issues and opportunities that can work against couple relationships. Although these forces do not necessarily create more conflict for homosexual than for heterosexual couples, this potential requires added skills to deal with conflict.

The noninstitutionalized nature of lesbian and gay male relationships has several significant effects on their conflicts. By *institution* we mean a basic and durable definition of correct conduct and meaning that both guides and constrains behavior. Institutions create, and are created by, the common norms and values around which social life is organized. The institution of marriage defines what a couple is by giving clear behavioral guidelines both for the married partners and for others with whom they interact; individuals act and react to each other within the conceptual guidelines of marriage.

Same-sex couples have to create their relationships without the benefit of the institutionalized social supports and norms that favor heterosexual coupling. Marriage is the only sexual relationship where partners can expect to receive public approval, through formalized rituals such as weddings and baby showers as well as a host of informal opportunities where couples can "do marriage." But gay and lesbian couples[1] (and heterosexual cohabitors) are left to their own devices. With such freedom, it is not clear how same-sex couples should look, even to themselves. Additionally, these couples have the problem of how to telegraph to others the shape and seriousness of their commitment. They must invent some "marital" rules, borrow others, and pick some to avoid. This is a difficult addition to the already difficult task any couple has in establishing a relationship that is durable and satisfying. And although we recognize that ready-made rules do not eliminate conflict in marriage, it seems fair to wonder in what ways the lack of an institutionalized relationship contributes to conflict for same-sex couples, as they bargain over issues that married people may take for granted.

Societal gender patterns, which allocate material and cultural resources differentially to men and women, also affect gay men and lesbians, who occupy different positions in the social structure by virtue of their genders. For example, more advantageous labor-market access confers greater economic power on men, giving them more money and mobility than lesbians. This difference has a direct impact not only on substantive issues of conflict, such as money, but also on the interpersonal bases of power that determine the processes of conflict in each type of couple. A double dose of same-gendered behavior, rather than gender-differentiated approaches, also gives a gendered flavor to the conflict issues each type of couple confronts. For example, men must often reconcile a tendency to compete with the need to cooperate in order to succeed as a couple, whereas women must work not so much on getting close as on maintaining their personal boundaries (Berzon, 1988; Blumstein & Schwartz, 1983; Clunis & Green, 1988; Pearlman, 1989; Zacks, Green, & Marrow, 1988).

In addition, we must take into account that, unlike the heterosexual world, which is organized around creating and maintaining families, gay microlevel institutions are organized around nothing of the sort. They are generally not even constructed in a way that supports the couple relationship. A case in point is the gay bar that, among other possibilities, creates

---

[1]When we refer to *couples* in this discussion, we mean romantic couples who live together rather than those involved in dating relationships. Of course, if these were married couples we could use the term *spouses* to indicate intent, but, being noninstitutionalized, it is not clear what specific term (*partners, lovers?*) would be appropriate. The definitional ambiguity of what constitutes a same-sex couple has been one of the many inconsistencies plaguing research in this area (Berger, 1990).

courtship opportunities. But unlike heterosexual bars, the "pool of eligibles" presents an incredibly diverse group, drawn together only because few other places to meet exist. The likelihood is that like will not meet like. Lesbian and gay institutions remain in a nascent form, largely subordinate to and often at odds with the dominant institutions of the broader culture.

Living at the margins of mainstream society means that same-sex couples are frequently at odds with heterosexual family and friends. As the level of kin support varies, so too do the levels and kinds of conflicts a couple is likely to experience. When a couple's relationship is not recognized, partners suffer from the added stresses of secrecy and isolation that increase their dependence on the relationship, but with less guidance and fewer models for their behavior.

Apart from the effects of the social environment, a couple's gender shapes the critical interactions giving form to interpersonal conflict. Men and women use distinct communication strategies because their goals and skills in interactions differ. The gender equality of same-sex couples does not solve the problems of power inequalities affecting cross-sex couples; instead, other personal and situational characteristics create power imbalances for gays and lesbians. Power itself may have different meanings for male and female couples, such that women and men are not likely to view the use of their interpersonal power in quite the same way. Gender and power therefore interact to affect the strategies couples rely on to engage and resolve conflict.

On several levels, then, we show how the gendered cultural and institutional contexts of same-sex couples shape both the issues and processes of their conflicts. We round out the discussion by examining the special conflict issues of domestic abuse and the impact of AIDS, and conclude by making suggestions for therapy and future research.

At times we make comparisons to heterosexual couples not because they are the standard by which all couples should be judged, but primarily because this strategy is useful analytically. Research has moved increasingly in the direction of studying gay and lesbian couples as types in the elaboration of theoretical issues about all intimate relationships (Risman & Schwartz, 1988). Nevertheless, the study of same-sex couples is decades behind the vast tradition in research on heterosexual couples. The impossibility of obtaining a representative sample or even one reflecting the entire range of diversity of lesbian and gay couples means that generalizations must be considered tentative and interpreted with caution. Urban, less closeted, and more educated couples tend to be overrepresented (Blumstein & Schwartz, 1983). Particularly in the area of conflict, the dearth of research about same-sex couples constrains us. Therefore, we often make assertions indirectly, by relying on the findings of the broader literatures on conflict and on same-sex couples, supplemented whenever possible by literature that handles these topics together. Perhaps these can serve as hypotheses for future research.

THE MECHANICS OF GENDER IN NONINSTITUTIONALIZED COUPLES

Although marriage is in flux, tradition still exerts considerable influence on the lives of heterosexual couples, from household economics to the obligations of kinship (Blumstein & Schwartz, 1983; Millman, 1991). Traditional marital roles can mitigate conflict when both partners agree on their domains of influence (e.g., instrumental vs. expressive). Alternatively, with changing gender expectations, prefashioned roles can also serve as a basis for conflict in married couples because the roles are becoming more of a negotiable source of contention. But compare with changing marital roles the flexibility and ambiguity of roles in gay and lesbian couples. Without a marital tradition, they are even freer to negotiate the allocation of roles in their relationships. Same-sex couples, therefore, have the opportunity to avoid some of the issues built into marriage by the gendered distribution of power and division of labor (Toder, 1979).

However, lesbians and gays are subject to at least two checks on their freedom to innovate. First, the extent to which they can afford to do so depends on how much initial conflict their relationships can endure. Married couples can afford to engage in more conflict because they have a contract that solidifies their relationships against breakup (indeed, this has been one of the criticisms leveled against marriage in that its security is a "license to abuse"). Without such a contract, same-sex couples have less security in their future as couples, perhaps part of the reason why same-sex couples may exhibit lower levels of conflict on average than heterosexual couples (Blumstein & Schwartz, 1983; Howard, Blumstein, & Schwartz, 1994). Rather than actually disagreeing less than married couples, same-sex couples may exercise a protective restraint to control conflict (or underestimate its existence) in order to survive as couples.

Second, gender itself constrains innovation and presents same-sex couples with unique sources of conflict. Gays and lesbians are prepared to assume the traditional, efficient, marital role division by gender (see the classic argument on role complementarity in Parsons & Bales, 1955). With no models for their relationships or for conflict management, a couple's gender, then, becomes an important ingredient in its conflict dynamics (Blumstein & Schwartz, 1983; Galvin & Brommel, 1991; Toder, 1979). Striking a balance between the demands of the relationship and outside pressures and interests is one of the most critical determinants of relationship viability and the kinds of adjustments needed between female and male couples. Peplau, Cochran, Rook, and Padesky (1978) conceived of these opposing centripetal and centrifugal forces in relationships as dimensions of attachment and autonomy; partners must accommodate needs for both interdependence and dependence.

Gender roles are relevant to this balancing act: They affect how same-sex couples accomplish the emotional work of maintaining the relationship. If neither partner makes the welfare of the couple a central concern by performing the duties of emotional caretaker, neglect of the relationship and outside attractions may lead partners to drift away from each other and eventually break up (Blumstein & Schwartz, 1983). In heterosexual couples, the emotional work typically falls more heavily on women (Cancian, 1987). Because women are socialized to do this job, lesbian couples are likely to have at least one and maybe two relationship-centered partners. This might seem to be a strong centripetal force. However, some researchers believe that two such partners may be prone to losing their personal boundaries, or "fusing," by constructing their identities too exclusively around the intimate relationship (Clunis & Green, 1988; Krestan & Bepko, 1980; Toder, 1979). Ironically, what might intuitively seem a benefit of role redundancy can cause some partners to rebel, retreat, or leave.

Fusion has been characterized as either pathological (Krestan & Bepko, 1980) or alternatively as a healthy adaptation whereby couples take refuge in their relationships from a hostile heterosexual world (Zacks, Green, & Marrow, 1988). In any case, when partners lack a measure of personal autonomy, individual idiosyncrasies and small disagreements are likely to assume an exaggerated importance. Differences become more difficult to tolerate as partners smother each other with unreasonable expectations and overattention to details. At the extreme, fusion may impel one or both partners to break free. Terminating the relationship may be the only way they know to reclaim separate identities from engulfment, or to abolish fears of abandonment with a preemptive strike (Clunis & Green, 1988).

Gay men are more likely to suffer from problems of individuation than engulfment (i.e., they have been taught that other men serve as a focus for competition). Self-disclosure, for example, may disable a competitive edge (Berzon, 1979). How do gay men come to value the role of emotional caretaker and develop the skills needed for the task, if presumably these aspects of relationships are less a part of their personal training and gender socialization? It is likely that at least one man must rise to the occasion and learn these skills for a relationship to continue to exist. But in this process, gay men are prone to conflict over how to reconcile ambition and commitment to work with the requirements of success in the private realm of their intimate relationships.

Of course, this explanation of gendered role division for relationship maintenance is oversimplified. In fact, some gay men do fuse, and some lesbians do compete. A person may exchange roles with his or her partner over the course of a relationship or switch roles from one relationship to another. However, research on the way same-sex couples handle careers, money, and housework provides further support for making a distinction between male and female couples and between the kinds of role conflicts that tend to be salient for each type of couple.

Income and Work

Conflicts over income and work provide clues about how power is derived and how the consequences of power imbalances are distinct for lesbian and gay couples. Same-sex couples may be more egalitarian than heterosexual couples, primarily because there is no gendered role division, but also because the differences between partners' incomes and educations are likely to be less, given that both partners are of the same sex (Harry, 1984). But notions of equality are relative: Being the same sex establishes a basis for partners to compare themselves to each other in a way that cross-sex partners cannot (e.g., a wife usually will not want to be as good a mechanic as her spouse). Same-sex partners can make direct comparisons; when the comparisons reflect less favorably on one partner than the other, tension and conflict may erupt.

As women in a world primarily run by men, lesbians have experienced the sting of inequality; therefore, they place importance on fairness and equality, and they try to bring these egalitarian principles to bear on their relationships. But ideology and reality are hard to bring together when partners have different resources. Avoiding dependence becomes difficult, particularly if one partner is economically dependent on the other (Blumstein & Schwartz, 1983; Roth, 1985). Given that women have less labor-market earning power relative to men, they tend to have more money problems than men (Toder, 1979).

However, the relationship of income to power for lesbians is not clear-cut. Whereas Caldwell and Peplau (1984) found that lower earning partners, as well as those who were less educated and more dependent on the relationship, were less powerful, Blumstein and Schwartz (1983) concluded that relative financial power did not generally establish the balance of power for lesbians (exceptions involved decisions about spending money on expensive items and recreational activities). Still, in a study of lesbian couples who had been together at least 10 years, money, or lack thereof, was the second most frequently mentioned current relationship problem (Johnson, 1990). The discomfort of both partners over one's dependence on the other creates difficulties: It is the awareness of financial inequality that tends to cause conflict, rather than the absolute level of income. Indeed, power imbalances in lesbian couples tend to correlate with lower satisfaction and expectations of future problems (Caldwell & Peplau, 1984). The lower income partner may even feel resentful of her partner's largesse. Indebtedness, rather than engendering gratitude, causes conflict. The higher earner also suffers because she may dislike feeling restricted about spending her money (Roth, 1985). Additionally, even though it is the dependent partner who reports feelings of inadequacy, the partner who earns more and is more ambitious and work centered is more likely to be the one to leave (Blumstein & Schwartz, 1983).

But even lesbians who manage to maintain financial equality are not immune to money conflicts. Couples who strive to be egalitarian are more ideologically motivated; value conflicts about how to spend money may be more relevant to understanding conflict in these couples. For example, women may disagree over whether to lead simpler lives or to spend their money freely (Clunis & Green, 1988). Unlike heterosexual couples who might seem to have a similar dilemma, this is fraught with added symbolism for lesbians. The "simple life" may be seen as one kind of challenge to mainstream materialism; the "free hand," a liberation from being dependent on male income for the good life. Thus, the issue becomes more than style or capability — it becomes an issue of identity and political philosophy, a potent mix.

Although gay men can enjoy a more comfortable standard of living than do lesbians, their economic advantage does not necessarily buy them harmony: Men more clearly link the couple's economic state with overall relationship satisfaction (Blumstein & Schwartz, 1983; McWhirter & Mattison, 1984). Despite high incomes among his respondents, Berger (1990) found that more than one third of them reported money problems. In clear contrast to lesbian and heterosexual couples, Blumstein and Schwartz (1983) found that gay male couples are the only type of couple where a man feels more successful when his partner's income is lower than his own. Heterosexual men do not ordinarily compete financially with their partners because they expect to earn more than women and usually do. In gay male couples, competing this way allows the "winner" to have more decision-making power (Blumstein & Schwartz, 1983; Harry, 1984).

But a man with less earning power may still retain a strong desire for independence and influence in making decisions (Blumstein & Schwartz, 1983). The power conferred on the higher earner can be especially threatening if the higher earner resists his partner's equal participation. Both differences in income and attitudes about money can cause long-term tension, conflict, and breakup (McWhirter & Mattison, 1984). As a result, couples can have a more difficult time establishing interdependence. Gay men without an egalitarian ideology, which fosters lesbian interdependence, struggle with issues of dominance. Blumstein and Schwartz (1983) found that gay men with lower incomes more often ended relationships, indicating that losing the financial competition may be especially difficult for men, creating conflict that leads to breakup.

In both lesbian and gay couples, neither partner tends to want a dependent or a provider role. Wary of dependence, both lesbians usually work because they must or because they love their jobs, but not because they wish to provide for the other. Gay men do not expect to be provided for, but each one wants his partner to contribute a fair share.

Money Management

Because pooling resources is considered a traditional element of marriage, most married couples combine their income in a common pot instead of maintaining separate finances. Although pooling necessitates negotiation over spending and is therefore associated with more conflict in a relationship, it also gives the relationship a shared financial anchor. With an uncertain future together, same-sex couples pool less often (Blumstein & Schwartz, 1983). An ideological goal of maintaining economic self-sufficiency also inhibits pooling, particularly among lesbians because of their hard-won economic independence. But not pooling eliminates a barrier to dissolution, makes the relationship seem less than a marriage, and creates the potential for more conflict when partners with income disparities must decide whose standard of living should prevail. Predictably, those who do not pool incomes experience higher breakup rates (Blumstein & Schwartz, 1983).

Thus, even though both gay men and lesbians have less conflict over money management than do married couples, when they do have serious disagreements, they are more likely to break up. This may be partially because the use, distribution, and rights of finances are less normed; it may also be because quick courtships and cohabitation may get them into hot arguments before they are a seasoned couple, more able to withstand a difference in economic theory or practice (Clunis & Green, 1988). Kurdek (1993) also found support for the argument that negotiating financial matters is central to a couple's interdependence, and, therefore, high conflict in this area tends to lead to dissolution in both same-sex and cross-sex couples.

Paid Work and Housework

Because almost all same-sex couples have two working partners, they frequently encounter issues about balancing the demands of paid work, housework, and the needs of the relationship. Work presents special challenges because scripts are not available to tell gay and lesbian couples whose work is more important, or, in the case of a career move, who should follow whom. Because neither partner in same-sex couples generally assumes the provider role, the careers of both partners often assume equal importance. Thus, like all dual-career couples, job circumstances often require partners to be away from each other. Spending time apart exposes partners to new alternatives to the relationship, whether a new partner or more immersion in work, and this can create conflict. Couples who spend more time apart also tend to have higher rates of dissolution (Blumstein & Schwartz, 1983; Clunis & Green, 1988).

Disagreements over household tasks mirror conflict over careers to some extent. But because this issue is literally "closer to home," where partners' lives intersect more substantially, conflicts in this area are both more likely and more consequential for future relationship stability (Kurdek, 1993). The immediacy of housework conflicts requires prompt confrontation, if not resolution.

Full-time homemaking has been traditionally associated with women and devalued in status. Few lesbians and gays simplify the division of tasks by taking over this role completely; fights can ensue over the relative amounts or assortment of tasks that each partner does. Blumstein and Schwartz (1983) found that partners in both male and female couples expect to do housework, and who does more is not related to the gender identities of the partners. For men this is largely a practical, not a political, matter, but lesbians may disagree over who does the "men's" versus the "women's" work around the house (Clunis & Green, 1988). Housework retains the stigma of its allocation to women in heterosexual relationships; partners are alert to assignments that imply lack of status in the relationship or in society.

COUPLING IN GAY AND LESBIAN COMMUNITIES

Although all couples are affected in some way by the dominant models of gendered conduct and role allocation, the impacts of gay and lesbian community institutions are truly unique to same-sex couples. The way couples enter their relationships and the environments in which they maintain them help shape the contours of their conflicts. This discussion deals primarily with the couple's relationship to the gay world — what brings them together, what keeps them together, and what pulls them apart.

The Question of Homogamy

A higher degree of homogamy between partners, or matching based on similarity, is thought to increase satisfaction and reduce conflict through its positive effects on empathy, communication, and the equitable division of power and labor (Howard, Blumstein, & Schwartz, 1994). But the structural organization of homogamy affects gay men, lesbians, and heterosexuals in different ways.

Same-sex couples, by mere virtue of being the same gender, would tend to be more homogamous than heterosexuals. But the stigma attached to homosexuality has made the search for intimate partners much more haphazard for most lesbians and gays. They tend to have smaller perceived pools of eligible partners than heterosexuals (Kurdek, 1991), not only because they are a minority but also because they are not always recognizable to each other due to variation in openness about their sexuality. The more closeted, the fewer available alternatives (Harry, 1984). The main interest that brings many gay people together is often their gayness, rather than similarity in other characteristics (Blumstein & Schwartz, 1983). A diverse pool of eligible partners creates greater variation in personality and status characteristics within gay and lesbian couples when compared with heterosexuals.

Partners in male couples frequently have large differences in age, education, and employment (Bell & Weinberg, 1978; Blumstein & Schwartz, 1983; McWhirter & Mattison, 1984). Dissimilarity in education may increase the likelihood of breaking up, suggesting that conflict resulting from mismatch can destroy a couple. A widely observed "incest taboo" limiting sexual contact between members of one's friendship groups, often combined with tastes for sexual partners who are dissimilar to oneself, further limit gay men's chances of meeting similar others (Bell & Weinberg, 1978; Warren, 1974).

Lesbians tend to place less emphasis on physical attraction, more on shared interests. Although lesbians have been characterized as more socially isolated than gay men, tending to reside less in "gay ghettos" where they might find eligible partners, participation in feminist political activities and other women's organizations enables many to establish contact with similar others (d'Emilio, 1983). Yet their political ideology has made them more open to pairing with others from divergent backgrounds (Sang, 1984). Class conflicts in lesbian relationships are a regular theme of lesbian popular literature. When women from working-class backgrounds pair with women from middle-or upper middle-class families, arguments about lifestyle or "assumption of privilege" are common and often lethal to the relationship.

Sexuality and Its Discontents

The organization of lesbians and gays into sexual communities has created nontraditional and gendered sexual values that make monogamy much more negotiable in homosexual than in heterosexual couples.

Lack of agreement on monogamy or agreement on nonmonogamy is one of the most common issues of conflict in lesbian couples (Clunis & Green, 1988; Toder, 1979). Johnson (1990) found that conflict over outside relationships was the reason women in long-term couples most often gave for considering breakup. A radical feminist ideology equating monogamy with patriarchal possessiveness legitimizes nonmonogamy more for lesbians than for heterosexual women (Peplau, 1991; Risman & Schwartz, 1988; Steen & Schwartz, in press), but nonmonogamy can stir up intense emotions. Besides creating jealousy, active nonmonogamy can imply an emotional and sexual competition between partners that leads to envy and resentment (Berzon, 1988).

Lesbians, like other women, tend to link sex and intimacy, with intimacy legitimizing sex. The large investments of time and emotions to create intimacy limit the frequency of sex with one's partner and work against nonmonogamy (Blumstein & Schwartz, 1983; Clunis & Green, 1988). But the close friendship circles that characterize lesbian communities provide substantial opportunities for women to develop intimacy with other women. Unlike gay men, lesbians appear to have less of an incest taboo such that friends, as well as ex-lovers, create more of a threat or the perception of threat to monogamy (Sang, 1984). Lower than desired levels of sexual intimacy among many lesbian couples also can create sexual interest in others (Johnson, 1990).

Monogamy is perhaps the single greatest area of difference between gay men, lesbians, and heterosexuals. Gay men have been the least sexually exclusive of all couples (Blumstein & Schwartz, 1983; Peplau, 1991), introducing into their relationships emotional complications conducive to conflict. Most research on gay nonmonogamy had been done prior to AIDS, but gay community norms still permit nonmonogamy despite health risks, or at least do not insist on monogamy as vehemently as in the heterosexual world. Gay men tend to be the least possessive of all couple types, and, as with lesbians, ideology supports a model of sexuality "uncontaminated" by Judeo-Christian marital traditions (Blumstein & Schwartz, 1983). Indeed, living in gay areas and having more gay friends are both associated with higher rates of nonmonogamy (Blumstein & Schwartz, 1983; Harry, 1984).

Blasband and Peplau (1985) showed how gay male couples may switch back and forth between sexual exclusivity and openness, with no fixed patterns or certainty for many couples that their relationships will not change (see also Kurdek, 1988). Ninety percent of their couples had discussed the issues at least somewhat, and most, quite a bit. Among those partners who were currently in "closed" couples (less than 50%), the median number of outside partners was three to five, indicating that even many of these couples had once been open or that partners were breaking the rules anyway.

Clearly, many gay men engage in continual conflict and negotiation over this issue. In an American couples study (see Blumstein & Schwartz, 1983), male couples tended to be the least sexually compatible of all types, probably both a cause and consequence of allowing outside sex. Additionally, those having outside sex in the last year were more likely to break up. These findings suggests three possibilities: Conflicts about nonmonogamy may lead to breakup; nonmonogamous partners may leave for a new partner; or nonmonogamy may signify conflicts in other areas of the relationship that lead to breakup.

Whereas McWhirter and Mattison (1984) reported that 95% of their sample was nonmonogamous, Berger (1990) demonstrated a reversal: Fully 96.4% of these couples reported monogamous relationships, and many had become so in response to AIDS. Although new norms favoring "safer sex" and the risks associated with multiple partners seem to have fostered a trend toward sexual exclusivity, it is likely that AIDS has not solved the conflicts but rather made the issues more complicated.

GAY COUPLING IN A STRAIGHT WORLD

Whereas homophobia makes a gay identity difficult for an individual, that difficulty is increased for a gay couple. Lesbian and gay couples invisible to kin have special difficulties, but being open does not guarantee support. Living "in the closet," isolated from even other same-sex couples, is likely in areas that are more conservative and less urbanized, where exposure to gay culture is minimal, support groups few or nonexistent, and personal exposure dangerous. Whether a couple perceives their relationship with the world outside as friendly or hostile affects their interpersonal conflict.

Secrecy and Social Support

Richardson (1989) documented how heterosexuals in secret romances develop unique expectations and norms as a consequence of the couple's isolation and secrecy. These relationships are often highly emotionally charged, invested with an almost magical quality where both partners feel uniquely understood by each other. For the secret to be kept, they sacrifice the social support of friends, co-workers, and family, who would usually provide "reality checks" — norms and sanctions to help both partners assess their own behavior.

These dynamics are not unlike the experiences of lesbian and gay couples. The difficulties involved in "coming out," or, alternatively, staying in the closet, are compounded when two persons must manage the process together. At stake is not only the knowledge of their couple status but also their identities as lesbians or gays. The stress of keeping the secret may take energy away from other problems in the relationship (Clunis & Green, 1988; Steen & Schwartz, in press).

Toder (1979) argued that partners at different stages in coming out experience the greatest amount of conflict. The less closeted partner may resent playing the role of friend rather than lover, particularly when he or she feels that the sanctity of the home is compromised by unaware visitors. Being out of the closet may be taken as a symbol of commitment to the relationship and its long-term viability. Not being openly gay is also bound to create ideological conflict in couples where one partner is highly committed to gay rights issues. But if the more open partner forces the issue or takes on a highly visible role as a gay person, the closeted one may also resent being "outed" by association (Roth, 1985).

More fundamental is whether a closeted partner is truly committed to a gay identity. Lesbians tend to be less exclusively homosexual than gay men (Kurdek, 1988), and women who drift in and out of their lesbian identities create an uncertainty in their partners that is disruptive to the relationship (Blumstein & Schwartz, 1974; Clunis & Green, 1988; Toder, 1979). Partners correctly fear that avoiding commitment to a gay identity makes leaving the relationship easier. Moreover, rejection of a gay identity can be seen as a larger rejection of the validity and goodness of homosexuality in general, and, by extension, of one's partner.

The couple relationship is at times the only context where lesbians and gays feel authentic and validated in all aspects of self. Isolation can heighten the importance the couple attaches to their relationship and increase their commitment and solidarity with each other. This extreme interdependence can be a source of deep comfort and security in a hostile environment. Conflicts may be truly neutralized through such mutual support, or only minimized at one time to recur later. Living in a social vacuum intensifies some couples' tendency to seek satisfaction through each other, making fusion more likely (Pearlman, 1989).

Couples may choose isolation, but it is more likely to result from perceived or real rejection by one's family and friends. Gays and lesbians report less family support than both married and cohabiting heterosexual couples (Kurdek & Schmitt, 1987), and Berger (1990) found that the conflict cited second most often among gay male couples was problems with family members. Partners disagreed about the sharing of secrets with family and split loyalties between one's partner and one's family.

Children

The presence of children complicates family matters still further. The paucity of literature on gay fathers and the fact that most gay parents with custody of their children are mothers limit our assertions somewhat to lesbians, although many conflicts around gay parenting may generalize to men as well as women. Limited evidence suggests that those gay fathers with custody of their children may be just as likely as lesbians to be in couple relationships (Harris & Turner, 1985–1986).

Custody issues often put pressures on the couple to remain closeted for fear that knowledge of her (or his) homosexuality will result in losing the children (Clunis & Green, 1988). Gay parents often feel pressure not to make mistakes with their children in order to keep custody, or even to disprove negative stereotypes about homosexuals and children (de Monteflores & Schultz, 1978).

Moore, Blumstein, and Schwartz (1994) provided evidence that the biological mother's partner may be disadvantaged in decision making and other aspects of power. When the partner loves children, the children become a resource to the biological mother. When the partner becomes a "second" mother, she does not have legal custody of the children. Her role is a privilege, not a right. She will likely find it in her interest to avoid conflict by giving in often to the priorities of the natural mother and children rather than assert her own.

Like most couples, gays and lesbians disagree over how to raise the children, but, uniquely, they must figure out what role the partner will play. Steen and Schwartz (in press) argued that without the organizational supports that lesbian mothers have, gay fathers are more isolated and may have more difficulty making a partner feel comfortable as co-parent. A nonbiological mother may resent the children's intrusion on the relationship, whereas the natural mother may equate her partner's feelings toward the children as a reflection of her partner's love for her (Toder, 1979). As the literature on heterosexual mothers illustrates, a mother's commitment to her children can potentially be used against her. For example, battered women often say that they stay in a destructive relationship because the children need the husband's income (Gelles, 1979; Martin, 1976). It is also true that a nonbiological parent unsympathetic to children can become more powerful in the relationship through the use of threats. For example, a lesbian mother who believes an angry partner might expose her sexual identity to an unfriendly ex-husband or court will take care not to behave in a way that might jeopardize custody.

GENDER, COMMUNICATION, AND CONFLICT

The microprocesses of communication show an intriguing mix of communication similarities and differences between homosexual and heterosexual styles of couple conflict. Differences found in conflict styles between husbands and wives are inconsistent, but gender patterns are evident in research that finds that husbands disengage more in conflict situations than wives, whereas wives seem to be able to tolerate conflict better and let it affect relationship satisfaction less (Gottman & Levenson, 1988; Rusbult, Johnson, & Morrow, 1986; although Raush, Barry, Hertel, & Swain, 1974, found that husbands attempt to resolve conflicts more than their wives). For more research an opposite-sex conflict, see Cahn (1992).

Pertinent to our overview of gay couples, the sex of the person with whom one is engaged in conflict seems to have a significant effect on the style used. Berryman-Fink and Brunner (1987) found that men reported competing more often than women, but when women were the target of the communication, both men and women were more accommodating. Somewhat consistent with these findings and research on married couples, Fitzpatrick and Winke (1979) found that male best friends negotiated less, using dogmatic assertions and repetition of points as conflict strategies instead, whereas women used rejection, empathic understanding, and emotional appeals with their same-sex best friends. Men's strategies were stronger than those of the women generally, with the exception of rejection, a strong strategy.

These studies provide evidence of a competitive dynamic that can emerge when two men are in conflict. In a same-sex couple, both men may be more interested in "winning" conflicts than resolving them. Neither may wish to give in, and consequently men can have difficulty agreeing or even listening to each other (Berzon, 1979, 1988; Steen & Schwartz, in press; Tannen, 1990). Ironically, the pressure to find quick solutions without taking feelings into account can actually prolong conflicts or cause the same issues to recur. However, both the women's and men's movements have provided many gay men with an awareness of a greater need for disclosure of feelings (Steen & Schwartz, in press). If they learn also to handle disclosures with greater sensitivity and trust, they may find more satisfying solutions to their conflicts.

Women may not necessarily have an easier time than men reaching agreement. They aspire to egalitarian norms that require consensus, but striking a perfect balance can be arduous and frustrating (Steen & Schwartz, in press). Women may be less likely than men to interrupt or to challenge in cross-sex conversations because they find that these strategies work against the goal of establishing intimacy (Tannen, 1990) and are personally threatening (Leet-Pellegrini, 1980; Zimmerman & West, 1975). This accommodating demeanor may hold for female–female interactions as well. Clunis and Green (1988) argued that because assertiveness is discouraged in women, they may be reluctant to express their own wants and needs. To avoid hurting their partners and losing support, lesbians may be less direct with each other, inhibiting problem solving. Instead, they may handle conflicts superficially, particularly in the early stages of the relationships, only to have them resurface later.

Female training to anticipate and satisfy the needs of others encourages partners to expect one another to be able to read minds. This notion creates unspoken assumptions and obligations that become the basis for conflict (Clunis & Green, 1988; Sang, 1984). Schullo and Alperson (1984) found that lesbians live up to the expectation of being understood by their partners more than other couples, indicating that some of their high ideals may be realistically justified. But relying on mind reading is risky; presumption of the partner's ability to automatically understand can thwart clear communication of wants and needs between partners, causing misunderstandings. Thus, it is not women's communication skills, but rather the norms associated with these abilities, that sometimes turn what is usually considered an advantage in conflict resolution into a liability. Excessive focus on emotions, including overanalyzing an issue, causes some partners to find themselves exhausted by continuing emotional intensity (Steen & Schwartz, in press).

The arguments presented here rely heavily on gender. However, a mounting body of evidence now both challenges and supplements gender-based explanations with a power-based model. Falbo and Peplau (1980) found that gender only played a role in determining power tactics among heterosexual couples, suggesting that gendered power differentials rather than gender per se were operating. Regardless of gender or sexual orientation, those who perceived themselves as more powerful tended to use the tactics of persuasion and bargaining, whereas low-power partners more often withdrew or used emotion to influence the other.

Howard, Blumstein, and Schwartz (1986) obtained similar results: Power generally determined which partner used strong autocratic and bullying tactics and which used the weaker tactics of supplication and manipulation, regardless of sexual orientation. Additionally, interaction with a male partner, by gay men or by heterosexual women regardless of the person's masculinity or femininity, was associated with the use of weaker tactics, indicating that men bring out this response in their partners. Thus, gender and power showed some interaction effects.

Power-based conversational dominance is further supported by Kollock, Blumstein, and Schwartz (1985), who found that more powerful partners interrupted more frequently than did the less powerful. The weaker the partner, the more successful the other was at interrupting. Some intriguing differences were found among couples that also provide support for the gender-based argument that men are more competitive, whereas women are more cooperative. Men in gay couples had lower rates of successful interruptions, suggesting that even less powerful male partners do not wish to yield and thereby lose the competition. Lesbians, on the other hand, had the lowest rate of attempted interruptions, perhaps because they find such controlling strategies unacceptable.

Taken together, these studies point strongly to power and gender exerting separate and combined effects on the strategies gay women and men employ in communication. For this reason, although both male and female couples might use similar tactics in their conflict behaviors because partners are the same gender, we are likely to see differences across couple types in both the intensity and frequency with which certain tactics are employed. These differences are further mediated within couples by the power discrepancies between partners. Gay men are more likely to engage conflicts by challenging and interrupting. At the same time, they try not to allow their partners to be successful at doing so, the weaker partner more often losing out. Resolution may be quicker, but not necessarily decisive in the long term. Lesbians, on the other hand, are more likely to skirt the issues. Once conflict is engaged, they may interrupt and challenge less than gay men, but instead rehash the issues to the point of weariness. Resolution may also take longer, with more time for feelings to be shared and heard, extra time that may be required for women to feel comfortable to express disagreement and find an equitable settlement.

VIOLENT CONFLICT

Almost exclusive focus on nonviolent conflict in same-sex couples has made the problem of domestic abuse all but invisible. This invisibility is reinforced by a cultural myth, believed by both homo- and heterosexuals, that same-sex couples are nonviolent (Hammond, 1989; Lobel, 1986). Lesbians in particular may believe that their relationships cannot be affected by the kind of aggression men perpetrate toward women (Renzetti, 1992), and society may also be less likely to view men as victims (Island & Lettelier, 1991). In addition, lesbian and gay communities are overwhelmed by AIDS, with far fewer resources for other concerns (Island & Letellier, 1991). These constraints create a silence inhibiting individuals from reporting problems (Lobel, 1986).

Although precise estimates are impossible, those obtained by self-report from lesbians show a degree of comparability to levels of abuse reported by heterosexual women. In a study comparing heterosexual and lesbian couples, 25% of lesbians and 27% of heterosexual women reported having been physically abused by partners in committed relationships (Brand & Kidd, 1986). Estimates of abuse for individual men range from 10% to 20% (Island & Letellier, 1991). The only study to compare lesbians and gay men systematically yielded rates of sexual coercion by current or most recent partners of 12% for gay men and 36% for lesbians (Waterman, Dawson, &

Bologna, 1989). The authors hypothesized that the difference in rates is because women are more sensitive to issues of sexual abuse and more likely to consider more acts as coercive. Men may be much less likely to report because of a belief that aggression between men is acceptable and, sometimes, unavoidable (Island & Letellier, 1991). The greater frequency with which men reciprocate violence, as Waterman, Dawson, and Bologna (1989) found, may indicate that men are more likely to believe that they should take responsibility for their own defense—reporting abuse to others may be considered a sign of weakness.

Battering seems to be connected to power imbalances, but who tends to have more power in the relationship, the abused or the abuser, is a matter of some confusion (Carlson, 1992; Renzetti, 1992; Waterman, Dawson, & Bologna, 1989). If a partner batters in order to compensate for a lack of power in other areas of the relationship, the battering itself may result in a shift in power over time in favor of the batterer. Renzetti (1992) found that half her subjects cited power imbalances as a problem, hypothesizing that power imbalances in either direction may work with other factors, such as conflicts over dependency and jealousy, to account for the violence.

The pressure of mutual dependence or fusion may be conducive to violence (Galvin & Brommel, 1991). The high value that women place on making their relationships work, sometimes at very high costs, seems to backfire in abusive relationships, because it encourages abused women to remain involved with their abusive partners. At the same time, Walker (1986) argued that lesbians fight back more than heterosexual women because lesbian partners have less of a size differential and community norms exist that encourage women to leave abusive situations.

Much less research has been done about abuse in male couples. Island and Letellier (1991) argued that a belief that violence or aggression is a natural part of being male may provide an excuse or justification for men to abuse or to tolerate being abused. Interestingly, they also identified the special role that AIDS may play in perpetuating an abusive relationship. If the batterer has AIDS, the behavior may be perceived as even more excusable out of sympathy for the person's suffering; the battering may even be excused as a consequence of dementia or other aspects of the disease. Alternatively, if the abused partner has AIDS, he may be dependent on his partner for support in his illness, and his physical condition may not allow him to leave.

CONFLICT IN THE TIME OF AIDS

AIDS may not often lead to violent conflict, but milder forms of conflict may arise for many of the same reasons. AIDS has changed the landscape of couple relationships, but none have been affected so drastically as gay male couples. The research about AIDS and gay men has been largely about individuals; the effects of AIDS on gay couples have been little studied.

Both single and coupled gay men report changes in behavior toward safer sex and greater monogamy (Berger, 1990; Siegel & Glassman, 1989). Gay men increasingly seek steady couple relationships as opposed to short-term sexual relationships; those already in relationships may feel their commitment strengthened (Bahr & Weeks, 1989; Carl, 1986; Gagnon, 1989), due to the health risks associated with finding new partners or changing partners frequently. In this way, the couple relationship may have increased in value in the gay community. But the negotiation of monogamy versus nonmonogamy may have only become more complicated. When the risks involve not only one's own life, but a partner's as well, the stakes run higher and so do emotions. The greater stress in being a gay man in the age of AIDS is likely to compound conflicts over sexuality. The fear of infecting or being infected with HIV may cause sexual difficulties in couples even when they agree on monogamy or nonmonogamy, especially if it is known that only one partner has tested positive for HIV, where guilt over that status can complicate feelings (Paradis, 1991). Yet in spite of these concerns, the greater emphasis placed on safer sex rather than monogamous sex may also cause many men to worry less about monogamy than about using condoms; Gochros (1992) argued that a gay sexual renaissance is occurring and people are once again believing that free sexual expression and joy is both a right and a need.

Living in a community in which many friends and sometimes former partners have died or are ill creates tremendous grief and anger, as well as uncertainty about the future. Paradis (1991) argued that many gay men have not been able to work through their grief, and that this block has affected their ability to be intimate. A person may be ambivalent about deepening feelings for a new partner for fear of losing him; one man may end up driving the other way as a self-protective measure to control the experience of loss, rather than let AIDS take a partner away.

AIDS has created a second stigma for gay men to face, whether or not they are living with HIV or AIDS. For those who are afraid to confront homophobia, the need to be closeted has increased; some couples have become more isolated, with all the potential stress that isolation poses (Paradis, 1991). Contracting AIDS forces some to come out to their families and co-workers with unpredictable results, yet if they hide their illness, they are cut off from crucial support (Weitz, 1990). Even those who once enjoyed tolerance or support of their sexuality can face ostracism with an AIDS diagnosis. These circumstances increase the need for a man with AIDS to depend on his partner. The diagnosis of one partner with HIV or AIDS sometimes motivates the other to end the relationship, although partners often do stay (Carl, 1986; Macks, 1987; Weitz, 1990). Conflict becomes likely as the person with AIDS is less able to focus on the needs of his partner; the demands of caring for a person with AIDS can easily monopolize most of the resources in the relationship (Gochros, 1992; Paradis, 1991). Alternatively, conflicts are sometimes suppressed in the interest of the ill person's health or out of sympathy (Carl, 1986).

For some, dealing with AIDS brings about increased closeness with partners, families, or both (Weitz, 1990). At the very least, relations between parents, siblings, the ill person, and his partner are likely to be clarified by an AIDS diagnosis. Families may blame a partner or try to prevent the men from seeing each other. A struggle between two separate family systems, straight and gay, can create conflicts for the couple, especially if the natural family is not accepting of their son's gayness, his relationship, or his friends. Perhaps more subtly, the existence of AIDS puts a pall on all gay relationships. To be sure, partners may value each other more, but the future feels so bleak in many gay communities that the happiness seems impossible.

SUMMARY

Conflict in lesbian and gay couples is, like all conflict between intimates, caused by a combination of personality, roles, the fit of institutional guidelines and constraints, and larger external forces that place critical pressures on couples and force them to make difficult decisions. All couples must find a way to negotiate and conclude conflict, satisfying both individual and collective desires. Same-sex couples, however, have specific additional pressures, and these relationship challenges are of interest not only to people concerned with gay populations, but also as a heuristic spur to the study of relationships in general.

Even though same-sex couples share many fundamental goals in common with heterosexual couples, same-sex couple conflicts are shaped by external and internal influences unique to noninstitutionalized relationships. Like heterosexual cohabitors, same-sex couples face ambiguity about how to create a relationship. The varying meanings couples give to their relationships set up the kinds of conflicts they will encounter. Although some gays and lesbians attempt to create a marriage, those who are critical of the structure of marriage treasure the opportunity to make their own rules and traditions. Either choice has pitfalls, but perhaps the most difficult challenge awaits couples where partners disagree on what the rules of their relationship should be. The degree of institutionalization is therefore the first variation we would like to suggest adding to the study of conflict.

The second is the degree to which location in the larger environment and specific subcultures shapes conflict—both issues and styles. Gays and lesbians find that their options for handling conflicts and other issues depend on whether they are closeted or open with straights about their relationships and whether they have greater or lesser contact with other gays and lesbians. Same-sex couples serve as a reminder that the internal workings of all relationships are sensitive or cultural contexts.

Third, gay and lesbian couples also provide a quasi-experimental setting to investigate what gender socialization and gendered roles bring to conflict. This research is relevant to understanding what aspects of masculine or feminine training help or hinder a couple, and where people find that differentiation serves utilitarian purposes. Additional research might explore how the gendered aspects of conflict in all types of couples respond to continuing changes in traditional gender roles.

These perspectives can inform research, policymaking, and therapy alike. Specific directions include further comparative research between types of heterosexual and homosexual couples, now particularly apropos, to test the effects of institutions on interpersonal relationships. Same-sex couples are beginning to obtain a status that, although far from institutionalized, gives them access to health benefits for partners of gay and lesbian employees, wedding announcements in the local papers, and other special "marital" rights. New research needs to determine what these privileges once reserved for heterosexual marriage do for same-sex couples.

Gay parenting has become increasingly common, but the first concerns of research have quite understandably been to determine the impact on children. It is now also time to investigate further how parenting affects lesbian and gay couples, especially considering that gay men are taking on the job of parenting with greater frequency.

In some ways, it could be argued AIDS has made past studies of gay male couples all but obsolete. Many studies of AIDS have focused almost exclusively on individual behavior as if decisions about sexual and emotional relationships occurred within a vacuum. With the prospect of a cure still quite distant, not only is there a need for research about the impact of AIDS on couple relationships, but especially research that takes into account the context of living in communities ravaged by AIDS.

We have emphasized conflicts to the detriment of satisfactions in same-sex couples, perhaps mistakenly giving the impression that gay and lesbian relationships are overly conflict-ridden and dysfunctional. Without a doubt, same-sex couples could benefit from the greater access to counseling services enjoyed by married couples. But many of the conflicts specific to lesbian and gay male couples are not unusual for them, given their unique circumstances. Knowing that there are other couples "like them" may be even more empowering because this realization enlarges a couple's frame of reference, helping them feel "normal" in a largely unsupportive world. Yet the obstacles themselves often provide a constant reminder to same-sex couples of the experimental nature of their challenge. This awareness of their relationships as a truly creative endeavor may also give lesbians and gays a more acute sensitivity about their own issues and styles and the difficulties they face as unconventional pioneers.

REFERENCES

Bahr, J. M., & Weeks, G. R. (1989). Sexual functioning in a nonclinical sample of male couples. *American Journal of Family Therapy, 17*, 110–127.

Bell, A. P., & Weinberg, M. S. (1978). *Homosexualities: A study of diversity among men and women.* New York: Simon & Schuster.

Berger, R. M. (1990). Men together: Understanding the gay couple. *Journal of Homosexuality, 19* (3), 31–49.

Berryman-Fink, C., & Brunner, C. (1987). The effects of sex of source and target on interpersonal conflict management styles. *Southern Speech Communication Journal, 53,* 38–48.

Berzon, B. (1979). Achieving success as a gay couple. In B. Berzon & R. Leighton (Eds.), *Positively gay* (pp. 30–40). Millbrae, CA: Celestial Arts.

Berzon, B. (1988). *Permanent partners: Building gay and lesbian relationships that last.* New York: Plume.

Blasband, D., & Peplau, L. A. (1985). Sexual exclusivity versus openness in gay male couples. *Archives of Sexual Behavior, 14*, 395–412.

Blumstein, P., & Schwartz, P. (1974). Lesbianism and bisexuality. In E. Goode & R. R. Troiden (Eds.), *Sexual deviance and sexual deviants.* New York: William Morrow.

Blumstein, P., & Schwartz, P. (1983). *American couples.* New York: Morrow.

Brand, P. A., & Kidd, A. H. (1986). Frequency of physical aggression in heterosexual and female homosexual dyads. *Psychological Reports, 59*, 1307–1313.

Cahn, D. (1992). *Conflict in intimate relationships.* New York: Guilford.

Caldwell, M. A., & Peplau, L. A. (1984). The balance of power in lesbian relationships. *Sex Roles, 10,* 587–600.

Cancian, F. M. (1987). *Love in America: Gender and self-development.* New York: Cambridge University Press.

Carl, D. (1986). Acquired immune deficiency syndrome: A preliminary examination of the effects on gay couples and coupling. *Journal of Marital and Family Therapy, 12* (3), 241–247.

Carlson, B. E. (1992). Questioning the party line on family violence. *Affilia, 7* (2), 94–110.

Clunis, D. M., & Green, G. D. (1988). *Lesbian couples.* Seattle, WA: Seal Press.

Dailey, D. M. (1979). Adjustment of heterosexual and homosexual couples in pairing relationships: An exploratory study. *Journal of Sex Research, 15*, 143–157.

d'Emilio, J. (1983). *Sexual politics, sexual communities.* Chicago: University of Chicago Press.

de Monteflores, C., & Schultz, S. J. (1978). Coming out: Similarities and differences for lesbians and gay men. *Journal of Social Issues, 34* (3), 59–71.

Falbo, T., & Peplau, L. A. (1980). Power strategies in intimate relationships. *Journal of Personality and Social Psychology, 38*, 618–628.

Fitzpatrick, M. A., & Winke, J. (1979). You always hurt the one you love: Strategies and tactics in interpersonal conflict. *Communication Quarterly, 27*, 3–11.

Gagnon, J. H. (1989). Disease and desire. *Daedalus, 118* (3), 47–77.

Galvin, K. M., & Brommel, B. J. (1991). *Family interaction: Cohesion and change.* New York: HarperCollins.

Gelles, R. J. (1979). *Family violence.* Beverly Hills, CA: Sage.

Gochros, H. L. (1992). The sexuality of gay men with HIV infection. *Social Work, 37,* 105–109.

Gottman, J. M., & Levenson, R. W. (1988). The social psychophysiology of marriage. In P. Noller & M. A. Fitzpatrick (Eds.), *Perspectives on marital interaction* (pp. 182–200). Philadelphia: Multilingual Matters.

Hammond, N. (1989). Lesbian victims of relationship violence. *Women and Therapy, 8,* 89–105.

Harris, M. B., & Turner, P. H. (1985–1986). Gay and lesbian parents. *Journal of Homosexuality, 12* (2), 101– 113.

Harry, J. (1984). *Gay couples.* New York: Praeger.

Howard, J. A., Blumstein, P., & Schwartz, P. (1986). Sex, power, and influence tactics in intimate relationships. *Journal of Personality and Social Psychology, 51,* 102–109.

Howard, J. A., Blumstein, P., & Schwartz, P. (1994). *Homogamy in intimate relationships: Why birds of a feather flock together.* Manuscript submitted for publication.

Island, D., & Letellier, P. (1991). *Men who beat the men who love them.* New York: Haworth Press.

Johnson, S. E. (1990). *Staying power: Long-term lesbian couples.* Tallahassee, FL: The Naiad Press.

Kollock, P., Blumstein, P., & Schwartz, P. (1985). Sex and power in interaction: Conversational privileges and duties. *American Sociological Review, 50,* 34–46.

Krestan, J., & Bepko, C. S. (1980). The problem of fusion in the lesbian relationship. *Family Process, 19,* 277–289.

Kurdek. L. A. (1988). Relationship quality of gay and lesbian cohabiting couples. *Journal of Homosexuality, 15,* 93–118.

Kurdek, L. A. (1991). Sexuality in homosexual and heterosexual couples. In K. McKinney & S. Sprecher (Eds.), *Sexuality in close relationships* (pp. 177–191). Hillsdale, NJ: Lawrence Erlbaum Associates.

Kurdek, L. A. (1993). *Areas of conflict for gay, lesbian, and heterosexual cohabiting couples: A dependence model analysis.* Manuscript submitted for publication.

Kurdek, L. A., & Schmitt, J. P. (1987). Perceived emotional support from family and friends in members of gay, lesbian, married, and heterosexual cohabiting couples. *Journal of Homosexuality, 14* (3/4), 57–68.

Leet-Pellegrini, H. M. (1980). Conversational dominance as a function of gender and expertise. In H. Giles, W. P. Robinson, & P. M. Smith (Eds.), *Language: Social psychological perspectives* (pp. 97–104). Oxford: Pergamon.

Lobel, K. (1986). *Naming the violence: Speaking out about lesbian battering.* Seattle, WA: Seal Press.

Macks, J. (1987). Meeting the psychosocial needs of people with AIDS. In C. G. Leukefeld & M. Fimbres (Eds.), *Responding to AIDS: Psychosocial initiatives* (pp. 25–38). Silver Springs, MD: NASW.

Martin, D. (1976). *Battered wives.* San Francisco: Glide Publications.

McWhirter, D. P., & Mattison, A. M. (1984). *The male couple: How relationships develop.* Englewood Cliffs, NJ: Prentice-Hall.

Millman, M. (1991). *Warm hearts and cold cash: The intimate dynamics of families and money.* New York: The Free Press.

Moore, M., Blumstein, P., & Schwartz, P. (1994). *The power of motherhood: A contextual evaluation of family resources.* Manuscript submitted for publication.

Paradis, B. A. (1991). Seeking intimacy and integration: Gay men in the era of AIDS. *Smith College Studies in Social Work, 61,* 260–274.

Parsons, T., & Bales, R. (1955). *Family socialization and interaction process.* Glencoe, IL: The Free Press.

Pearlman, S. F. (1989). Distancing and connectedness: Impact on couple formation in lesbian relationships. *Women and Therapy, 8*, 77–88.

Peplau, L. A. (1991). Lesbian and gay relationships. In J. C. Gonsiorek & J. D. Weinrich (Eds.), *Homosexuality: Research implications for public policy* (pp. 177–196). Newbury Park, CA: Sage.

Peplau, L. A., Cochran, S. D., Rook, K., & Padesky, C. (1978). Loving women: Attachment and autonomy in lesbian relationships. *Journal of Social Issues, 34*, 7–27.

Raush, H. L., Barry, W. A., Hertel, R. K., & Swain, M. A. (1974). *Communication, conflict, and marriage.* San Francisco: Jossey-Bass.

Renzetti, C. M. (1992). *Violent betrayal: Partner abuse in lesbian relationships.* Newbury Park, CA: Sage.

Richardson, L. (1989). Secrecy and status: The social construction of forbidden relationships. In B. J. Risman & P. Schwartz (Eds.), *Gender in intimate relationships* (pp. 108–119). Belmont, CA: Wadsworth.

Risman, B., & Schwartz, P. (1988). Sociological research on male and female homosexuality. *Annual Review of Sociology, 14*, 125–147.

Roth, S. (1985). Psychotherapy issues with lesbian couples. *Journal of Marital and Family Therapy, 11*, 273–286.

Rusbult, C. E., Johnson, D. J., & Morrow, G. D. (1986). Impact of couple patterns of problem solving on distress and nondistress in dating relationships. *Journal of Personality and Social Psychology, 50*, 744–753.

Sang, B. (1984). Lesbian relationships: A struggle toward partner equality. In T. Darty & S. Potter (Eds.), *Women-identified women* (pp. 51–65). Palo Alto, CA: Mayfield.

Schullo, S. A., & Alperson, B. L. (1984). Interpersonal phenomenology as a function of sexual orientation, sex, sentiment, and trait categories in long-term dyadic relationships. *Journal of Personality and Social Psychology, 47*, 983–1002.

Siegel, K., & Glassman, M. (1989). Individual and aggregate level change in sexual behavior among gay men at risk for AIDS. *Archives of Sexual Behavior, 18* (4), 335–348.

Steen, S., & Schwartz, P. (in press). Communication, gender, and power: Homosexuals as a case study. In M. A. Fitzpatrick & A. L. Vangelist (Eds.), *Perspectives on family communication.* Beverly Hills, CA: Sage.

Tannen, D. (1990). *You just don't understand: Women and men in conversation.* New York: Ballantine Books.

Toder, N. (1979). Lesbian couples: Special issues. In B. Berzon & R. Leighton (Eds.), *Positively gay* (pp. 41–55). Millbrae, CA: Celestial Arts.

Walker, L. (1986). Battered women's shelters and work with battered lesbians. In K. Lobel (Ed.), *Naming the violence: Speaking out about lesbian battering* (pp. 198–201). Seattle, WA: Seal Press.

Warren, C. A. B. (1974). *Identity and community in the gay world.* New York: Wiley.

Waterman, C. K., Dawson, L. J., & Bologna, M. J. (1989). Sexual coercion in gay male and lesbian relationships: Predictions and implications for support services. *Journal of Sex Research, 26*, 118–124.

Weitz, R. (1990). Living with the stigma of AIDS. *Qualitative Sociology, 13*, 23–38.

Zacks, E., Green, R., & Marrow, J. (1988). Comparing lesbian and heterosexual couples on the circumplex model: An initial investigation. *Family Process, 27*, 471–484.

Zimmerman, D. H., & West, C. (1975). Sex roles, interruptions, and silences in conversations. In B. Thorne & N. Henley (Eds.), *Language and sex: Difference and dominance.* Rowley, MA: Newbury House.

2 Physically Aggressive Conflict in Romantic Relationships

Sally A. Lloyd
Miami University, Oxford, Ohio

Beth C. Emery
Middle Tennessee State University

The occurrence of aggression in romantic relationships is a complex phenomenon, involving a range of behaviors from coercion and intimidation to beatings to rape. Physical aggression has been defined as "the use or threat of physical force or restraint carried out with the intention of causing pain or injury to another" (Sugarman & Hotaling, 1989, p. 4). Physical aggression in marriage, cohabitation, and courtship is alarmingly prevalent. On a yearly basis, physical aggression (including slapping, pushing, kicking, punching beating stabbing, threatening, or using a weapon) occurs in 16.1% of marriages, 35% of cohabiting relationships, and 30% of dating relationships (Stets & Henderson, 1991; Stets & Straus, 1990b; Straus & Gelles, 1990).

Much of the research on aggression in intimate relationships has concentrated on describing the personality factors and characteristics of both the aggressive male and the victimized female (Lloyd, 1991).[1] However, as noted by Cate and Lloyd (1992), such intra-individual factors are relatively poor predictors of aggression; the weight they are given in the literature may

---

[1]We have combined the literature on aggression in marriage and aggression in courtship, in order to speak more generically about aggression in intimate, romantic, heterosexual relationships. This should not be interpreted as an indication that we believe that the dynamics of aggression are exactly the same in courtship and in marriage, although the literature shows a great deal of similarity between the interpersonal dynamics of aggression during courtship and during marriage. We chose to combine these literatures, because there are interesting insights on the interpersonal nature of aggression from both studies of courtship and studies of marriage. At the present time, both sets of literature are needed to build a more comprehensive understanding of the dynamics of aggression.

be due to the legacy of the psychiatric/medical model. Recent work indicates that interpersonal factors are better at differentiating relationships that contain aggression from relationships wherein no aggression occurs. Fortunately, the fields of family studies, communication, and psychology are beginning to view physical aggression as a communicative act (Lloyd, 1993; Planalp, 1993). Research clearly indicates different interpersonal patterns, as measured through observational coding of communication (Margolin, John, & Gleberman, 1988), behavioral self-report assessment of daily interaction (Lloyd, 1993), and survey assessment of communication and relationship patterns (Bird, Stith, & Schladale, 1991; Infante, Sabourin, Rudd, & Shannon, 1990; O'Leary, 1988). Infante, Chandler, and Rudd (1989) made this point most eloquently:

> A communication approach to the problem of interspousal violence is illuminating because it reveals that when violence occurs it is not an isolated event in people's lives, but is embedded firmly in the process of interpersonal communication which people use to regulate their daily lives. (p. 174)

This chapter embodies the development of nine "tenets" that explicate an interpersonal and communicative perspective on aggression in romantic relationships. These tenets are built on the work of scholars who have emphasized a relational perspective on aggression. Although we are emphasizing the interpersonal and communicative dynamics that are associated with the presence of aggression in relationships, we feel it is important to also acknowledge the larger context, particularly the cultural factors that tend to sustain and reinforce the use of aggression against women by the men who love them.

Before proceeding with the tenets, we should address how we have conceptualized aggression in romantic relationships. Although both males and females perpetrate physically aggressive acts in their intimate relationships (Straus & Gelles, 1990), women's use of aggression largely occurs in the context of self-defense or response to males' use of aggression (Saunders, 1988). Due to the greater size and strength of men, women are clearly at greater risk of injury; women sustain 95% of the injuries that occur in situations of domestic violence (Stets & Straus, 1990a). From these realities, we have conceptualized the problem of aggression in intimate relationships in terms of men's physical abuse of women. However, as some of our previous work (cf. Emery & Lloyd, in press) demonstrates, we do not deny that women behave aggressively in close relationships, nor that men at times sustain injuries from such aggression. Rather, in this chapter we have framed the phenomenon of physical aggression in terms of its most likely occurrence — we believe that most often women are the victims, and men are the aggressors.[2] Our emphasis on examining the larger contexts of gender and relationships is integrally tied to our conceptualization of women as the likely victims of aggression.

TENET 1: AGGRESSION IS A POTENT CONFLICT NEGOTIATION STRATEGY

Conflict is a component of almost any relationship, and romantic relationships are no exception to this rule. Although there are frequent occasions for differences of actions, opinions, or goals to arise, such differences may be suppressed rather than expressed (Roloff & Cloven, 1990). As a result, when conflict does occur, it often covers accumulated grievances as well as the issue at hand (Zillmann, 1990). As differences build up, so do negative affect, shame, and hostility. Such emotions may contribute to intense and escalated conflict, a ripe context for the eruption of physical aggression. Conflict can be constructive, helping to resolve differences and bring partners closer together, or conflict can be destructive, ending in emotional abuse and/or physical violence (Cahn, 1990; Retzinger, 1991). Recent evidence corroborates a strong association between the amount and intensity of conflict and physical aggression in romantic relationships (Coleman & Straus, 1990; Lloyd, 1990b; Riggs, 1993).

Physical aggression can be conceptualized as a conflict negotiation strategy (Lloyd, Koval, & Cate, 1989). Certainly, the typical examination of conflict does not speak to aggression as a negotiation strategy. Indeed, the very use of the term *negotiation* implies the use of more positive and forward-looking strategies, such as compromise, discussion, and disclosure. However, there is utility in conceptualizing aggression as a conflict negotiation strategy. First, aggression often occurs in the context of a relational argument or disagreement, whether covert or overt. Second, aggression is the ultimate way to get what one wants, that is, if one cannot "talk" the

---

[2]The direction of aggression (i.e., who behaved aggressively first) as well as the issue of victimization are notably blurred in much of the literature. Most often, questions about the extent of aggression are asked in terms of the overall frequency of particular acts without reference to who typically initiates the aggression. While it may be possible to assess who initiated aggression the first time, or during the most recent incident, such questions are still limited, for they fail to acknowledge the context of the relationship. For example, a wife who has been severely battered over an extended period of time may reach the point where she initiates aggression against her husband in order to relieve tension an | get the battering over with. We would argue vehemently against portraying this woman as ..ie "perpetrator" in this relationship. Only an examination of the overall history of her relationship can inform us of the long-term dynamics of the situation.

partner into seeing one's viewpoint and complying with a request, aggression can be used to force compliance through physical threat or harm. Finally, aggression may be used as a last resort when other conflict negotiation strategies have failed (Lloyd, Koval, & Cate, 1989).

Aggression is a highly potent conflict strategy for a variety of reasons, not the least being that it often works. If the aim of engaging in conflict is achieving one's desires or meeting one's needs, and if aggression helps to ensure that one "wins," then aggression will be reinforced to the extent that winning is more important than the emotional and physical well-being of the partner (Zillmann, 1990). And because aggression is a punishment-oriented strategy, it is inherently more effective than reward-oriented strategies in getting one's way (deTurck, 1987). To the extent that a conflict episode involves a dynamic of the strong against the weak, then physical aggression allows men to fall back on their ultimate authority and physical strength to get what they want (Zillmann, 1990, p. 201). In other words, physical aggression may be used to force cooperation or compliance, particularly when the aggressor believes that the victim will not be able to resist or retaliate (deTurck, 1987; Zillmann, 1990). Physical aggression is a means to an end; its unchallenged use can lead to its incorporation as a pattern of behavior (Stets, 1992).

Often physical aggression is negatively reinforced as well. This cycle begins with the perception of an aversive act. For example, a man may perceive that his partner is nagging him; he experiences this as an aversive situation, and may feel anxious and aroused. If he uses physical aggression to stop this aversive stimulus, and if aggression serves to halt the behavior, then aggression will be reinforced by the cessation of the aversive behavior and the reduction of arousal (Dutton, 1988; Patterson, 1985). In particular, repeated noncompliance of the partner may result in an aversive situation that may lead to use of physical aggression (deTurck, 1987).

In addition, the release of tension and the following of aggression with positive emotions and actions may also inadvertently reinforce the likelihood of the future use of physical aggression. Walker (1979) described a three-part cycle of battering: the buildup of tension, the battering incident, and the honeymoon phase. Inherent in this cycle are the powerful reinforcers of tension release (the buildup of tension may be very aversive to both the perpetrator and the victim of aggression) as well as extremely positive profession of love and begging for forgiveness during the post-battering honeymoon.

Thus, factors from the efficacy of physical aggression in getting one's way to the cessation of an aversive stimulus combine to make aggression one of the most potent conflict negotiation strategies. This potency is accompanied by profoundly negative implications for the relationship, from psychological terror to physical injury and sometimes even homicide.

TENET 2: AGGRESSION IS OFTEN PRECIPITATED BY RELATIVELY INSIGNIFICANT ACTS

In relationships characterized by the use of physical aggression, almost anything can trigger an argument that results in an episode of aggression. In our qualitative analysis of the motivations for violence in dating relationships, a significant theme was the unpredictability of the aggressive behavior (Emery & Lloyd, in press). Many women talked about their partner's aggression in phrases such as "anything would set him off"; the reason for the aggression differed from one incident to the next. Events as simple as watching a movie together, bringing up a problem at the "wrong" time, or joking around were identified as precipitators of aggression.

Similarly, interviews with battered women indicate that trivial reasons such as perception of nagging, phone calls from friends, questioning their husbands' decisions, spending money on their own, wearing a certain style of clothing, etc., could incite a partner's abusive tirades (Blixeth, 1987; Walker, 1979). Although both the argument and the subsequent aggression may be brought on by relatively insignificant events, the underlying issues may be much larger and pervasive ones: problems in distance regulation (addressed in the next tenet) and control (addressed in tenet six).

TENET 3: PHYSICAL AGGRESSION MAY BE INSTIGATED BY PHYSIOLOGICAL AROUSAL AND PROBLEMS IN DISTANCE REGULATION

Zillmann (1990) discussed the role of physiological arousal and emotion in aggression in romantic relationships. The link between a disagreement and aggression begins with feelings of acute anger that emanate from a feeling of threat or endangerment to the self or the relationship. These threats produce intense feelings of anger, which are accompanied by elevated sympathetic excitation in the autonomic nervous system. Such intensified anger can lead to aggression, particularly when sympathetic excitation is at a high level due to the residual effects of several simultaneous arousing experiences (Zillmann, 1990). For example, financial stress, problems at work, and frustration over a felt inability to communicate could combine with a perceived irritating action on the part of the spouse to produce high levels of excitation. Similarly, verbal aggression may produce over time an accumulation of negative arousal, which leads to an intensification of emotion (Infante, Chandler, & Rudd, 1989). And in the absence of social control or potential retaliation, aggression may ensue (Zillmann, 1990).

Due to socialization patterns, men may be predisposed to label arousal as anger (Dutton, 1988). Extreme excitedness and feelings of anger may impair, overwhelm, or short-circuit the processes that normally inhibit the use of aggression. This excitation reduces the ability to utilize complex cognitive coping strategies, leading to the use of strategies that have worked in the past, such as physical aggression (Zillmann, 1990). The use of aggression may also be linked to a cognitive style characterized by lower levels of rational thinking and self-control (Eisikovits, Edleson, Guttman, & Sela-Amit, 1991) as well as to modeling of aggression in the family of origin (O'Leary, 1988).

Subsequent use of aggression may, however, be more under the control of the aggressor than it first appears. Stets (1988) argued that initially, aggression may be an impulsive action; however, she noted that over time, through a process of reinforcement and success, aggression becomes instrumental, particularly as a way to enact control of the female partner.

We believe that the primary threats that induce physiological arousal and excitation are related to issues of distance regulation. Distance regulation is defined as the process of negotiating the level of intimacy in the relationship, and the subsequent definition of rights of influence and control of one partner over the other. Many of the precipitators of aggression noted earlier can be placed within a distance regulation framework, for example, jealousy, interaction with friends, the form and frequency of sexual intimacy, and challenges to the authority of the aggressor (Blixeth, 1987; Stets, 1988). Thus, a feeling of threat may arise from the perceived violation of unspoken rules about relationship closeness and interaction. Partners may learn that aggression is an effective strategy for maintaining a comfortable distance in the relationship (Follette & Alexander, 1992).

Dutton (1988) wrote of distance regulation in terms of an optimal zone. This zone represents the amount of emotional closeness that is comfortable for the individual; both too little and too much distance may induce anxiety and arousal. Dutton and Browning (1988) noted that for husbands this arousal is often translated into anger rather than fear, and may lead to a response of physical aggression. They found that abandonment scenes produced anxiety and nonconstructive reasoning in physically aggressive men.

Likewise, Retzinger's (1991) work on the disruption of social bonds in precipitating conflict fits into a distance regulation framework. Retzinger (1991) emphasized the role of real or perceived rejection by the partner in producing shame (broadly defined as anxiety, humiliation, embarrassment) and subsequent aggression. Threats to the bonds with the partner can lead to shame, which, if unacknowledged, leads to an anger-shame-rage cycle that may erupt into physical aggression.

Another indication of problematic distance regulation is enmeshment in the relationship. Enmeshment, defined as a level of cohesiveness that prohibits normal separation and individuation, appears to characterize some relationships that contain aggression (Dutton & Painter, 1981; Lloyd, 1992; Weitzman & Dreen, 1982). Interaction may be marked by rigidity and structured patterns of communication, both of which serve to reduce flexibility in coping with disagreements (Margolin, Burman, & John, 1989).

Finally, patterns of attachment may be related to physical aggression. Mayseless (1991) hypothesized that individuals with histories of insecure attachment may be prone to the use of physical aggression in response to distance regulation issues. Avoidant individuals, due to a need for self-reliance, may try to enact a great deal of control over the intimacy level of their relationships in an attempt to avoid the danger of rejection. Anxious/ambivalent individuals may be very jealous and possessive, desiring closeness with their partners; at the same time, they are angry and ambivalent about their attachment and dependency. Both types of individuals may utilize aggression as a means of ensuring that a comfortable emotional distance is maintained with the partner.

TENET 4: THE VICTIM OF AGGRESSION IS IN A NO-WIN SITUATION

We believe that the dynamics of aggression place the female victim in a particularly vulnerable position when it comes to responding to the aggression of her male partner. Without his commitment to cease all aggressive behavior, from a safety standpoint it appears as though her only recourse is to leave the relationship temporarily or permanently. Although we are not saying that men who enact physical aggression toward their romantic partners cannot cease, we do assert that the female victim of such aggression cannot be expected to stop it.

A female victim's response in the short run (i.e., during the episode of aggression) may be retaliation and self-defense. Such a response may backfire to the extent that it provides her partner an easy justification for further aggression (Feld & Straus, 1990). Furthermore, a response of self defense provides a simple justification for blaming her for the aggressive episode, since as a society we believe that women are only worthy of our sympathy when they remain nonaggressive (Breines & Gordon, 1983).

The other side of the coin would be a response of conciliation or withdrawal. Although conciliation or withdrawal may help the aggressor cease his aggression during a particular episode, in the long run they may inadvertently increase the likelihood of aggression in the future, through the dynamics of reinforcement (see Tenet 2). If conciliation and withdrawal are perceived by the aggressor as the cessation of an aversive stimuli, as gaining her compliance, or as getting what he wants, then he will be more likely to use aggression again. Thus, the victim of aggression is in a no-win situation—if she responds with self-defensive aggression, the aggression of her partner may escalate, and if she responds with conciliation or withdrawal, her partner's use of aggression is inadvertently reinforced.

The key to stopping aggression in romantic relationships may be twofold. First, the commitment to cease the aggression must be present on the part of the aggressor (Willbach, 1989). Second, couples must develop functional, constructive conflict negotiation patterns that promote relationship growth and prevent escalated and intensely emotional conflict (Cahn, 1990; Infante, Sabourin, Rudd, & Shannon, 1990).

TENET 5: AGGRESSION IS A TACTIC OF CONTROL THAT EMANATES FROM A PATRIARCHAL SOCIETY

Physical aggression can be conceptualized as a tactic of control. It may embody literal physical control of the woman (e.g., holding her down), as well as symbolic control (e.g., denying autonomy of thought and behavior) (Ferraro, 1988; Stets & Pirog-Good, 1990). Although they may not use the word *control*, it is clearly a theme in the explanations given by men for their use of physical aggression against their romantic partners. Dutton (1988, p. 38) noted that male aggressors describe three power-related themes: the need to dominate the female, fear of the female gaining independence, and attempts to coerce the female into adopting the male's rules for the relationship. Stets (1988) noted three challenges to control that are related to aggression: challenges to male authority, interaction with friends, and spending decisions. Ptacek (1988) conceptualized men's justifications for the use of aggression as responding to a perceived failure of the woman to fulfill the "obligations of a good wife." Physical aggression may also be used as a tactic to intimidate, "strike fear into," or discipline the partner (Emery & Lloyd, in press).

Thus far we have noted that arousal and perceived threat may instigate the use of physical aggression in romantic relationships, and that underlying the use of aggression is the issue of control. Our analysis would be incomplete, however, if we failed to go one step further and examine the roots of control in relationships. We believe that the roots of control can be laid squarely at the door of the patriarchal nature of society in general and romantic relationships in particular. Patriarchy is embodied in the social realities of the greater access of men to material and symbolic resources, the devaluing of women's work (especially work that relates to connection and caring) and women as persons, and women's socialization toward financial and emotional dependence on men. As a class, men hold power and dominion over women (Bograd, 1988; Harding, 1987).

Patriarchal norms endorse the use of physical aggression as a legitimate tactic of social control of women (Bograd, 1988). The popular media is rife with characterizations of "macho" males who control others with physical aggression. The resulting message is that it is natural and acceptable for males to dominate. Ultimately, the threat of physical aggression (whether at the hands of romantic partners or strangers) serves to restrict women's lives and options (Kelly, 1988). Control within the romantic relationship is merely an extension of the control men wield in society. Once a woman becomes involved in a relationship, she is viewed as subject to the dominion of her partner (Lloyd, 1991).

Although physical aggression is generally regarded as a negative concept, males tend to be more accepting of its use than are females (Emery, Cate, Henton, & Andrews, 1987). This may be due to an assimilation of patriarchal privileges and attitudes as well as the differences in consequence and injury for men versus women. The reality of physical injury further places women in a subordinate position (Kelly, 1988).

Yllo and Straus (1990) cited changes in sex roles and the balance of power as explanations for the need to control women and the subsequent use of physical aggression. They indicated that families with patriarchal norms have twice the incidence of aggression against women as those with egalitarian norms. Physical aggression against women has been found to be more common in situations where there is a discrepancy within the social context of the abuse, that is, between women's high structural status (defined by economic, political, and legal statuses) and a cultural or social norm that advocates their subordination (Yllo & Straus, 1990).

TENET 6: PHYSICAL AGGRESSION IS OFTEN ACCOMPANIED BY OTHER NEGATIVE INTERACTION IN THE RELATIONSHIP

Recently, a series of studies have begun to examine the interaction patterns that characterize romantic relationships that contain aggression. This line of research is very fruitful, for aggression is clearly associated with other negative interaction patterns, and, indeed, these other negative interactions may occur more frequently than physical aggression itself (Holtzworth-Munroe, Jacobson, Fehrenbach, & Fruzzetti, 1992).

Margolin and her colleagues have conducted behavioral observation of interaction in aggressive versus nonaggressive marriages. In the laboratory, in comparison to verbally aggressive, withdrawing, and nondistressed couples, physically aggressive husbands displayed greaᵗer levels of offensive negative behavior (e.g., threat, blame) and negativ₁ voice; their wives displayed a tendency to escalate offensive negative behavior during the middle of the discussion, followed by de-escalation during the final stages.

Physically aggressive couples displayed significantly fewer positive behaviors (e.g., positive physical touch, smiling) than did the nondistressed couples (Margolin, John, & Gleberman, 1988). These researchers identified a possible cycle of attack and defend, a behavioral pattern that increases the probability of escalation of conflict. Nonaggressive couples appear to enact patterns that help to de-escalate conflict, whereas physically aggressive couples do not utilize such de-escalation techniques (Burman, John, & Margolin, 1992).

In home observations of a marital conflict, Margolin, Burman, and John (1989) noted that marriages characterized by physical aggression were higher in overt hostility and lower in problem-solving skills, particularly by the end of the discussion. Physically aggressive husbands were also characterized by high defensiveness, and by a pattern of increasing withdrawal and despair as the conflict progressed. Margolin, Burman, and John (1989) characterized this pattern as an attempt to withdraw from an unpleasant situation; unfortunately, since these couples have few problem-solving skills, they are left with few alternatives for constructive conflict when their withdrawal attempts are unsuccessful.

Finally, in an examination of diary descriptions of naturally occurring conflicts, Margolin, John, and O'Brien (1989) noted that physically aggressive husbands and their wives showed greater contingency of their behavior. Specifically, an initial anger reaction (defined as an active feeling of anger linked to irritation, criticism, disapproval, etc.) followed by reciprocal anger from the spouse increased the likelihood of further anger responses. Withdrawing, verbally aggressive, and nondistressed couples in the study were noteworthy in their relative absence of contingent patterns of behavior.

Using Huston, Robins, Atkinson, and McHale's (1987) measurement of daily interaction, Lloyd (1992) assessed rates of both positive and negative behaviors in marriages that contain aggression. Aggressive-distressed marriages contained significantly higher levels of negative interaction; surprisingly, they also contained high levels of positive interaction. Lloyd (1992) hypothesized that the high levels of both positive and negative interaction may be an indication of highly intense attachments or enmeshment in the marriage. Distressed marriages, on the other hand, contained low levels of both positive and negative interaction; Lloyd (1992) described these marriages as withdrawn.

Lloyd (1990b) also assessed conflict strategies in aggressive marriages. Problem-solving skills in the aggressive marriage were poor, characterized by more nonconstructive approaches to conflict (including verbal attack, anger, and withdrawal) and fewer constructive approaches (such as negotiation and initiating a problem-solving discussion). Rather than letting minor arguments drop without a resolution, aggressive couples appeared to strive to reach a resolution of all their disagreements (Lloyd, 1990b).

Riggs (1993) noted a similar tendency to react to any problem as a disagreement among aggressive premarital couples. Partners in physically aggressive courtships exhibit more negative affect, conflict, indirect styles of negotiation, confrontation, blaming the partner, and expression of anger (Bird, Stith, & Schladale, 1991; Gryl, Stith, & Bird, 1991; Lloyd, Koval, & Cate, 1989). These partners are also distinguished by their use of persistence as a negotiation strategy, high investment in the relationship, and the belief that the partner can be changed (Lloyd, Koval, & Cate, 1989).

Infante, Chandler, and Rudd (1989) have developed a model of physical aggression in romantic relationships that emphasizes the role of skill deficiencies and verbal aggression. Physically aggressive couples are characterized by low levels of argumentativeness; that is, they feel less skilled at arguing, they are less willing to argue, and they are less competent communicators (Infante, Chandler, & Rudd, 1989; Infante, Sabourin, Rudd, & Shannon, 1990). This argumentative skill deficiency leads to a greater use of verbal aggression. Verbal aggression is catalytic to physical aggression, particularly when the verbal aggression entails character attack, swearing, competence attacks, and threats (Infante, Sabourin, Rudd, & Shannon, 1990). Such escalation of verbal into physical aggression is believed to occur in a context of undissipated anger and hostility (Infante, Chandler, & Rudd, 1989).

Many conceptualizations of aggression in romantic relationships emphasize relationship distress as a precursor to aggression (O'Leary, 1988). However, Lloyd (1990b, 1992) described a subset of aggressive marriages that were also high in marital satisfaction. These relationships were characterized by high levels of positive interaction and low levels of negative interaction; indeed, they were very similar to nonaggressive-nondistressed marriages. Lloyd (1993) noted that if the aggression in these marriages continues, the aggression eventually erodes the quality of the relationship. Similarly, O'Leary et al. (1989) noted the presence of aggression in relationships that are otherwise described as satisfying and positive.

Overall, interaction in the aggressive relationship can be characterized as enmeshed, conflictual, reactive, nonspontaneous, volatile, and unpredictable (Lloyd, 1992; Margolin, John, & O'Brien, 1989). However, although relationships that contain aggression may be characterized by other negative interaction patterns, it is clear that marital dissatisfaction is not always a feature of the aggressive marriage (Lloyd, 1992).

TENET 7: AGGRESSION IS NOT A UNITARY PHENOMENON

Unfortunately, most of the descriptions of aggression in romantic relationships discuss aggression as a unitary phenomenon—that is, as though all aggressive relationships were the same (Lloyd, 1990a). However, a number of studies clearly demonstrate that there is a great deal of variability from one relationship to the next, even if both are characterized by aggressive interaction patterns. Indeed, even a comparison of women who have experienced aggression in a dating relationship once versus women who have experienced aggression multiple times yields a very different dynamic, with the former being most similar to women who have never experienced aggression (Follingstad, Rutledge, Polek, & McNeill-Hawkins, 1988). Although only a few scholars have approached aggression in romantic relationships from the perspective of multiple patterns (see, for example, Deschner, 1984; Follingstad, Laughlin, Polek, Rutledge, & Hause, 1991; Lloyd, 1990a; Snyder & Fruchtman, 1981), all are in agreement that the patterns of aggression are varied and complex.

Two recent studies are illustrative here. Lloyd (1990a) demonstrated that a priori groupings of relationships as aggressive, distressed, nondistressed, etc., may mask important differences among them. In a cluster analysis of marriages based on frequency and severity of aggression and level of marital satisfaction, Lloyd (1990a) identified eight types of marriages. Some of these types were "predictable"; for example, there were non-distressed-nonaggressive and distressed-nonaggressive types. However, rather than lumping all aggressive couples into one category, the use of an inductive method like cluster analysis yielded multiple types of aggressive relationships, ranging from nondistressed-aggressive to distressed-mildly aggressive to distressed-severely aggressive to extremely distressed-mildly aggressive.

Follingstad, Laughlin, Polek, Rutledge, and Hause (1991) created a typology of battered women using multiple variables, from severity of abuse to reason for staying in the relationship. They discovered five types of battered women, ranging from women who experienced high frequency and severity of aggression, were in long-term abusive relationships, and were likely to have experienced abuse as a child, to women who experienced high frequency of aggression initially in the relationship, with decreasing aggression over time.

Such typologies of aggressive relationships both clarify and complicate the current literature on aggression. Contradictory findings may indeed be a function of the inadvertent description of multiple types of relationships that contain aggression as though they were unitary. However, since the multiplicity of aggression has been ignored, current literature may be somewhat inaccurate and even misleading. In addition, describing the various types of romantic relationships that contain aggression has important implications for designing multiple intervention strategies (Follingstad, Laughlin, Polek, Rutledge, & Hause, 1991).

TENET 8: THE TRAJECTORY OF AGGRESSION IS VARIED FROM COUPLE TO COUPLE

One important facet often overlooked in the research is the fact that physical aggression does not necessarily herald the demise of the relationship (Lloyd, 1990a). Indeed, estimates from shelter programs indicate that 50% to 80% of battered wives return to their husbands, even though particularly severe violence and injury have occurred (Ferraro & Johnson, 1983). Granted, in the long run aggressive relationships may dissolve; however, in the short run they are stable.

The fact that the ongoing nature of relationship aggression is often overlooked may be a matter of practicality, for longitudinal study of aggressive relationships is difficult at best. Retrospective accounts given by women seeking shelter indicate that physical aggression increases in severity and frequency over time (Ferraro & Johnson, 1983; Walker, 1979). This upward trajectory has been accepted as the norm; authors often caution that while aggression may begin with pushing and shoving, relatively noninjurious aggressive behaviors, it is likely to become more life threatening and frequent over time. However, since the upward trajectory of aggression has been derived from studies of what are probably the more severe forms of wife abuse, does such a trajectory characterize all aggressive relationships?

Several studies challenge the notion of an upward trajectory of physical aggression for all couples. O'Leary et al. (1989) examined the stability of aggression from one month premarriage to 30 months of marriage. They reported low, yet statistically significant, stability of aggression across the three years of the study. However, there was considerable movement in and out of aggressive and nonaggressive categorizations; for example, although at premarriage 31% of the men were aggressive, only 8% were classified as aggressive at all three waves of the project.

Feld and Straus (1990) recontacted a subsample of the 1985 National Family Violence Survey 12 months later to assess changes in aggression. According to their analyses, minor assaults between spouses tended to encourage subsequent severe aggression. However, again there was considerable movement from aggressive to nonaggressive categorizations. For example, 58% of husbands who enacted a minor assault and 33% of husbands who enacted a severe assault in 1985 reported enacting no assaults in 1986. Similarly, Lloyd (1993) found that 30% percent of couples reporting aggression at the first point of data collection reported no aggression 18 months later; 18% of couples reporting no aggression at the first point of data collection indicated that they had experienced aggression during the subsequent 18 months.

What do these studies tell us about the trajectory of aggression? Again, physical aggression in relationships is not unitary. Clearly, for some couples aggression is a relatively stable feature of the relationship; in the study by Lloyd (1993), 32% of the sample reported aggression at both time one and time two. However, aggression may be less stable than early studies of severely battered women have implied. Most likely, there are multiple patterns of the trajectory of aggression, with one type being severe, increasing aggression over time; another type representing more sporadic aggression; and still other types being characterized by declines in aggression over time.

Second, given that these longitudinal studies are assessing stable relationships — that is, only relationships that remained intact across the time of the study are analyzed — the fact that aggression declines or disappears for some couples should not be unexpected. The presence of such negative behavior as physical aggression may be an indication of relationship trouble; if it were to continue unabated, one would expect the relationship to dissolve. Relationships in which the level of aggression declined over time would be expected to remain intact.

Finally, the findings of these longitudinal studies of aggression should not be used in any way to diminish the plight of battered women. The dynamics of relationships that contain severe battering, coercion, and verbal abuse may be different from the dynamics of relationships that contain more occasional (and yet still troubling) aggression. However, in either type of relationship, appropriate intervention is called for, whether that intervention seeks primarily to provide safety to the battered woman or halt the occurrence of aggression and other negative features of the relationship.

TENET 9: MANY FACTORS IN THE BROADER SOCIAL CONTEXT OF ROMANTIC RELATIONSHIPS SERVE TO SUSTAIN THE USE OF PHYSICAL AGGRESSION

Any examination of conflict and physical aggression requires an exploration of the social context within which romantic relationships exist. This context includes patriarchy (addressed in tenet six), the power of romance, socialization for relationships, and the influence of privacy norms. All of these contextual factors in one way or another may serve to ensure that physical aggression will proceed unchecked.

Feelings of love and romance have a great influence on expectations for appropriate behavior in intimate relationships. Lloyd (1991) conceptualized romanticism as a powerful contributor to dating conflict and aggression. The assumptions that "love conquers all" and that intimate relationships are problem free is a romantic ideal that is both erroneous and dangerous. Romanticism allows partners to downplay physical aggression by attributing it to situational or external circumstances (anger, stress, alcohol, etc.) rather than the aggressive partner (Henton, Cate, Koval, Lloyd, & Christopher, 1983). Follingstad, Rutledge, Polek, & McNeill-Hawkins (1988) found that women who reported romanticizing relationships experienced aggression earlier in the relationship and that those who reported stronger feelings of romantic love were also more likely to experience ongoing aggression. Victims and aggressors tend to overlook, reframe, and/or forgive the aggression based on rationalizations of love (Henton, Cate, Koval, Lloyd, & Christopher, 1983). Romanticism serves as a constraining factor by encouraging individuals to remain in abusive relationships (Lloyd, 1991).

Gender-based patterns of socialization for relationships are also important contextual factors. A key relationship theme for men is maintaining control, whereas the predominant theme for women is dependence on the relationship (Lloyd, 1991). The theme of maintaining control may justify a man's use of aggression to gain compliance from his partner. The theme of dependency may encourage women to rationalize aggression away and remain in destructive relationships, for this theme emphasizes that any relationship is better than no relationship (Lloyd, 1991).

Men and women may also be socialized to approach conflict in different ways. For example, women tend to view the continued discussion of a conflict issue as a "pursuit of resolution" and contributing to greater feelings of love and commitment, whereas men perceive it as "rehashing the same old issue" and a detraction from the relationship (Lloyd, 1987). These patterns may result from the belief that relationship maintenance and conflict resolution are the responsibility of women. Our society emphasizes the importance of relationships for women to the exclusion of all else (career, personal safety, etc.). The success or failure of the relationship, then, is on the woman's shoulders (Breines & Gordon, 1983).

Norms of privacy also contribute to perpetuating aggression. Through this norm, intervention from third parties (including the police) is discouraged, which in turn serves to minimize social action against aggressive behavior (Dutton, 1988; Zillmann, 1990). In addition, aggression is most likely to occur in the privacy of the home, where it is less likely to be detected or reported by either victims or outsiders (Dutton, 1988).

The cultural norm of privacy may create isolation. A couple's isolation from support networks is consistently cited as characteristic of physically aggressive marital and dating relationships (Dutton, 1988; Stets & Straus, 1990b; Walker, 1979). Isolation from friends, family, and community deters the possibility of any negative labeling of the aggressive behavior, thereby keeping the relationship intact and reputation of the aggressor unsullied. Even when there is a social network in place, members of the man's peer group may be aggressive or supportive of such behavior (DeKeseredy, 1988; Gwartney-Gibbs, Stockard, & Bohmer, 1987). The importance of a supportive network to the victim is paramount, for support and assistance from family and/or friends appears to be a pivotal factor in helping a woman leave an aggressive dating partner (Emery & Lloyd, in press).

CONCLUSIONS

This chapter outlines nine tenets that describe the dynamics of physically aggressive conflict in romantic relationships. We view these tenets as a series of "working hypotheses"; although there is support for each tenet in the literature, there is still room for further explication and scrutiny of these ideas. Two basic ideas underlie much of this chapter. First, we have emphasized the interpersonal dynamics associated with physical aggression, and second, we have tried to emphasize the importance of examining interpersonal dynamics in context.

Several nagging questions remain. One of the more important has to do with explaining why one man engages in physically aggressive behavior toward the woman he purports to love, and yet another man does not, even though both may be involved in a conflictual relationship, or have witnessed aggression between their parents, or hold stereotypical notions about the roles of men and women, etc. Thus far, very few researchers have been able to shed light on this question (our work included). Although we can outline a plethora of variables that are correlated with physical aggression, as of yet we have not found many answers to the question of why some men can stop short of crossing the line and using physical aggression even in the face of a highly physiologically arousing, intense, aversive conflict situation. Certainly, this is an important question for future research.

Many other research questions can be culled from the tenets. Further work on the trajectory of aggression over time is sorely needed, as is a greater understanding of the multiple types of aggressive relationships. Work in these areas has implications for therapy. If we can determine what is related to a decrease in aggression in romantic relationships, then perhaps we can better assist batterers in their quest to eliminate aggression as a response to conflict with their romantic partners. As the many types of aggressive patterns are identified, interventions can be better tailored to the needs of the individual partners. For example, if the relationship contains severe battering, the need for shelter and safety for the woman is of tantamount importance. However, if the aggression is more sporadic and less severe, and if the male partner can control the impulse to aggress, conjoint therapy may be the most appropriate intervention.

Prevention, however, holds the key to ending physically aggressive conflict in romantic relationships. Prevention should include a variety of efforts, such as conflict management and interpersonal skills training, elimination of adversarial attitudes between the sexes, efforts to increase equality between the sexes, and work to reduce the romantic (and sometimes blinding) veneer of intimate relationships (Lloyd, 1990b).

ACKNOWLEDGMENTS

An earlier version of this chapter was presented at the International Network on Close Relationships, Milwaukee, June 1993. The authors would like to express their gratitude to Dudley Cahn for his helpful comments on an earlier version of this paper. The first author would also like to gratefully acknowledge the support of the Harry Frank Guggenheim Foundation; all of her work on aggression in marriage described in this chapter was supported by two research grants from the Foundation.

REFERENCES

Bird, G. W., Stith, S. M., & Schladale, J. (1991). Psychological resources, coping strategies, and negotiation styles as discriminators of violence in dating relationships. *Family Relations, 40*, 45–50.

Blixeth, E. D. (1987). *Uncharged battery*. New York: Warner.

Bograd, M. (1988). Feminist perspectives on wife abuse: An introduction. In K. Yllo & M. Bograd (Eds.), *Feminist perspectives on wife abuse* (pp. 11–27). Newbury Park, CA: Sage.

Breines, W., & Gordon, L. (1983). The new scholarship on family violence. *Signs, 8*, 490–531.

Burman, B., John, R. S., & Margolin, G. (1992). Observed patterns of conflict in violent, nonviolent, and nondistressed couples. *Behavioral Assessment, 14*, 15–37.

Cahn, D. D. (1990). Confrontation behaviors, perceived understanding, and relationship growth. In D. D. Cahn (Ed.), *Intimates in conflict: A communication perspective* (pp. 153–166). Hillsdale, NJ: Lawrence Erlbaum Associates.

Cate, R. M., & Lloyd, S. A. (1992). *Courtship*. Newbury Park, CA: Sage.

Coleman, D. H., & Straus, M. A. (1990). Marital power, conflict, and violence in a nationally representative sample of American couples. In M. A. Straus, & R. Gelles (Eds.), *Physical violence in American families* (pp. 287–304). New Brunswick, NJ: Transaction.

DeKeseredy, W. S. (1988). *Woman abuse in dating relationships: The role of male peer support*. Toronto: Canadian Scholars Press.

Deschner, J. (1984). *The hitting habit: Anger control for battering couples*. New York: The Free Press.

deTurck, M. A. (1987). When communication fails: Physical aggression as a compliance gaining strategy. *Communication Monographs, 54*, 106–112.

Dutton, D. G. (1988). *The domestic assault of women*. Boston: Allyn & Bacon.

Dutton, D. G., & Browning, J. J. (1988). Power strategies and intimacy anxieties as causative factors of violence in intimate relationships. In G. Russell (Ed.), *Violence in intimate relationships* (pp. 163–176). New York: PMA.

Dutton, D. G., & Painter, S. (1981). Traumatic bonding: The development of emotional attachment in battered women and other relationships of intermittent abuse. *Victimology, 6,* 139-155.

Eisikovits, Z. C., Edleson, J. L., Guttman, E., & Sela-Amit, M. (1991). Cognitive styles and socialized attitudes of men who batter: Where should we intervene? *Family Relations, 40,* 72-77.

Emery, B. C., Cate, R. M., Henton, J. M., & Andrews, D. (1987). *Perceived legitimizing factors in premarital violence.* Paper presented at National Council on Family Relations, Atlanta, November.

Emery, B. C., & Lloyd, S. A. (in press). A feminist perspective on the study of women who use aggression in close relationships. In D. L. Sollie & L. A. Leslie (Eds.), *Feminism and the study of family and close relationships: Conceptual, personal, and methodological issues in current research.* Newbury Park, CA: Sage.

Feld, S. L., & Straus, M. A. (1990). Escalation and desistance from wife assault in marriage. In M. A. Straus & R. Gelles (Eds.), *Physical violence in American families* (pp. 489-505). New Brunswick, NJ: Transaction.

Ferraro, K. J. (1988). An existential approach to battering. In G. Hotaling, D. Finkelhor, J. Kirkpatrick, & M. Straus (Eds.), *Family abuse and its consequences* (pp. 126-138). Newbury Park, CA: Sage.

Ferraro, K. J., & Johnson, J. M. (1983). How women experience battering: The process of victimization. *Social Problems, 30,* 325-339.

Follette, V. M., & Alexander, P. C. (1992). Dating violence: Current and historical correlates. *Behavioral Assessment, 14,* 39-52.

Follingstad, D. R., Laughlin, J. E., Polek, D. S., Rutledge, L. L., & Hause, E. S. (1991). Identification of patterns of wife abuse. *Journal of Interpersonal Violence, 6,* 187-204.

Follingstad, D. R., Rutledge, L. L., Polek, D. S., & McNeil-Hawkins, K. (1988). Factors associated with patterns of dating violence toward college women. *Journal of Family Violence, 3,* 169-182.

Gryl, F. E., Stith, S. M., & Bird, G. W. (1991). Close dating relationships among college students: Differences by use of violence and by gender. *Journal of Social and Personal Relationships, 8,* 243-264.

Gwartney-Gibbs, P., Stockard, J., & Bohmer, S. (1987). Learning courtship aggression: The influence of parents, peers, and personal experiences. *Family Relations, 36,* 276-282.

Harding, S. (1987). Is there a feminist method? In S. Harding (Ed.), *Feminism and methodology.* Bloomington, IN: Indiana University Press.

Henton, J. M., Cate, R. M., Koval, J. E., Lloyd, S. A., & Christopher, F. S. (1983). Romance and violence in dating relationships. *Journal of Family Issues, 4,* 467-582.

Holtzworth-Munroe, A., Jacobson, N., Fehrenbach, P. A., & Fruzzetti, A. (1992). Violent married couples' attributions for violent and nonviolent self and partner behaviors. *Behavioral Assessment, 14,* 53-64.

Huston, T. L., Robins, E., Atkinson, J., & McHale, S. M. (1987). Surveying the landscape of marital behavior: A behavioral self-report approach to studying marriage. In S. Oskamp (Ed.), *Family processes and problems* (Vol. 7, pp. 45-71). Newbury Park, CA: Sage.

Infante, D. A., Chandler, T. A., & Rudd, J. E. (1989). test of an argumentative skill deficiency model of interspousal violence. *Communication Monographs, 56,* 163-177.

Infante, D. A., Sabourin, T. C., Rudd, J. E., & Shannon, E. A. (1990). Verbal aggression in violent and nonviolent marital disputes. *Communication Quarterly, 38,* 361-371.

Kelly, L. (1988). How women define their experiences of violence. In K. Yllo & M. Bograd (Eds.), *Feminist perspectives on wife abuse* (pp. 114-132). Newbury Park, CA: Sage.

Lloyd, S. A. (1987). Conflict in premarital relationships: Differential perceptions of males and females. *Family Relations, 36,* 290-294.

Lloyd, S. A. (1990a). Asking the right questions about the future of marital violence research.

In D. Besharov (Ed.), *Family violence: Research and public policy issues* (pp. 93–107). Washington, DC: AEI.

Lloyd, S. A. (1990b). Conflict types and strategies in violent marriages. *Journal of Family Violence, 5*, 269–284.

Lloyd, S. A. (1991). The dark side of courtship. *Family Relations, 40*, 14–20.

Lloyd, S. A. (1992). *Physical aggression and distress in marriage: The role of everyday marital interaction.* Manuscript submitted for publication.

Lloyd, S. A. (1993). *Physical aggression and marital quality: Predicting changes over time.* Technical report to the Harry Frank Guggenheim Foundation, New York, June.

Lloyd, S. A., Koval, J. E., & Cate, R. M. (1989). Conflict and violence in dating relationships. In M. Pirog-Good & J. Stets (Eds.), *Violence in dating relationships: Emerging social issues* (pp. 126–142). New York: Praeger.

Margolin, G., Burman, B., & John, R. S. (1989). Home observations of married couples re-enacting naturalistic conflicts. *Behavioral Assessment, 11*, 101–118.

Margolin, G., John, R. S., & Gleberman, L. (1988). Affective responses to conflictual discussion in violent and nonviolent couples. *Journal of Consulting and Clinical Psychology, 56*, 24–33.

Margolin, G., John, R. S., & O'Brien, M. (1989). Sequential affective patterns as a function of marital conflict style. *Journal of Social and Clinical Psychology, 8*, 45–61.

Mayseless, O. (1991). Adult attachment patterns and courtship violence. *Family Relations, 40*, 21–28.

O'Leary, K. D. (1988). Physical aggression between spouses. In V. Van Hasselt, R. Morrison, A. Bellack, & M. Hersen (Eds.), *Handbook of family violence* (pp. 31–55). New York: Plenum.

O'Leary, K. D., Barling, J., Arias, I., Rosenbaum, A., Malone, J., & Tyree, A. (1989). Prevalence and stability of physical aggression between spouses: A longitudinal analysis. *Journal of Consulting and Clinical Psychology, 57*, 263–268.

Patterson, G. R. (1985). A microsocial analysis of anger and irritable behavior. In M. A. Chesney & R. H. Rosenman (Eds.), *Anger and hostility: Behavioral and cardiovascular disorders* (pp. 83–100). Washington, DC: Hemisphere.

Planalp, S. (1993). Communication, cognition, and emotion. *Communication Monographs, 60*, 3–9.

Ptacek, J. (1988). Why do men batter their wives? In K. Yllo & M. Bograd (Eds.), *Feminist perspectives on wife abuse* (pp. 133–157). Newbury Park, CA: Sage.

Retzinger, S. M. (1991). *Violent emotions.* Newbury Park, CA: Sage.

Riggs, D. S. (1993). Relationship problems and dating aggression: A potential treatment target. *Journal of Interpersonal Violence, 8*, 18–35.

Roloff, M. E., & Cloven, D. H. (1990). The chilling effect in interpersonal relationships: The reluctance to speak one's mind. In D. D. Cahn (Ed.), *Intimates in conflict: A communication perspective* (pp. 49–76). Hillsdale NJ: Lawrence Erlbaum Associates.

Saunders, D. G. (1988). Wife abuse, husband abuse, or mutual combat. In K. Yllo & M. Bogard (Eds.), *Feminist perspectives on wife abuse* (pp. 90–113). Newbury Park, CA: Sage.

Snyder, D. K., & Fruchtman, L. A. (1981). Differential patterns of wife abuse: A data-based typology. *Journal of Consulting and Clinical Psychology, 49*, 787–885.

Stets, J. E. (1988). *Domestic violence and control.* New York: Springer-Verlag.

Stets, J. E. (1992). Interactive processes in dating aggression: A national study. *Journal of Marriage and the Family, 54*, 165–177.

Stets, J. E., & Henderson, D. A. (1991). Contextual factors surrounding conflict resolution while dating: Results from a national study. *Family Relations, 40*, 29–36.

Stets, J. E., & Pirog-Good, M. A. (1990). Interpersonal control and courtship aggression. *Journal of Social and Personal Relationships, 7*, 371–394.

Stets, J. E., & Straus, M. A. (1990a). Gender differences in reporting marital violence and its medical and social consequences. In M. A. Straus & R. J. Gelles (Eds.), *Physical violence in American families* (pp. 151–166). New Brunswick, NJ: Transaction.

Stets, J. E., & Straus, M. A. (1990b). The marriage license as a hitting license: A comparison of assaults in dating, cohabiting, and married couples. In M. A. Straus & R. J. Gelles (Eds.), *Physical violence in American families* (pp. 227–243). New Brunswick, NJ: Transaction.

Straus, M. A., & Gelles, R. J. (1990). How violent are American families? Estimates from the national family violence resurvey and other studies. In M. A. Straus & R. J. Gelles (Eds.), *Physical violence in American families* (pp. 95–112). New Brunswick, NJ: Transaction.

Sugarman, D. B., & Hotaling, G. T. (1989). Dating violence: Prevalence, context, and risk markers. In M. A. Pirog-Good & J. E. Stets (Eds.), *Violence in dating relationships: Emerging social issues* (pp. 3–32). New York: Praeger.

Walker, L. E. (1979). *The battered woman*. New York: Harper & Row.

Weitzman, J., & Dreen, K. (1982). Wife beating: A view of the marital dyad. *Social Casework, 63*, 259–265.

Willbach, D. (1989). Ethics and family therapy: The case management of family violence. *Journal of Marital and Family Therapy, 15*, 43–52.

Yllo, K. A., & Straus, M. A. (1990). Patriarchy and violence against wives: The impact of structural and normative factors. In M. A. Straus & R. J. Gelles (Eds.), *Physical violence in American families* (pp. 383–402). New Brunswick, NJ: Transaction.

Zillmann, D. (1990). The interplay of cognition and excitation in aggravated conflict among intimates. In D. D. Cahn (Ed.), *Intimates in conflict: A communication perspective* (pp. 187–208). Hillsdale, NJ: Lawrence Erlbaum Associates.

3 Managing Conflict in Intimate Intercultural Relationships

Stella Ting-Toomey
California State University at Fullerton

Conflict is inevitable in all phases of social and personal relationship development. From a Western cultural perspective, conflict is, in and of itself, not a negative phenomenon. It is how we resolve or manage conflict that will affect the quality of our relationships. However, from an Eastern (e.g., Japan) or a Middle Eastern (e.g., Saudi Arabia) cultural perspective, the opening sentence is problematic. Conflict is often perceived by people in many non-Western cultures as a high-risk, costly relational phenomenon. For them, conflict is not necessarily "inevitable"; it can be proactively avoided or managed before it actually takes on the reality of conflict. Conflict, according to the root word *conflictus* in Latin, means to "strike together" or to strike against one another. Similarly, the term *conflict* in Japanese (i.e., *shótótsu*) and Chinese (i.e., *chóngtu*) means "positional collision" or intensive, antagonistic struggle.

Unfortunately, although there has been a blossoming interest concerning the study of intimate conflict in personal relationship development (for an extensive review, see Cahn, 1992) in recent years, the role of culture in intimate conflict has been virtually ignored. Human beings, however, are first and foremost cultural beings before they are beings in interpersonal relationships. Individuals first learn the implicit scripts of interpersonal relationship development within the webs of their culture. More specifically, people learn the values, norms, and rules of appropriate or inappropriate conflict conduct, and effective or ineffective conflict behavior within the primary socialization process of their culture.

There are three reasons why it is important to understand conflict differences and similarities in intercultural personal relationships: (a) The

47

changing demographic trends of the U.S. population indicate that within the next 50 years, one in every three U.S. Americans will be a person of nonwhite heritage (Thurnstone, 1992) and, thus, the chance of intercultural encounters increases exponentially; (b) intercultural and interracial marriage rates within the United States and on a global level have increased dramatically since World War II; and (c) by probing deeper into how individuals in different cultures approach and manage intimate conflict, we may gain new insights to enhance our own options in approaching and managing conflict differently. Understanding intimate conflict across cultures contains both theoretical and practical implications for interpersonal and marital researchers, counselors, social workers, students and teachers, and conflict mediators, to name only a few examples.

Overall, the purpose of this chapter is to call attention to the central role that culture plays in our assumptions of intimate conflict in cross-cultural and intercultural personal relationship development. Briefly, culture is defined here as a complex, symbolic frame of reference (e.g., history, traditions, values, beliefs, collective perceptions, norms, symbols, and meaning patterns) that is shared to varying degrees by members of a larger society and that is passed on from one generation to the next (see Ting-Toomey, in press, for a detailed discussion). Because there is a dearth of studies on either cross-cultural or intercultural intimate conflict, implications concerning intercultural intimate conflict are drawn from the general literature on cross-cultural personal relationship development. The chapter is developed in three sections. First, intimate conflict assumptions and intimate conflict processes are introduced and relevant cross-cultural personal relationship and conflict studies are reviewed. Second, based on the reviewed research findings of cross-cultural personal relationships, practical implications for engaging in effective management of intercultural intimate conflict are drawn. Third, recommendations for future theorizing and researching about intercultural intimate conflict are proposed.

INTIMATE CONFLICT: AN ORGANIZING FRAMEWORK

Intimate conflict is defined in this chapter as the implicit or explicit verbal and/or nonverbal struggling process within, between, or among two or more interdependent parties when they perceive incompatible conflict bases, processes, and/or outcomes in the course of their personal relationship development process. This definition attempts to incorporate intrapersonal dissonance and interpersonal interaction struggle in the management of intimate conflict. Although for many Western cultures intimate conflict is an overt phenomenon, in many non-Western cultures the experience of intimate conflict can be very subtle and elusive. A personal relationship, in this context, can include close friendship, a dating relationship, or a marital relationship. A personal relationship is conceptualized here as any close relationship that exhibits a certain degree of relational interdependence (i.e., the degree to which the partners are dependent on and committed to the relationship for tangible and intangible resources). The organizing framework of intimate conflict proposed in this chapter has three major clusters: conflict assumptions, conflict processes, and managing intercultural intimate conflict. The framework is presented in Fig. 3.1.

Two assumptions guide the development of the organizing framework: (a) The specific factors in the conflict assumptions influence the meanings and the conflict behavioral patterns in the conflict processes, and vice versa, and (b) the combined conflict assumptions and conflict processes affect the effective management of intercultural intimate conflict. No specific predictive pathways are specified in the framework because actual empirical studies in either cross-cultural or intercultural intimate conflict are still at the infancy stage. However, recommendations for future theorizing, researching, and practicing effective management of intercultural intimate conflict will be proposed. Before we discuss the factors of cross-cultural intimate conflict in more detail, we need to review briefly the existing theoretical frames of intimate conflict in the interpersonal communication literature.

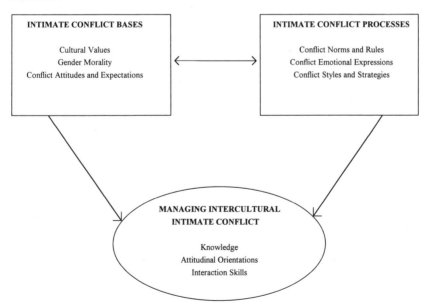

FIG. 3.1. Managing intercultural intimate conflict factors: An organizing framework.

Theoretical Frames

Theoretically, three approaches have been identified by Cahn (1992; see also Cahn, 1990) as explanatory frameworks that guide our understanding of intimate conflict in the U.S. culture: cognitive-exchange, rules-interventionist, and systems-interactionist. A fourth approach, the dialectical perspective (Baxter, 1988, 1990; Montgomery, 1993) is also a viable option to explain conflict in personal relationships. Overall, cross-cultural interpersonal research studies (especially studies that are reported in this chapter) have followed the cognitive-exchange theoretical approach, with a heavy emphasis on interdependence theory. A few selected cross-cultural interpersonal studies, however, have followed the rules-interventionist tradition (e.g., Ting-Toomey, 1991).

To explain briefly, the cognitive-exchange tradition emphasizes the importance of perceived rewards, costs, comparison of alternative choices, and degree of interdependence in close relationships. The rules-interventionist tradition, in contrast, focuses on the importance of rela-tional expectations and conflict rules that regulate appropriate and inap-propriate conflict behaviors in the relational system. Although the cognitive-exchange tradition emphasizes relational partners as rational, calculating beings in the conflict management process, the rules-interventionist tradi-tion emphasizes the emotionally charged, rule-governed conflict negotiation process. The latter tradition also calls attention to the important role of third-party intervention (e.g., the use of conflict mediators) in re-establishing boundaries and rules in the intimate conflict situation. The systems-interactionist tradition (e.g., Gottman, 1979, 1991; Ting-Toomey, 1983), on the other hand, emphasizes the importance of delineating the verbal and nonverbal patterns of intimate conflict that impact on the quality of the relationship. Finally, the dialectical perspective (Baxter & Simon, 1993) emphasizes the importance of managing dialectical tensions (such as autonomy-connection, closedness-openness, and predictability-novelty dialectics) and relational contradictions in personal relationships.

Although these four approaches have provided us with powerful, explan-atory frames to understand the relationship between sets of intimate conflict concepts in Western-based nations (e.g., Australia and the United States), major questions concerning these four traditions remain to be addressed in the cross-cultural intimate conflict arena. For example, to what extent are these theoretical frames generalizable to other non-Western cultures? How can we best uncover functionally equivalent and non-equivalent interpersonal conflict concepts in different cultures? How can we use the interpersonal conflict research findings in nonethnocentric ways of practice? With these questions in mind, we now turn to a discussion of the factors that shape intimate conflict in individualistic and collectivistic cultures. We return to answer the questions raised here in the recommendations' section of the chapter.

Intimate Conflict Assumptions

In order to understand intercultural intimate conflict, we have to first understand the basic assumptions of intimate conflict from a cross-cultural point of view. "Intimate conflict assumptions" can include implicit cultural values, morality, relational attitudes, and expectations that influence intimate conflict negotiation processes. The implicit "theories" or assumptions we hold in "locating" and processing intimate conflict within our own cultures have a profound influence on how we manage intercultural intimate conflict (see Fig. 3.1). Our cultural lenses, in sum, influence the ways we view conflict and mediate conflict processes.

The term *cross-cultural* is used throughout this chapter to refer to a personal relationship or intimate conflict that is comparative in nature (e.g., comparing mate selection attitudes in cultures X, Y, and Z), whereas the term *intercultural* is used to refer to intimate conflict encounter that entails two (or more) conflict parties from different cultural communities (e.g., intimate conflict that involves a Japanese and German romantic couple). In this section, major factors and findings that contribute to cross-cultural intimate conflict are reviewed. The discussion is based on inferences from studies in cross-cultural heterosexual dating or marital relationships (because of available data) in the recent years.

Cultural Values. To understand differences and similarities in intimate conflict across cultures, it is necessary first to have a perspective to explain why and how cultures are different or similar. A cultural variability perspective refers to how cultures vary on a continuum of variations in accordance to some basic dimensions or core value characteristics. While there are many dimensions in which cultures differ, one dimension that has received consistent attention from both cross-cultural communication researchers and psychologists around the world is individualism-collectivism. Countless cross-cultural studies (Hofstede, 1980, 1991; Schwartz & Bilsky, 1990) provide theoretical and empirical evidence that the value orientations of individualism and collectivism are pervasive in a wide range of cultures.

The value dimension of individualism-collectivism, as existing on a continuum of value tendency differences, can be used as a beginning point to understand some of the basic relational differences and similarities in individualistic-based or group-based cultures. Essentially, individualism refers to the broad value tendencies of a culture in emphasizing the importance of individual identity over group identity, individual rights over group rights, and individual needs over group needs. In contrast, collectivism refers to the broad value tendencies of a culture in emphasizing the importance of the "we" identity over the "I" identity, group obligations over individual rights, and ingroup-oriented needs over individual wants and desires. Ingroups tend to influence a wide variety of interpersonal situations in collectivistic cultures more so than individualistic cultures. The characteristics of perceived common fate, common outside threat, proximity, and/or perceived similarity (e.g., in demographic attributes, activities, preferences, institutions, religious beliefs) often serve as important determinant of the ingroup/outgroup boundary (Triandis, 1989, p. 509).

Macrolevel factors such as ecology, affluence, social and geographic mobility, migration, cultural background of parents, socialization, rural/urban environment, mass media exposure, education, and social change have been identified by Triandis (1988, 1990) as some of the underlying factors that contribute to the development of individualistic and collectivistic value tendencies. High individualistic value tendencies have been found in the United States, Australia, Great Britain, Canada, the Netherlands, and New Zealand, to name only a few. High collectivistic value tendencies have been uncovered in Indonesia, Columbia, Venezuela, Panama, Ecuador, and Guatemala, to name only a few (Hofstede, 1991). In intercultural communication research (e.g., Gudykunst & Ting-Toomey, 1988), Australia, Canada, and the United States have been identified consistently as cultures with predominant individualistic value tendencies, whereas (comparatively speaking) empirical evidence revealed that China, Taiwan, Korea, Japan, and Mexico can be identified as cultures that subscribe to predominant collectivistic, group-based values. In addition, within each culture different ethnic or speech communities can also display distinctive low (i.e., individualistic) and high (i.e., collectivistic) community sharing value tendencies. For example, members of first-generation Asian and Latin American immigrant cultures in the United States may retain some strong group-oriented, communal sharing characteristics.

In a capsule description, the core building block of individualism-collectivism lies in its relative emphasis on the importance of the "independent self" or the "interdependent self" orientation. In using the terms *independent construal of self* and *interdependent construal of self* to represent individualistic versus group-oriented identity, Markus and Kitayama (1991) argued that the placement of our sense of self-conception in our culture has a profound influence on our communication with others. They argued that the sense of individuality that accompanies this independent construal of self includes a sense of "oneself as an agent, as a producer of one's actions. One is conscious of being in control over the surrounding situation, and of the need to express one's own thoughts, feelings, and actions of others. Such acts of standing out are often intrinsically rewarding because they elicit pleasant, ego-focused emotions (e.g., pride) . . . the acts of standing out, themselves, form an important basis of self-esteem" (p. 246). Conversely, the sense of self-conception that accompanies an interdependent construal of self includes an: "Attentiveness and responsiveness to others that one either explicitly or implicitly assumes will be reciprocated by these others. . . . One is conscious of where one belongs with respect to others and assumes a receptive stance toward these others. . . . Such acts of fitting in and accommodating are often intrinsically rewarding, because they give rise to pleasant, other-focused emotions (e.g., feeling of connection) while diminishing unpleasant ones (e.g., shame)" (p. 246). Thus, the identity locus of independent versus interdependent construal of self frames our existential and affective experience and serves as an anchoring point in terms of how we view ourselves and our communicative actions.

Dion and Dion (1988), in reviewing the various individual and cultural perspectives to the study of romantic love, concluded that the "high divorce rate that characterizes [U.S.] American society is due in good part to the culture's exaggerated sense of individualism" (p. 286). They observed further that for U.S. Americans, romantic love often poses an existential dilemma. Although many U.S. individuals (especially coming from a Eurocentric value system) desire to "lose" themselves in a love relationship, they also have to struggle with the dialectical tensions of autonomy and connection that face the relationship. Conversely, for many individuals in the collectivistic cultures (e.g., China and Japan), the experience of being "in love" is contextualized and constructed within other social and personal network relationships (e.g., work relationships, extended family relationships, and close friendships).

Overall, intimate partners in individualistic cultures have to spend enormous time and energy dealing with personal privacy and autonomy issues on one hand, and relatedness and connection on the other. Comparatively speaking, intimate partners in the collectivistic cultures have to learn to work out their relational commitment to their loved ones or spouses on one hand, and deal effectively with their family and social/personal network issues on the other. For individualists, the autonomy-connection dialectic is viewed often by intimate partners as consisting of "me-you" oppositional forces. For collectivists, autonomy and connection are viewed often as complementary essences (e.g., from the Chinese Taoist conceptualization of *yin* and *yang*) that contribute to the relational whole. The dialectical tensions that exist in collectivistic, intimate relationships are evoked often through the couple's relational commitment being at odds with ingroup loyalties and obligations (e.g., toward family group, extended family group, work group, and/or caste group).

Drawing from the literature concerning individualistic and collectivistic value tendencies, we can summarize several observations here. For the independent construal of self-individualists, intimate conflict often means:

(a) Working out autonomy or privacy issues while learning to deal with connection or interdependence in the relationship (and vice versa), (b) experiencing the loss of personal freedom while feeling the pressures of relational constraint, and (c) clarifying the pulls and tugs of personal commitment and relational commitment in the relationship. For the interdependent construal of self-collectivists, intimate conflict often means: (a) Working out connection as a couple and separation from immediate family, extended family, and/or network influences; (b) dealing with the couple's identity while fulfilling ingroup role obligations; and (c) redefining and reassessing personal/relational commitment and social role commitment. While cultural values assert a strong influence on the meaning of intimate conflict in different cultures, gender belief systems within and between cultures also profoundly influence the intimate conflict negotiation process.

Gender Morality.   The incorporation of gender is critical in any serious attempt to understand the intimate conflict negotiation process between females and males. Gender identity-based issues can serve as additional explanatory bases of cross-cultural gender-linked intimate conflict behavior. Culture is viewed, however, as the widespread intrinsic webs in which gender roles are defined and modified. As Bem (1993), in her newly developed enculturated-lens theory, observed:

> Just as [U.S.] American society constructs me-firsters by situating people in a culture whose discourses and social practices are organized around the lens of radical individualism, so, too, does it construct conventionally gendered women and men by situating people in a culture whose discourses and social practices are organized around the lens of androcentrism [i.e., male-centeredness] and gender polarization. . . . These social practices program different and unequal social experiences for males and females; they also transfer the androcentric and gender-polarizing lens of the culture to the psyche of the individual. (p. 143)

Although the term *program* is a strong word to use to explain the cumulative yet subtle enculturation experiences of males and females in the U.S. society, there is no doubt that culture does play a strong role in defining and shaping the stereotyped expectations of gendered role behavior. The term *gender* is used throughout this chapter (as a parallel term to *culture*) to refer to the gender-based belief system that is developed from the primary sex role socialization process of individuals in a particular society. This belief system influences how individuals in different societies define and hold expectations of "femaleness," "maleness," or both. The term *sex difference* will be used (especially in accordance with the selected studies) whenever research finding have used biological sex difference as the basis of differentiation. The findings of female–male differences and similarities in cross-cultural personal relationship development can help us to understand intergender, intimate conflict with more depth and richness.

Although Bem (1993) proposed a macrostructural theory of female and male-gendered role development based on the assumptions that men and women are placed in markedly unequal positions in the U.S. societal structure, and that the androcentric social practices have priviledged the male point of view, Gilligan (1982) attempted to present a more balanced approach in her viewing of the gendered "voices." According to Gilligan (1988), two distinctive voices signal the differences in female and male conceptualizations of moral issues in the United States. Based on her research, Gilligan (1988) argued that U.S. males and females have developed different ways of thinking about what constitutes a "moral problem and how such problems can be addressed or solved" (p. xvii). Gilligan (1988) elaborated that: "Self, others, and the relationship between them — can be organized in different ways, depending on how "relationship" is imagined and constructed. From the perspective of someone seeking or loving justice, relationships are organized in terms of equality [or equity]. . . . From the perspective of someone seeking or valuing care, relationship connotes responsiveness or engagement, a resiliency of connection that is symbolized by a network or web" (pp. xvii–xviii). Morality problems as framed in the morality of justice revolve around conflicting claims between self and others, and can be resolved by invoking impartial rules, principles, or standards. Conversely, morality problems as cast in the morality of caring revolve around issues of relationships, and they can be approached through the activities of caring (Lyons, 1988). Thus, while the morality of justice is grounded in an independent construal-of-self world view, the morality of caring is grounded in an interdependent construal-of-self system. Both females and males can subscribe to either the morality of justice or morality of caring, or both—depending on the influence of culture, family socialization process, personality characteristics, self-conception issues, developmental consciousness, etc.

Overall, according to the work of Gilligan and others (Gilligan, Ward, & Taylor, 1988; Tannen, 1990; Wood, 1986), whereas European American males in the U.S. culture tend to subscribe to the morality of justice ideology, European American females tend to engage in the morality of caring ideology (see Bem's critique, 1993). In the cross-cultural personal relationship arena, VanYperen and Buunk (1991), for example, uncovered greater U.S. male and female differences (with a mixed sample of Asian Americans, European Americans, and African American students in Hawaii and Pennsylvania) in their orientations toward intimate relationships than in a Dutch sample in the Netherlands. Overall, they found that U.S.

females tend to consider strong-mindedness and getting along with in-laws as positive contributions, and inattentiveness and antisociability as negative contributions to an intimate relationship, more so than the U.S. males. No significant male and female orientations, however, are uncovered in the Dutch sample. In another study (Stimpson, Jensen, & Neff, 1992), results revealed that females in China, Korea, Thailand, and the United States prefer a more caring morality than males. They explain their results in terms of both sex role socialization differences and biological and reproductive differences.

Based on the findings of previous cross-cultural gender-related studies, we can draw out some specific implications concerning intimate conflict here. Potential intergender misunderstanding and conflict may arise when individuals (and predominantly, perhaps, males) rely primarily on: (a) Using the morality of justice principles to interpret an intimate conflict situation, (b) applying impartial rules and standards to manage a conflict episode, (c) separating the discussion of conflict substantive issues from socioemotional issues because of their justice stance, and (d) holding different relational criteria such as relational equity and relational fairness in defining a satisfying, intimate relationship. Concurrently, potential intergender conflict may occur when individuals (and predominantly, perhaps, females) rely primarily on: (a) Using the morality of caring principles to define an intimate conflict situation, (b) using relational attachment and relational network responses in negotiating a conflict episode, (c) viewing conflict substantive issues integratively with socioemotional issues because of their connected stance, and (d) holding different relational criteria such as relational sociability and relational responsiveness in defining a satisfying, intimate relationship. Intergender conflict can be effectively managed when both sexes realize that possible differences in viewing conflict negotiation patterns exist and that both can widen their conflict conceptualizations and repertoires through mindful observations and conscious learning and unlearning processes. In addition, rather than focusing on gender polarities, both sexes need to realize that common grounds do exist between the two gender groups. While culture influences the degree of differentiation and overlap between female's and male's role expectations and behavior, the power of skillful interpersonal negotiation can help to transform societal constraints (especially in individualistic cultures more so than in collectivistic cultures) concerning intercultural and intergender polarization.

Relational Attitudes and Expectations.   Moving beyond cross-cultural gender morality, more specific differences and similarities have also been found in the areas of attitudes and expectations toward romantic love, romantic stability, and mate selection preferences across cultures. *Rela-*

tional attitudes and expectations are defined here as the general inclinations/ feelings and anticipatory tendencies of "how things should reasonably occur" concerning different relationship types or stages. Both cultural values and gender morality influence relational attitudes and expectations in interpersonal relationships. Expectation violations and hence conflicts are likely to occur when relational partners hold fundamentally different attitudes and expectations of how to approach romantic love and how to communicate in romantic love relationships.

In a study that compares individualistic and collectivistic orientations (i.e., the United States and China) toward romantic love, Gao (1993) observed that for the U.S. romantic couples involved in the study, sharing interests and activities served as important intimacy barometers; for the Chinese romantic couples, shared perceptions concerning the exchange of intellectual intimacy (partners helping each other to clarify ideas and thoughts) acted as an important dimension in Chinese romantic relationship development. In a related study, Gao (1991) also uncovered four common romantic communication themes that cut across the two cultures: mutuality of openness, involvement, shared nonverbal meanings, and positive relational assessment. She observed that although cultural variations may exist in relational initiation and major relationship transitional stages, more cultural similarities may exist in the relational stability stage between individualistic and collectivistic cultures. Thus, the role of relational stage can serve to mitigate either culture or gender differences, or both.

Whereas Gao's (1991, 1993) work focused on general relational differences and similarities in romantic couples in China and the United States, Chang and Holt (1991) focused on the Chinese indigenous concepts such as *yuan* (relational karma) and *kuan-hsi* (interlocked ties) in developing both social and personal relationships. It should not come as a surprise that for many "traditional-oriented" collectivists (e.g., India or Taiwan), relational karma serves as a strong motivational basis (or spiritual reason) for couples to either stay together (regardless of the relational sufferings) or exit the relationship (i.e., especially from the Chinese Buddhist conceptualization in perceiving that relational *yuan* is over). Whereas members of Western cultures often tend to emphasize the controllability and the predictability aspects of interpersonal relationship development (and, hence, generating enormous relational stress and personal pressure), members of Eastern cultures often tend to emphasize the conjoint effect of both personal effort and relational karma in resolving personal relationship issues.

In a different line of research, Simmons and associates (Simmons, Vom Kolke, & Shimizu, 1986; Simmons, Wehner, & Kay, 1989) revealed that German and U.S. respondents scored higher in their attitudes of valuing romantic love than did Japanese respondents. It appears that while romantic love is treasured where kinship ties are weak (as in some individualistic cultures), romantic love is diluted where kinship ties are strong (as in some collectivistic cultures). In times of loneliness, members in collectivistic, group-oriented cultures often can find solace and comfort via family or close social/friendship networks. Their orientations, thus, toward romantic love are less intense (see Gao's 1993 study, in which Chinese couples reported less passionate love in romantic relationships than did U.S. romantic couples) and they tend to emphasize companionship love more so than passionate love. In addition, we can also infer that when romantic couples encounter intimate conflict in collectivistic cultures, family and close social/personal networks become actively involved in the conflict mediation process, more so than do comparable romantic couples in individualistic cultures.

Whereas collectivists would tend to seek advice from informal, third-party mediators (e.g., siblings, close friends, or even supervisory mentors) concerning major relational crisis decisions, individualists would tend to seek counsel from formal, third-party help (e.g., therapists and counselors) in resolving their major relational or marital crises. For collectivists, close friends are the ones that have a wholistic picture of the ebbs and flows of the history of intimate conflict situation; therefore, collectivists view it natural to turn to friends (or family members) for conflict advice and empathy. Conversely, individualists often view close friends as not able to stay "objective", thus, it is more natural for individualists to turn to "neutral" professional experts for help to resolve major relational crises and pains. For collectivists, going to therapists or counselors for relational or family advice and counseling means "airing the dirty laundry" in the public arena, and can potentially cause the couple or the family to lose tremendous face.

From romantic love to sexual jealousy, Buunk and Hupka (1987) compared emotional reactions to various forms of sexual jealousy in seven nations: Hungary, Ireland, Mexico, the Netherlands, the former Soviet Union, the United States, and the former Yugoslavia. Results indicate that in all of these nations, flirting and sexual involvement of one of the partners with an interloper evokes strong negative emotional reaction and conflict. Concurrently, behaviors such as dancing, hugging, and kissing lead to different jealousy intensity in different cultures. In all instances, females are more upset when their partners kiss someone else than are males. In addition, males react more negatively to sexual fantasies of their partners about another person than do females. Overall, although cultural and sex difference variations have been uncovered in this study, the cultural and gender meanings that are attached to baseline concepts such as "jealousy" and "flirting" need to be addressed more interpretively and systematically.

Finally, in an ambitious cross-cultural study project, Buss and collabo-rators (Buss, 1989; Buss et al., 1990) conducted a study of mate preferences in 37 samples. Overall, the greatest cultural variation is found in the attitude of premarital chastity. In addition, respondents in China, India, Iran, and Nigeria have been found to occupy the "traditional" collectivistic view of mate selection preferences, whereas respondents in the Netherlands, Great Britain, Finland, and Sweden have been found to occupy the "modern" individualistic view of mate selection preferences.

Overall, however, results of Buss et al.'s (1990) study indicate that there are remarkable similarities of mate selection preferences among the 37 samples. Nearly all samples placed mutual attraction–love as the top-rated characteristic (it is important to note here that the concept of "relational karma" or many cultural indigenous concepts were not included as mate selection criteria on the self-report survey). In addition, nearly all samples placed tremendous value on the mate characteristics of dependability, emotional stability, kindness–understanding, and intelligence. In terms of overall male and female differences, males tended to evaluate potential mates in terms of physical appearance, youth, and health. Females tended to evaluate potential mates in terms of earning potential, ambition, and industriousness. The authors used a resource exchange/reproductive perspective to explain the differences in findings between genders.

To briefly summarize here, findings from several major cross-cultural personal relationship studies indicate that both significant differences and commonalities exist in individuals' attitudes toward different romantic relationship constructs. In individualistic cultures, most individuals typically "fall in love" first (which sometimes involves intensive dating procedure) and then get married. However, for members in many collectivistic cultures (e.g., in India, Iran, and Northern Nigeria, in which arranged marriages are still the norm), they get married and then learn to fall in love and also carry out basic marital responsibilities and obligations. For individualists, their attitudes toward romantic love are high and intense and they expect passion from the feelings of being in love. For collectivists, their attitudes toward romantic love are pragmatic, caring, and responsibility-based, and they expect a sense of harmonized companionship from the feelings of being in love. Thus, intercultural intimate conflict can occur when individualistic spouses do not live up to the relational expectations of the collectivists, and, likewise, when collectivistic spouses do not live up to the romantic ideals of their individualistic partners. In addition, while individualistic spouses believe in actively managing and controlling the relational conflict process, collectivistic spouses often believe in relational karma or fate in accepting and flowing with the ups and downs of the relationship. Finally, while individualistic partners prefer to turn to professional help in resolving major relational crises and problems, collectivistic spouses prefer to either "wait the crisis out" or turn to close friends or family members for solace and comfort. Thus, even in the third-party help-seeking arena, special attention needs to be paid to the different attitudes and expectations that intercultural partners hold toward the role of third-party mediation process.

The selective studies reviewed thus far have highlighted both cultural and gender differences and similarities in personal relationship development values, morality, attitudes, and expectations. While differences in intimate conflict do exist between individualistic and collectivistic perspectives, considerable commonalities and convergent points also exist. More important, it appears that mutual attraction–love and other positive relational qualities can mitigate the effect of culture and gender on intimate conflict negotiation processes. We now turn to a discussion of the actual negotiation processes of cross-cultural intimate conflict.

Intimate Conflict Processes

The intimate conflict processes include the factors of conflict norms and rules, conflict emotional expressions, and conflict styles and strategies. Intimate conflict negotiation processes are guided by the implicit conflict norms and rules of a culture, the appropriate and inappropriate emotional expressions of intimate conflict in relationship to the context, and the conflict styles and strategies that constitute the intimate conflict negotiation process.

Intimate Conflict Norms and Rules.   Drawing from the literature of both social and personal relationship conflict, we can infer that a relational equity model guides intimate conflict management in many individualistic cultures and a communal orientation model underscores intimate conflict negotiation in many collectivistic cultures. The term *relational equity model* emphasizes the importance of utilizing equity norms and rules in resolving social and personal conflict issues. In addition, a relational equity model stresses the importance of romantic couples in weighing the costs and benefits of the overall personal relationship, gauging the costs of intimate conflict against overall relational investment size, and comparing attractive available alternatives in the horizon (Rusbult, 1987). A relational equity model is also more outcome oriented rather than process oriented in intimate conflict. On the other hand, a communal orientation model refers to the importance of the use of equality norms and rules to uphold group and relational harmony (or facework issues) during social and intimate conflict situations. In either social or intimate conflict, the model emphasizes the importance of weighing the costs and benefits of family and personal network reactions, lifelong relational goals, a sense of indebtedness, and long-range obligatory reciprocity in different conflict relational situations. It is also more process oriented than outcome oriented.

For example, results in the social conflict literature (for a review, see Ting-Toomey, 1994a) indicate that individualists often use the norm of equity (self-deservingness norm) to resolve task-oriented conflicts, whereas collectivists tend to use the equality norm (equal distribution norm) to uphold harmony in the task-oriented interaction group. In addition, Leung and Bond (1984) and Leung and Iwawaki (1988) indicated that U.S. individualists typically prefer to use the equity norm in dealing with reward allocation system in group conflict interaction. In comparison, Chinese collectivists oftentimes prefer to use the equality norm to deal with ingroup members and thus avoid group disharmony. However, like their individualistic cohorts, collectivists prefer the application of the equity norm when competing with members of the outgroups, especially when the conflict involves competition for scarce resources in the system. In a recent set of studies, Leung and associates (Bond, Leung, & Schwartz, 1992; Leung, Au, Fernandez-Dols, & Iwawaki, 1992) further argued that expectancies based on animosity reduction (i.e., perceived capability of a procedure in reducing animosity between the disputants) and process control (i.e., perceived control over the development of disputes) act as cultural-general predictors of conflict procedure preferences.

In the intimate conflict arena, it has been found that U.S. Americans appear to subscribe to an equity orientation in intimate relationships more than do the Dutch (VanYperen & Buunk, 1991). Those who feel that their relational partners contribute equitably to the relationship reported more relationship satisfaction than those who feel underbenefited and overbenefited. However, for the Dutch sample, overbenefited individuals tended to report a higher level of relationship satisfaction than did underbenefited individuals. No difference was uncovered between the two samples concerning the communal orientation to intimate relationship. In a related line of research (Rusbult, 1987; see also Healey & Bell, 1990) concerning relational equity and conflict responses, findings in the United States reveal that large relational investment size encourages the use of "constructive" conflict responses (such as assertive "voice" and active "loyalty") and discourages the use of "destructive" responses (such as "exit" and "neglect"). On the other hand, attractive alternatives encourage the use of "active" conflict responses (such as voice and exit—"shape up or ship out") and that no alternatives promote the use of "passive" conflict responses (such as neglect and passive loyalty). In addition, U.S. males tend to prefer the use of neglect and exit responses in dealing with intimate conflict more than do U.S. females. U.S. females prefer the use of voice and loyalty responses more than do U.S. males in negotiating intimate conflict interaction.

Although no specific cross-cultural EVLN (i.e., exit, voice, loyalty, and neglect conflict response) studies (i.e., to the best of my knowledge) have been conducted in the collectivistic cultures, we can make some predictions here. Drawing from the individualism-collectivism cultural variability perspective, we can speculate that romantic or married couples who subscribe to collectivistic values would tend to use passive conflict responses (such as neglect and passive loyalty) more so than active responses in handling relational dissatisfaction (i.e., when the intimate conflicts are within tolerable conflict thresholds). In addition, within a collectivistic community, males and females would display distinctive intimate conflict responses—males would tend to use more passive conflict responses and females would tend to use more active conflict responses. Cultural gendered socialization process and power inequity between females and males can serve as possible explanatory bases for the latter observation. Thus, the underlying logics and meanings that account for such differences often outweigh behavioral differences or similarities (e.g., the use of withdraw or avoidance responses can mean a control move or a harmonizing intimate conflict move) observed between the cultures or gender groups. It will not be surprising, however, when the recurring intimate conflict patterns become so intolerable that the romantic couples would use action-oriented responses such as voicing (and, perhaps, lobbying of network help), physical violence, and even surprising leave-taking exit behavior as the final resolution of the prolonged intimate conflict episode.

Finally, in individualistic cultures, many couples would tend to take a "monochronic time" (i.e., a discrete, linear approach; Hall, 1983) view in settling intimate conflict, whereas in group-oriented cultures, many couples would tend to take a "polychronic time" (i.e., a continuous, spiral, lifelong approach; Hall, 1983) view in dealing with different intimate conflict disputes. For individualists, time is a precious commodity that should not be wasted; for collectivists, time is a fluid stream that one learns to flow with good friends and loved ones by both sides. Persons who subscribe to a monochronic rhythmic pattern would tend to work on developing clear goals and instrumental solutions to end the intimate conflict situation. They are more outcome oriented in attempting to resolving the conflict situation and they tend to take a more short-time, closure viewpoint in wanting to end the conflict. In comparison, persons who operate with a polychronic rhythmic pattern would tend to emphasize the process (e.g., from avoidance to seemingly contradictory compromising moves) in which the intimate conflict is being negotiated. They work at delicate facework moves of give and take—reciprocating and compensating in different areas beyond the immediate conflict situation. They also tend to take a long-term viewpoint in resolving different conflict issues.

Conflict Emotional Expressions.   Intimate conflict is, essentially, an emotionally laden experiential phenomenon. According to Markus and Kitayama (1991), individuals who subscribe to the independent construal of self-perspective would often tend to engage in ego-based emotional expressions, whereas individuals who operate from an interdependent construal of self-perspective would often tend to engage in other-focused emotional expressions. Ego-based emotions can include the protection of self-pride, vulnerabilities, and hurts. Other-focused emotions can include the concerns with the intimate partner's feelings, vulnerabilities, and emotional reactions.

In two extensive, detailed reviews (Mesquita & Frijida, 1992; Russell, 1991) of cultural variations and emotions, clear cross-cultural emotional expression and decoding differences (and also similarities) were identified by the reviewers. Drawing from the reviewers' lines of arguments and rich cultural examples, we can infer that cultural norms do exist in regulating the expression of "aggressive" or "negative" emotional reactions such as anger, fear, hostility, jealousy, resentment, and sadness in intimate conflicts in different cultures (for culture-specific examples, see Mesquita & Frijida, 1992). We can also infer from their discussions and from the work of Markus and Kitayama (1991) (see also the work of Matsumoto, Wallbott, & Scherer, 1989) that masking or downplaying facial expression techniques are used in monitoring the display of aggressive emotions in many Asian, collectivistic cultures (e.g., in Japan and Korea) during either social or intimate conflict negotiation stages.

Drawing from the abundant examples from the two reviews (especially pertaining to different collectivistic communities) and Markus and Kitayama's (1991) work, several observations can be made. First, although for many Western, individualistic cultures open emotional expressions are viewed as caring and engaging signals in dealing with intimate conflict, for many Asian, collectivistic cultures restrained emotional composures are viewed as self-disciplined, mature signals in handling intimate conflict (especially in terms of stereotyped male role performance). However, for many Middle Eastern cultures effusive emotional expressions and the use of layered language to signal displeasures and anger are employed. Facework emotional expression styles — from understated styles to effusive, expressive styles — underscore collectivistic conflict emotional expressions. Second, although basic conflict emotions such as anger, fear, and sadness can be viewed as pancultural conflict emotions, cultural display rules of when to express what nonverbal emotions (and to whom in what context) differ from one cultural community to the next. Third, facework-related emotions (e.g., emotions of shame, disgust, contempt, feeling insulted, being embarrassed, dignity, honor, etc.) are important bargaining resources in both social and intimate conflict in individualistic and collectivistic cultures. Although how members in different cultures define and interpret the meanings of face-related insults, dignity and/or honor can vary from one cultural group to the next, and from one ethnic group to the next (for a discussion on face, see the next section; see also Ting-Toomey, 1994b).

Finally, in testing self-report emotional expression patterns of intimate relationships in three cultures (France, Japan, and the United States) from a cultural rules' approach, Ting-Toomey (1991) uncovered that French and U.S. American respondents tended to report a significantly higher level of love commitment and disclosure maintenance activities in their relationships in comparison to their Japanese counterparts. In addition, U.S. American respondents reported a higher degree of relational ambivalence in comparison to the Japanese sample. The French sample reported the lowest degree of intimate conflict in comparison to the Japanese and the U.S. samples. Overall, females reported a significantly higher degree of love commitment, disclosure maintenance, and interpersonal conflict problems than did their male cohorts. Results are explained from the individualism-collectivism and low- and high-context viewpoints.

Conflict Styles and Strategies. Conflict styles and strategies refer to the patterned responses of managing conflicts in a variety of communicative situations. In addition to individualism-collectivism, Edward T. Hall's (1976, 1983) low-context and high-context communication framework may help to enrich our understanding of intimate conflict style variations. According to Hall (1976), human transaction can be basically divided into low-context and high-context communication systems: "HC [high context] transactions featured preprogrammed information that is in the receiver and in the setting, with only minimal information in the transmitted message. LC [low context] transactions are the reverse. Most of the information must be in the transmitted message in order to make up what is missing in the context" (p. 101). In general, low-context communication refers to communication patterns of linear logic interaction approach, direct verbal interaction mode, disciplined to relaxed nonverbal emotional expressions, and sender-oriented persuasive value (Ting-Toomey, 1985). High-context communication (on a continuum of differences) refers to communication patterns of spiral logic interaction approach, indirect verbal negotiation mode, understated nonverbal nuances (e.g., for some Asian, collectivistic cultures) or animated/effusive emotional expressions (e.g., for many African, Latin American, and Middle Eastern, collectivistic cultures), and interpreter-sensitive value (Ting-Toomey, 1985). Low-context (LC) communication patterns have been typically found to be predominant in individualistic cultures, and high-context (HC) communication patterns have been found to be predominant in collectivistic cultures.

For individualistic LC romantic couples, the bargaining resources in intimate conflict typically revolve around individual pride and self-esteem, individual space and attention, individual "I" assertive emotions, and, more important, the approach or style of dealing with intimate conflict itself. Comparatively, for collectivistic HC couples, the negotiation issues in intimate conflict typically revolve around the couple's love and commitment for each other in competition with their extended ingroup loyalty and obligations. Additionally, especially for collectivists, the relational level of dealing with conflict is often involved directly or indirectly with the meanings of face and facework management strategies in intimate conflict.

In a capsule summary, Ting-Toomey (1988) argued in her face-negotiation theory that although the concept of face exists in all cultures, how people interpret and manage face (from face loss to face gain, from face saving to face giving) issues differ across cultural, gender, and relational lines. Face, in her theory, is defined as the claimed sense of self-respect in any social and personal interactive situations. Her theory also delineates 12 theoretical propositions to account for the relationship among cultural variability, facework, and specific conflict styles. Based on the line of facework research (see, for example, Cohen, 1991; Ting-Toomey, Gao, Trubisky, Yang, Kim, Lin, & Nishida, 1991) in relating individualism-collectivism with facework concerns and conflict styles, clear evidence indicates that whereas individualists tend to be more self-face oriented in managing conflict, collectivists tend to be more other-face oriented in negotiating conflict. In addition, U.S. respondents have been found to use more dominating, competing conflict strategies than Japanese and Korean respondents. Finally, Chinese and Taiwanese respondents have been found to use more compromising, obliging, and avoiding conflict strategies than their U.S. counterparts in managing task-oriented, social conflict. The generalizability of this line of research, however, awaits to be further tested in different cross-cultural intimate conflict relationship settings and in different gender variability settings.

In this section, the assumptions of intimate conflict, norms and rules, emotional expressions, and conflict styles and strategies in individualistic and collectivistic cultures have been explored. Overall, there are more empirical studies that have tested the possible differences and similarities of managing social conflict in individualistic and collectivistic cultures than intimate conflict studies. Taken as a whole, the underlying intimate conflict assumptions, the intimate conflict norms and rules, and conflict emotional expressions and styles all act as a powerful package to affect the triggering points, the processes, and the outcomes of intimate conflict in different cultures. Table 3.1 presents cross-cultural intimate conflict assumptions concerning individuals who subscribe to either individualistic or collectivistic value tendencies.

MANAGING INTERCULTURAL INTIMATE CONFLICT: PRACTICAL IMPLICATIONS

The selective studies reviewed in the last section and the implications drawn from these studies have highlighted cultural and gender differences and

TABLE 3.1
Managing Cross-Cultural Intimate Conflict*

Key Concepts	Individualistic Values	Collectivistic Values
Identity	Independent construal of self	Interdependent construal of self
Conflict primary dialectic	Me-you dialectic	We-they dialectic
Gender morality	Morality of justice	Morality of connectedness
Relational model	Relational equity	Communal orientation
Conflict resources	Self-face, control	Mutual-face, harmony
Conflict norms	Equity principles	Ingroup principles
Conflict issues	Separate task and socio-emotional dimensions	Integrate task and socio-emotional dimensions
Conflict resolution tempo	Short-term view	Long-term view
Conflict emotional expressions	Conflict emotional openness	Conflict emotional restraint or conflict emotional effusiveness
Conflict styles and strategies	Direct, controlling, and dominating styles	Indirect, obliging, and avoiding styles
Third-party intervention	Seek formal intervention	Seek informal intervention

*Note. From Ting-Toomey (in press). Reprinted by permission.

similarities in intimate conflict. We can draw out some practical implications in this section for romantic couples and practitioners who are interested in practicing effective intimate conflict management. Effective management of intimate conflict across cultural and gender lines contain three basic dimensions: knowledge, attitudinal orientations, and interaction skills. We first discuss these dimensions in that order.

Intimate Conflict Knowledge

Of all the dimensions of managing intercultural intimate conflict, knowledge is the most critical dimension that underscores the other dimensions of effective intimate conflict management. Without cultural-sensitive knowledge, romantic couples cannot learn to uncover the implicit "ethnocentric lenses" or assumptions they use to interpret and evaluate events in their romantic conflict situations. They would not be able to be self-reflexive about their own ethnocentric or androcentric (or gynecentric) attitudinal states. Without the rudiments of cultural and gender knowledge, romantic couples would not know how to communicate appropriately, effectively, and creatively across cultural and gender lines. Knowledge here refers to the process or condition of in-depth understanding of certain phenomena via a range of information gained through conscious learning and personal experiences and observations. Overall, the knowledge base in this chapter focuses on a discussion of individualistic and collectivistic value tendencies and gender morality issues in the construction of intimate conflict in female–male personal relationships. In addition, cultural-specific knowledge and personal experiential knowledge would also complement and enrich our understanding of intimate conflict across specific cultural and gender boundaries.

In approaching intimate conflict, intercultural romantic couples should keep in mind that intimate partners (they can be both males and females) who subscribe to an individualistic, independent construal of self-perspective would tend to: (a) Emphasize a "me–you" dialectical pull model of intimate conflict; (b) view intimate conflict issues as revolving around privacy/independence issues on one hand, and romantic connection/interdependence issues on the other; (c) use the morality of justice to invoke rules and equity in the relationship; (d) approach intimate conflict from a relational equity framework (e.g., calculating rewards, benefits, and possible alternatives); (e) emphasize the separation of substantive issues and relational issues in managing intimate conflict; (f) desire to seek out formal, third-party experts for help in resolving intimate conflict problems because of their neutral stance; (g) often approach intimate conflict from a monochronic, linear viewpoint; (h) emphasize the importance of accomplishing clear, intimate conflict outcomes and goals and the importance of conflict closure; (i) stress emotional openness in intimate conflict; and (j) emphasize verbal directness and conflict controlling strategies (i.e., one up/one down messages) in managing intimate conflict. It is critical to point out that gender variations (and also personality and contextual variations) exist in the subscription of the independent construal of self-, individualistic perspective.

On a continuum of differences, romantic couples (they can be both females and males) whose partners subscribe to a collectivistic, interdependent construal of self-perspective would tend to: (a) Experience relational dilemmas of a "we-they" dialectical pull model of intimate conflict; (b) view intimate conflict issues as issues revolving the couple as a unit on one hand and extended family and personal/social network problems (e.g., unwanted relational advice and interference) on the other; (c) use the morality of caring or connectedness to frame and evaluate the intimate conflict situation; (d) operate from a communal, face-oriented grid in assessing intimate conflict; (e) view both substantive issues and relational, face-related issues in intimate conflict as tightly intertwined; (f) prefer to seek informal third parties' counsel and advice because of their holistic knowledge of the relational, conflict situation; (g) approach intimate conflict from a polychronic, rhythmic pace; (h) emphasize the importance of the fluid process of compromising and countercompromising the intimate conflict negotiation procedure; (i) not express their conflict emotions overtly or openly; and (j) use avoiding or obliging conflict styles to gloss over intimate conflict and often emphasize conflict endurance and patience. Again, gender variations (and personality and contextual variations) exist in the subscription of the interdependent construal of self-, collectivistic perspective toward intimate conflict.

Although differences in intimate conflict exist between the individualistic and collectivistic perspectives, it is important to remember that considerable common grounds also exist. More important, it appears that mutual attraction-love, and other positive relational qualities, can moderate the effect of culture and gender on intimate conflict negotiation processes. However, if couples do not develop an in-depth knowledge base concerning the implicit "theories" and the "root causes" of intercultural and intergender conflict as experienced by their romantic partners, the fundamental problems of the intimate conflict may continue to linger indefinitely in their relationships and conflict spirals may continue to occur.

In terms of the knowledge base for the conflict practitioners (such as conflict mediators, counselors, and marital therapists), here are some suggestions: (a) Remember that members from different cultures hold fundamental different assumptions of approaching third-party help; (b) cultural members (especially from collectivistic cultures) often do not have clear knowledge and expectations of third-party intervention procedures; (c) conflict practitioners need to articulate the goals of the counseling or mediation procedure clearly and learn to mediate and forge linkages between contrastive cultural values (such as individualism and collectivism); (d) knowledge about face interactive issues (such as face giving and face saving, or face protecting and face compensating) and ingroup network face issues is a must — especially in dealing with collectivistic clients; (e) affirm the importance of the role of culture in approaching intimate conflict; (f) learn how cultural values shape female and male roles in a particular culture; and (g) learn the sources (and, perhaps, the ethnocentric or androcentric biases) of one's mediation or therapeutic training techniques and honestly assess such techniques to see if they are culturally inclusive and sensitive to the needs of diverse groups and persons. In short, an effective conflict practitioner often serves the role of an intercultural mediator or broker who mediates between the needs of members of two contrastive cultures. She or he also learns to develop a superordinate "third culture" (e.g., emphasizing relational superordinate goals and possible common cultural linkages) for the couple so that they have a common dialogue or common ground on which to proceed.

Attitudinal Orientations

Attitudinal orientations refer to our cognitive and affective predispositions with regard to communicating with people who are different (or similar). In modifying and managing our attitudinal orientations in intercultural and intergender intimate conflict, we can work at cultivating the following attitudinal schema: mindfulness, attitudinal flexibility, attitudinal responsiveness, and intergroup depolarization process.

Mindfulness. The concept of *mindfulness* can serve as the first effective step in raising our attitudinal awareness of differences and similarities that exist in intercultural or intergender intimate conflict. Langer's (1989) concept of mindfulness helps individuals to tune in conscientiously to their habituated mental scripts and be meta-aware of their own expectations and biases. According to Langer, if mindlessness is the "rigid reliance on old categories, mindfulness means the continual creation of new ones. Categorization and recategorization, labeling and relabeling as one masters the world are processes natural to children" (p. 63).

To engage in a mindfulness state, an individual needs to learn to (a) be open to new information, (b) create new categories, and (c) be aware that multiple perspectives typically exist in viewing a basic phenomenon (Langer, 1989, p. 62). New information concerning intercultural intimate conflict can be acquired through attending intercultural conflict workshops, intercultural and interethnic readings, personal experiences and observations, and, more important, the willingness to suspend judgments concerning the intimate conflict situation. Creating new categories means learning to acquire culturally sensitive and gender-sensitive vocabularies and concepts, and to be able to engage in conflict discourse inclusively and nondefensively. Finally, being aware that multiple perspectives exist means individuals, as active learners, can accommodate and apply divergent viewpoints (such as both individualistic and collectivistic perspectives) in analyzing and experiencing an intimate conflict situation.

Attitudinal Flexibility. With mindfulness and conscious practice of the mindfulness state, romantic couples should be able to develop a flexible mindset to deal with conflict problems more creatively and contextually. Attitudinal flexibility means, at the same time, that the romantic couples now understand the cultural and gender constraints on the interpretation and the communication processes of intimate conflict, they are not trapped by such constraints. Rather, they are able to renegotiate the cultural or gender boundaries of their conflict situation—displaying cultural and gender respect for differences in values when needed and, simultaneously, forging their private culture and developing their own norms and rules in their relationships.

Attitudinal Responsiveness. Attitudinal responsiveness means that romantic couples are able to affirm the cultural ways of being and the gendered ways of responding in their relationships. During intimate conflict situations, they learn to observe cultural signals of communicating and they are sensitive to both the verbal and nonverbal nuances of their romantic partners. They are also able to pay close attention to the relational and the meta-relational (i.e., reflective of culture and gendered socialization processes of being or doing) assumptions of their partners and are able to empathsize and experience their world view and their belief systems of how to communicate appropriately and effectively in the intimate conflict negotiation process.

Intergroup Depolarization Process.   Whether we are discussing female--male differences or cross-cultural differences, we are all at one point human beings first, then cultural beings and gendered beings. However, because of the unconscious programming of our enculturation process, we learn first to be ethnocentric beings and androcentric or gynecentric (female-centeredness, Bem, 1993) beings before coming back full circle, to learn to become genuinely free-spirited, human beings. By learning first the patterns of differences and similarities between the sexes or between cultures, we can develop sensitivity and understanding for why things occur the way they do. Ultimately, however, we have to go back full circle to realize that, indeed, genuine human bonds can be forged and genuine intimate relationships can be developed between females and males, between males and males, and between females and females across cultural and ethnic lines.

Perhaps moving beyond the concept of mindfulness, the concept of *soulfulness* (Moore, 1992) may help to explain this point here. Moore (1992) pondered:

> To the soul, memory is more important than planning, art more compelling than reason, and love more fulfilling than understanding. We know we are well on the way toward soul when we feel attachment to the world and the people around us and when we live as much from the heart as from the head. We know soul is being cared for when our pleasures feel deeper than usual, when we can let go of the need to be free of complexity and confusion, and when compassion takes the place of distrust and fear. Soul is interested in differences among cultures and individuals, and within ourselves it wants to be expressed in uniqueness if not in outright eccentricity. (pp. 304–305)

To develop a sense of soulfulness is to develop a sense of connection with ourselves and with others. It calls for a special art of "placemaking"—for including self and other in the same sacred space, equally, and through genuine collaborative dialogue. Although the soul knows no color, it nevertheless radiates brilliant hues and tones because of its existential diversity of the basic human experiences.

Interaction Skills

Interaction skills refer to our communication abilities to use our knowledge wisely and display our attitudinal orientations flexibly and responsively (via explicit verbal and nonverbal messages) in a wide variety of communication situations. Many communication skills are useful to promote a sense of cultural and intergender inclusiveness and to manage intimate conflict effectively. We will discuss four specific skills here: responsive listening, perception checking, value clarification sharing skills, and face-management interaction skills.

Responsive listening means making a strong commitment to listen despite the fact that you are both clearly entangled in an intensive conflict situation. When you make a strong commitment to listen, you are physically and emotionally present with your romantic partner despite the fact that intimate conflict is in progress. Responsive listening is attending to the words and the nonverbal nuances that your romantic partner is signaling to you. Interestingly, the Chinese character for "listening" or "ting" means "focused listening with your ears, eyes, and heart" without distractions. In responsive listening you have to signal to your partner that you are genuinely listening and that you display verbal and nonverbal congruent messages in your responsive listening process.

Perception checking is another intimate conflict management skill that can be actively practiced by both partners in the intimate conflict situation. Perception checking means actively using paraphrases (i.e., restating the partner's previous message in your own words) to check out whether you are interpreting the thoughts and feelings of your partner accurately. Perception checking also needs to be conducted in a culturally-sensitive manner. For individualists, perception checking typically emphasizes the use of explicit verbal messages. For collectivists, however, they may emphasize indirect inquiries, probing statements, and even silence as a reflective perception-checking skill.

Practicing values' clarification and sharing skills mean that both partners have to constantly underestimate that they actually understand where their relational partner is coming from, even if they have known each other for a long period of time. Romantic partners have to assume the responsibilities of cultural ambassadors in teaching their partners about their own cultural/ethnic values and norms and their gendered values and norms if they deem these values and beliefs as salient to their core identities and beings. They have to learn to clarify for their partners their cultural values (especially during peaceful moments of their relationship lives rather than during the intimate conflict process) and their gendered beliefs systems. They also should engage in progress reports of their own changes and transformed beliefs systems at different points in their relationship.

Finally, all relational partners and conflict practitioners should learn facework management skills in dealing with social or intimate conflict. Facework management skills basically address the fundamental core issue of human self-respect. All human beings like to be respected and be approved of in their daily interaction with their colleagues and their loved ones. However, how they manifest such self-respect needs and concerns, and how others accord them with respect and dignity may differ from one culture to the next, and may also differ between the sexes (see, for example, Tannen, 1990; and Ting-Toomey, 1994b).

Romantic couples and conflict practitioners should be able to use the skills of responsive listening, perception checking, values' clarification, and facework management in a wide variety of conflict negotiation sessions. Improving conflict interaction skills can improve our basic attitudinal orientations in conflict, and, vice versa, transforming our attitudinal orientations can help us to display our conflict interaction skills more consistently and effectively. Knowledge, however, is viewed as the grid in which flexible conflict learning attitudes and creative interaction skills can be developed.

Additionally, on a more specific level, conflict intervenors or mediators should learn to: (a) Sequence long warm-up sessions for collectivists who need therapeutic or mediation help; (b) ask for family and extended family background information concerning their reactions to the intimate conflict; (c) observe nonverbal signals and indirect, verbal messages that are implicitly expressed by the collectivists; (d) monitor power imbalance between the intercultural romantic couples; (e) schedule separate therapeutic sessions for wives and husbands and solicit cultural information concerning female and male roles in the family and workplace in their respective societies; (f) show facework-sensitivity skills; (g) discern any language and also verbal and nonverbal communication problems between husbands and wives; (h) actively imagine how the cultural context (and also how the immigration experience) frames the conflict perspectives of the clients; (i) actively paraphrase their cultural and personal points of view; and (j) schedule long exit-closure sessions and follow-up sessions so that the clients do not feel abandoned "out in the cold" all of a sudden.

In addition, the conflict mediators or therapists may have to refer the conflict case to other competent, bilingual conflict mediators or therapists if they sense that the clients have language problems. Overall, all conflict intervenors should take a mandatory course in intercultural communication before mediating intercultural conflict. More importantly, all intercultural conflict intervenors have to develop a sense of personal ethics that is sensitive to their multicultural clients' needs and the needs of the community at large. Although many intercultural intimate conflicts may indeed involve genuine cultural and intergender value clashes, many intimate conflicts may also revolve around familiar, basic interpersonal relationship issues such as fundamental relational respect, love, commitment, power, and passion.

INTERCULTURAL INTIMATE CONFLICT: THEORETICAL AND RESEARCH RECOMMENDATIONS

This chapter focuses on a discussion of how culture and gender construct and frame intimate conflict in personal relationship development. Future theorizing on intercultural intimate conflict can proceed along the following lines. First, future theorizing on the relationship between culture (or ethnicity or gender) and intimate conflict can benefit the most by focusing on the identity-negotiation process (see, for example, Ting-Toomey, 1993a). This would involve examining the conditions that lead to a salient identity construction process and how certain aspects of individuals' identities influence their approach to intimate conflict negotiation. Additionally, a cultural-sensitive dialectical approach in accounting for the relationship between interactive self and intimate conflict strategies offers numerous theoretical possibilities.

Second, it is critical that more effort should be paid to uncovering underlying triggering points that constitute explosive, intimate conflict interaction. What triggers intimate conflict in one culture may deem to be nonsalient in other cultures. In addition, more attention should be given to the cross-cultural and gendered threshold points of accommodating and tolerating different kinds of intimate conflict in different personal relationships and in different contexts (e.g., public versus private). More attention also should be paid concerning the cultural ways of emotional expressions in reacting to different types of intimate conflict.

Third, more concerted theoretical effort is needed to investigate the role of emotional expressions (or repressions) during intercultural intimate conflict. What conflict-related emotions are appropriate or inappropriate to be displayed in different cultures? What conflict-related emotions are experienced as universal feelings, and what conflict-related emotions are deemed as cultural-specific feelings in different cultural communities? How do grieving and healing processes of intimate conflict differ across cultures?

Fourth, we also need to seek answers to the questions of: What constitute the verbal and nonverbal conflict interaction patterns of intercultural intimate conflict? Do satisfied couples structure and negotiate intercultural conflict in a certain manner that are distinctly different from that of dissatisfied couples? Do the two groups go through different conflict negotiation phases or similar phases? Do intercultural couples who are happily married display a higher level of perceptual accuracy concerning their intimate conflicts than intercultural couples who are unhappily married? Do happily married, intercultural couples develop a "third culture" that transcends their respective cultures? What are the resources or communication strategies they use to develop a complementary, third culture outlook in their marriages and to reconcile their various cultural, religious, and even gender differences? To the best of my knowledge, no systematic interaction analysis studies have yet been conducted on marital couples from diverse ethnic and cultural backgrounds and, thus, the generalizability of the results on marital interaction research can only apply to primarily European American couples to the neglect of African American couples, Asian American couples, Latino American couples, Native Indian couples, mixed-marriage couples, and mixed-heritage couples. Of course, even within a broad cultural or ethnic label such as African American, culture-of-origin diversity and individual diversity exist. This latter point, however, should not deter us from seeking out complex interaction patterns with complex solutions.

Finally, more culturally sensitive relational outcome variables such as relational acceptance, relational fatalism, and relational longitudinal viewpoint (i.e., adding to the already existing variables of relational satisfaction, quality, and commitment) should be incorporated in the study of relationships between intercultural intimate conflict and intimate conflict outcomes. Most of the present relational outcome variables in existing interpersonal and marital communication literature follow strongly an independent construal of self-individualistic outlook. A stronger communal-oriented, collectivistic model is urgently needed to balance the picture of female and male relatedness across different cultural and ethnic domains.

Methodologically, more triangulated research efforts are needed to uncover cultural indigenous concepts that assume high salience in interpersonal conflict management in different cultural communities. Intensive case study, ethnographic interviewing, discourse analysis, and diary and log methods, in conjunction with experimental and survey methods, can help to yield different types of data set to enrich our understanding of cultural-specific intimate conflict process. Of course, each research method also comes with its inherent strengths and problems that need to be untangled as much as possible before the researchers walk into the field to collect data.

Multicultural/multiethnic and mixed-sex teams may be one of the ways to help to untie some of the ethnocentric knots that hinder theorizing and research on intercultural and interethnic conflict. With genuine, collaborative efforts in a face-to-face multicultural dialogue format, the field of intercultural and interethnic conflict can be advanced productively and constructively. In addition, the incorporation of theorists and researchers from interdisciplinary areas would also help to bring new and alternative insights into this multicultural, collaborative dialogue effort. Finally, more studies need to be designed to capture the turning points of intercultural intimate conflict in the relational trajectory of the couple's relationship life stage and, also, to test how such turning points influence their mixed-heritage children and their conceptualizations of intercultural intimate conflict.

In this chapter, I have only scratched the surface of cross-cultural and intercultural intimate conflict. Although most theorizing effort in interpersonal intimate conflict follows an independent construal of self-, individualistic tradition, a volume on intimate conflict such as this book will help to open a window on the immense diversity of the different ways of knowing and different ways of being in managing intimate conflict in diverse forms of social and personal relationship.

REFERENCES

Baxter, L. (1988). A dialectical perspective on communication strategies in relationship development. In S. Duck (Ed.), *Handbook of personal relationships* (pp. 257-273). New York: Wiley.

Baxter, L. (1990). Dialectical contradictions in relationship development. *Journal of Social and Personal Relationships*, 7, 69-88.

Baxter, L., & Simon, E. (1993). Relationship maintenance strategies and dialectical contradictions in personal relationships. *Journal of Social and Personal Relationships*, 10, 225-242.

Bem, S. (1993). *The lenses of gender: Transforming the debate on sexual inequality.* New Haven, CT: Yale University Press.

Bond, M., Leung, K., & Schwartz, S. (1992). Explaining choices in procedural and distributive justice across cultures. *International Journal of Psychology*, 27, 211-225.

Buss, D. (1989). Sex differences in human mate preferences: Evolutionary hypotheses tested in 37 cultures. *Behavioral and Brain Sciences*, 12, 1-49.

Buss, D. et al. (1990). International preferences in selecting mates: A study of 37 cultures. *Journal of Cross-Cultural Psychology*, 21, 5-47.

Buunk, B., & Hupka, R. (1987). Cross-cultural differences in the elicitation of sexual jealousy. *The International Journal of Sex Research*, 23, 12-22.

Cahn, D. (Ed.). (1990). *Intimates in conflict: A communication perspective.* Hillsdale, NJ: Lawrence Erlbaum Associates.

Cahn, D. (1992). *Conflict in intimate relationships.* New York: Guilford.

Chang, H. C., & Holt, G. R. (1991). The concept of *yuan* and Chinese interpersonal relationship. In S. Ting-Toomey & F. Korzenny (Eds.), *Cross-cultural interpersonal communication* (pp. 28-57). Newbury Park, CA: Sage.

Cohen, R. (1991). *Negotiating across cultures: Communication obstacles in international diplomacy.* Washington, DC: U.S. Institute of Peace.

Dion, K. L., & Dion, K. K. (1988). Romantic love: Individual and cultural perspectives. In R. Sternberg & M. Barnes (Eds.), *The psychology of love* (pp. 264-287). New Haven, CT: Yale University Press.

Gao, G. (1991). Stability in romantic relationships in China and the United States. In S. Ting-Toomey & F. Korzenny (Eds.), *Cross-cultural interpersonal communication* (pp. 99-115). Newbury Park, CA: Sage.

Gao, G. (1993, May). *An investigation of love and intimacy in romantic relationships in China and the United States.* Paper presented at the International Communication Association convention, Washington, D.C.

Gilligan, C. (1982). *In a different voice: Psychological theory and women's development.* Cambridge, MA: Harvard University Press.

Gilligan, C. (1988). Remapping the moral domain: New images of self in relationship. In C. Gilligan, J. Ward, & J. Taylor (Eds.), *Mapping the moral domain* (pp. 3–20). Cambridge: Harvard University Press.

Gilligan, C., Ward, J., & Taylor, J. (Eds.). (1988). *Mapping the moral domain.* Cambridge, MA: Harvard University Press.

Gottman, J. (1979). *Marital interaction: Experimental investigations.* New York: Academic.

Gottman, J. (1991). Predicting the longitudinal course of marriages. *Journal of Marital and Family Therapy, 17,* 3–7.

Gudykunst, W., & Ting-Toomey, S. (1988). *Culture and interpersonal communication.* Newbury Park, CA: Sage.

Hall, E. T. (1976). *Beyond culture.* New York: Doubleday.

Hall, E. T. (1983). *The dance of life.* New York: Doubleday.

Healey, J., & Bell, R. (1990). Assessing alternative responses to conflict in friendship. In D. Cahn (Ed.), *Intimates in conflict: A communication perspective* (pp. 25–48). Hillsdale, NJ: Lawrence Erlbaum Associates.

Hofstede, G. (1980). *Culture's consequences: International differences in work-related values.* Beverly Hills, CA: Sage.

Hofstede, G. (1991). *Cultures and organizations: Software of the mind.* London: McGraw-Hill.

Langer, E. (1989). *Mindfulness.* Reading, MA: Addison-Wesley.

Leung, K., Au, Y.-F., Fernandez-Dols, J. M., & Iwawaki, S. (1992). Preference for methods of conflict processing in two collectivistic cultures. *International Journal of Psychology, 27,* 195–209.

Leung, K., & Bond, M. (1984). The impact of cultural collectivism on reward allocation. *Journal of Personality and Social Psychology, 47,* 793–804.

Leung, K., & Iwawaki, S. (1988). Cultural collectivism and distributive behavior. *Journal of Cross-Cultural Psychology, 19,* 35–49.

Lyons, N. (1988). Two perspectives: On self, relationship, and morality. In C. Gilligan, J. Ward, & J. Taylor (Eds.), *Mapping the moral domain* (pp. 21–48). Cambridge, MA: Harvard University Press.

Markus, H., & Kitayama, S. (1991). Culture and the self: Implications for cognition, emotion, and motivation. *Psychological Review, 98,* 224–253.

Matsumoto, D., Wallbott, H., & Scherer, K. (1989). Emotions in intercultural communication. In M. Asante & W. Gudykunst (Eds.), *Handbook of international and intercultural communication* (2nd ed., pp. 225–246). Newbury Park, CA: Sage.

Mesquita, B., & Frijda, N. (1992). Cultural variations in emotions: A review. *Psychological Bulletin, 112,* 179–204.

Montgomery, B. (1993). Relationship maintenance versus relationship change: A dialectical dilemma. *Journal of Social and Personal Relationships, 10,* 205–224.

Moore, T. (1992). *Care of the soul: A guide for cultivating depth and sacredness in everyday life.* New York: HarperCollins.

Rusbult, C. (1987). Responses to dissatisfaction in close relationships: The exit-voice-loyalty-neglect model. In D. Perlman & S. Duck (Eds.), *Intimate relationships: Development, dynamics, and deterioration* (pp. 209–237). Newbury Park, CA: Sage.

Russell, J. (1991). Culture and the categorization of emotions. *Psychological Bulletin, 110,* 426–450.

Schwartz, S., & Bilsky, W. (1990). Toward a theory of the universal content and structure of values. *Journal of Personality and Social Psychology, 58,* 878–891.

Simmons, C., Vom Kolke, A., & Shimizu, H. (1986). Attitudes toward romantic love among American, German, and Japanese students. *The Journal of Social Psychology, 126,* 327–336.

Simmons, C., Wehner, E., & Kay, K. (1989). Differences in attitudes toward romantic love of French and American college students. *The International Journal of Social Psychology, 129,* 793–799.

Stimpson, D., Jensen, L., & Neff, W. (1992). Cross-cultural gender differences in preference for a caring morality. *The Journal of Social Psychology, 132,* 317–322.

Tannen, D. (1990). *You just don't understand: Women and men in conversation.* New York: Morrow.

Thurnstone, M. (1992). The quiet immigration: Foreign spouses of U.S. citizens, 1945–1985. In M. Root (Ed.), *Racially-mixed people in America* (pp. 64–76). Newbury Park, CA: Sage.

Ting-Toomey, S. (1983). An analysis of verbal communication patterns in high and low marital adjustment groups. *Human Communication Research, 9,* 306–319.

Ting-Toomey, S. (1985). Toward a theory of conflict and culture. In W. Gudykunst, L. Stewart, & S. Ting-Toomey (Eds.), *Communication, culture, and organizational processes* (pp. 71–86). Beverly Hills, CA: Sage.

Ting-Toomey, S. (1988). Intercultural conflict styles: A face-negotiation theory. In Y. Kim & W. Gudykunst (Eds.), *Theories in intercultural communication* (pp. 213–235). Newbury Park, CA: Sage.

Ting-Toomey, S. (1991). Intimacy expressions in three cultures: France, Japan, and the United States. *International Journal of Intercultural Relations, 15,* 29–46.

Ting-Toomey, S. (1993). Communicative resourcefulness: An identity negotiation perspective. In R. Wiseman & J. Koester (Eds.), *Intercultural communication competence* (pp. 72–111). Newbury Park, CA: Sage.

Ting-Toomey, S. (1994a). Managing intercultural conflicts effectively. In L. Samovar & R. Porter (Eds.), *Intercultural communication: A Reader* (7th ed., pp. 360–372). Belmont, CA: Wadsworth.

Ting-Toomey, S. (Ed.). (1994b). *The challenge of facework: Cross-cultural and interpersonal issues.* Albany, NY: State University of New York Press.

Ting-Toomey, S. (in press). *Effective intercultural communication.* New York: Guilford.

Ting-Toomey, S., Gao, G., Trubisky, P., Yang, Z., Kim, H. S., Lin, S.-L., & Nishida, T. (1991). Culture, face maintenance, and styles of handling interpersonal conflict: A study of five cultures. *The International Journal of Conflict Management, 2,* 275–296.

Triandis, H. (1988). Collectivism vs. individualism: A reconceptualization of a basic concept in cross-cultural psychology. In G. Verma & C. Bagley (Eds.), *Cross-cultural studies of personality, attitudes, and cognition* (pp. 60–95). London: Macmillan.

Triandis, H. (1989). The self and social behavior in different cultural contexts. *Psychological Review, 96,* 506–520.

Triandis, H. (1990). Cross-cultural studies of individualism and collectivism. In J. Berman (Ed.), *Nebraska symposium on motivation* (pp. 41–133). Lincoln, NE: University of Nebraska Press.

VanYperen, N., & Buunk, B. (1991). Equity theory and exchange and communal orientations from a cross-cultural perspective. *The Journal of Social Psychology, 13,* 5–20.

Wood, J. (1986). Different voices in relationship crises. *American Behavioral Scientist, 27,* 273–301.

4

Mediating Peer Conflicts in Education Contexts: The Maintenance of School Relationships

Nancy A. Burrell
University of Wisconsin

Dudley D. Cahn
SUNY College at New Paltz

Conflict is typically defined as an expressed struggle between interdependent parties based on the perception of incompatible goals (Hocker & Wilmot, 1992; Putnam & Poole, 1987). However, not all conflicts are alike. Conflicts vary according to intensity, number of parties, degree of interdependence, importance of outcomes, power imbalances, and so on. In addition, some conflicts are categorized as disputes. Moore (1986) suggested that emerging conflicts are disputes in which participants acknowledge the dispute, realize that most issues have been clarified, but are unable to enact workable problem-solving or negotiation processes. For the purpose of this chapter, we define *dispute* as a conflict that has reached a point where the parties are unable to resolve the issues by themselves due to a breakdown in communication, and normal relations are unlikely until the dispute is resolved. Because mediation may restore communication and normalize relations, it is often used to resolve disputes (Volpe & Witherspoon, 1992).

Mediation is the intervention into a dispute by an impartial third party who has no authority/power in the decision-making process. A mediator's immediate goal is to build a cooperative context for negotiation, encouraging disputants to collaboratively create their own agreement. Ideally, a mediator's long-term goal is to educate disputants about their future conflict needs and their ability to create additional solutions to problems (Folberg & Taylor, 1984; Keltner, 1987; Kressel & Pruitt, 1985; Moore, 1986).

Because disputes have plagued school systems at all levels, many educators have taken an interest in mediation. "Since the establishment of school-based mediation in the early 1980s, school projects are now recognized as a successful part of school reform" (Dreyfuss, 1990, p. 24). School officials have found that mediation programs empower students to resolve student-to-student disputes. Mediation training gives students more knowledge to make choices, generate options, make decisions, communicate, and solve problems (Dreyfuss, 1990). The purpose of this chapter is to characterize various school-based mediation programs, by discussing the history, philosophy, training, and program implementation. School-based mediation utilizes members from the community to promote programs, train mediators, and evaluate training and program effectiveness.

HISTORY OF SCHOOL-BASED MEDIATION

Mediation in the school setting began in New York City, when teachers became active in nonviolence training during civil rights actions of the 1960s. The Quakers began an educational project (Children's Project for Friends), and their goal was to link nonviolence training with conflict resolution techniques for children. In 1972, this project became the Children's Creative Response to Conflict (CCRC). Student training helped to develop skills in cooperation, communication, affirmation, and conflict resolution.

By the late 1970s, other educators were focused on peace and global education, integrating the impact of nuclear war into their lesson plans. Teachers encouraged students to explore the roots of global violence. In the 1980s, these same educators formed a group, Educators for Social Responsibility (ESR), a national association committed to teaching nonviolence and social awareness. In short, the national agenda for this group was to promote peace and socially conscious education, which closely aligned with the Quakers' educational goals.

At about the same time, members in the San Francisco mediation community recognized the need to incorporate conflict resolution training into school curricula. Helena Davis wrote the first Conflict Manager curriculum for the elementary schools based on her strong convictions that fourth and fifth graders were developmentally ready for mediation training (Cheatham, 1988). According to Cohn and her associates, "The development of competent relations with peers has long been viewed as one of the most important psychosocial tasks of childhood" (Cohn, Patterson, & Christopoulos, 1991, p. 315). Researchers suggest that successful peer relations are important indices of social competence and, when lacking, predict later adjustment problems (Coie, Dodge, & Kupersmidt, 1990). This elementary curriculum has been extended and revised for middle and high school programs.

In 1984, at a small conference involving community mediators, peace educators, and ESR members, the group recognized that their efforts were isolated and what was needed was a national network. Thus, the National Association for Mediation in Education (NAME) was formed to become the integrator for resource and curricula materials (Cheatham, 1988).

To summarize, there are a number of successful school mediation programs around the country, such as New York's Children's Creative Response to Conflict (CCRC) and San Francisco's Community Board Program (CBP). The primary goal of all of these programs is to reverse the high rates of in-school aggression. Although conflicts at the elementary, middle, and high school levels differ in type, intensity, and complexity, the goal of every mediation program is to help students resolve their conflicts productively.

An inherent assumption in all of the school mediation training programs is that although conflict is a part of everyday life, individuals can grow from conflictual interactions. This growth occurs in practicing and enacting communication and other skills that promote creative problem solving (Burrell & Bankier, 1992; Levy, 1989). Students, teachers, and administrators who participate in the training programs soon recognize that there is no one "right" answer/solution but, rather, multiple ways to resolve problems. In short, training programs focus on the need to creatively explore solutions to conflict so that all disputants are satisfied with the outcome. Mediation training may begin as early as the third grade, and is reinforced up to and throughout high school. In other words, most school systems use conflict training at elementary, middle, and high school levels. Overall, training activities are designed to promote cooperation, communication skills, and self-esteem.

Pedagogical Assumptions

Promoters of school mediation programs envision a change in learning climates by teaching responsible cooperation. Responsible cooperation "is internally motivated, a positive consequence to a positive choice" (Bluestein, 1988, p. 33). Rather than solving students' problems, students are challenged to make responsible decisions and recognize the implications/consequences of their choices. According to Bluestein (1988), "Every time we solve a problem for our students, we rob them of a chance to practice responsibility and interfere with their learning and growth" (p. 161). Furthermore, a guiding principle for problem solving in the classroom is that the person with the problem is responsible for its resolution.

Teaching responsible decision making begins in a "peaceable classroom," which refers to a warm, caring environment that reflects cooperation, communication, tolerance, positive emotional expression, and conflict resolution (Kreidler, 1984; 1990). Current social conflicts should be discussed in classrooms in ways that are balanced and developmentally appropriate. Students need to learn to participate responsibly in democracy. Students in a peaceable classroom learn how to define *peace* according to their own values, to examine their definitions from many angles, and to learn the concrete skills in living according to those definitions. Teaching concepts of peace and conflict reflects a pedagogy based on cooperative problem solving, conflict resolution, listening to other points of view, community building, decision making, and critical thinking.

School-Based Mediation Models

There are several types of mediation models, which vary according to how formal or informal the dispute is dealt with and how immediate the conflict resolution process is enacted. For example, the playground model uses conflict managers to intervene at the time a dispute occurs. Using this informal mediation model, students help their peers resolve their problems during recess, at lunch, or before/after school. Conversely, many schools use a more formal intervention process, in which: (a) the conflict is referred to mediation by an administrator, teacher, or student; (b) those students named in the referral are approached about the possibility of using mediation to resolve their dispute; and (c) if students mutually agree to follow the procedures for mediation described by the student mediator, the session takes place (Burrell & Vogl, 1990). Because schools' needs vary, program trainers/advisors individually tailor the intervention process, selection and training of school mediators, and program operation. Using the Milwaukee Public School System and SUNY–The College at New Paltz as exemplars, school-based peer mediation programs are discussed.

Mediation in Milwaukee

School-based mediation was introduced to several pilot schools in the Milwaukee Public School System in 1985. Because of the disruptive and sometimes violent school climates, several concerned administrators and teachers approached the Milwaukee Mediation Center to elicit help in developing and implementing a training program for elementary, middle, and high school students. The directors of the mediation center recognized that they were not curriculum specialists, yet they were intrigued about promoting the mediation process within the schools and community. The solution was to train key administrators, human resource personnel, and teachers at elementary, middle, and high school levels. This small group worked closely with the directors and each other to develop and coordinate training materials for their respective schools.

It should be noted, however, that the student-mediation program was not immediately embraced by the school system (i.e., school board, superintendent, administrators, teachers, students, and parents). In fact, eight years later, about one third of the system's schools are still attempting to implement mediation training/programs. Because of budget cuts, loss, and/or change in personnel, and resistance to another "new" program, school-based mediation has grown slowly in Milwaukee. What follows is a summary of how to initiate a mediation program, in addition to a description of the training program.

Initiating a school-based mediation program.   When starting a mediation program, whether it is in the elementary, middle, or high school, there are three steps to ensure a successful program (Bankier, 1992). First, the staff needs to agree that the philosophy of teaching students peacekeeping skills is important. Because students will be out of class for the training (which takes 12 to 15 hours) as well as during mediation sessions, the staff needs to agree that these peacekeeping skills are just as important as reading, writing, and math. In short, in order for the program to succeed, it is critical that parents, administrators, and faculty at each school support the implementation and maintenance of the mediation process (Araki, 1990).

The second step involves training the staff. Ideally, the whole staff should be trained so that everyone understands and appreciates the mediation process. The obvious long-term goal is to empower students to resolve their own disputes rather than relying on adults to intervene in what sometimes may seem petty and inconsequential conflicts to outsiders. According to Maxwell (1989), "It is the self-empowering aspect of mediation—the fact that disputants actively participate and make decisions about issues and problems that are central to their own lives—that establishes mediation as an important tool in the fostering of self-regulation, self-esteem, and self-discipline" (p. 151). Promoters of school-based mediation programs point to the notion that students should be given a greater role in determining their own destiny (Araki, 1990; Maxwell, 1989). Teachers can also begin to implement some of the conflict resolution skills in their classroom. Staff training centers on understanding conflict, learning and practicing the mediation process, learning techniques to train students, and how to implement a schoolwide program.

Finally, the third step is identifying coordinators who will take charge in implementing the schoolwide program (e.g., training students for 12 to 15 hours; Bankier, 1992). Coordinators not only train students, but also promote the mediation process throughout the school and community. In short, coordinators function as part public relations personnel and part training/development personnel. The first year is critical to the success or failure of the program. According to Araki (1990), "90 percent of the success factor of any pilot project hinges on the start-up phase" (p. 53). Most coordinators work at building a base of support to help promote their programs because they are committed to the view that "the school is a microcosm of its larger community . . ." (Araki, 1990, p. 52).

The Training Program for Milwaukee Public Schools. Coordinators combine procedures/activities from several established conflict resolution programs (e.g., the Community Board Program, Wakefield Peer-Mediation Program, and the Children's Creative Response to Conflict). For example, conflict training from the Community Board Program emphasizes that the starting point in finding a resolution to conflict is the active participation of the disputants. In other words, it is crucial that disputants communicate directly to one another: why the dispute is important, what it means to them, what emotions it has generated, what fears and angers exist, and what attitudes and impressions they have of the other disputant. To summarize, each of these programs emphasizes the importance of communication, a nonviolent approach to conflict, and creative problem solving.

Training begins with a discussion about the importance of communication during conflict interactions. Unfortunately, in most disputes, participants' communication has deteriorated or totally broken down. A critical role, then, of the mediator is to facilitate the communication process by encouraging disputants to communicate directly to each other. It is in this direct communication that several things happen. First, each disputant learns something about the dispute from the other's perspective. Second, each disputant sees how the other disputant could have misunderstood his or her actions, motives, and intents. Third, each disputant learns what is at stake for the other and what the conflict means to him or her. Each disputant comes to appreciate the significance of the relationship that generated the dispute in the first place. Finally, teachers and students learn how to become empowered to express and resolve their own conflicts, thereby improving the quality of their own lives (Kemmis, 1993; Sadalla, Henriquez, & Holmberg, 1987).

Next, factors that influence effective communication are emphasized, especially active listening. Several exercises are used that illustrate how stereotypes influence our perceptions of others and the importance of clarification in the communication process. Also, several activities are engaged in to reinforce paraphrasing skills and the use of positive verbal and nonverbal listening cues (e.g., "yes," "O.K.," "uh-huh," forward lean, head nodding). Student trainees view videotapes of positive communication skills, and demonstrations are conducted to help them identify poor listening cues. In short, they learn about the importance of communication and its impact during conflictual interactions.

The process of mediation is presented, and various roles a mediator can assume are described. To reinforce the need for neutrality, participants role play school conflicts that they have experienced and discuss communicative techniques/strategies that reflect unbiased/neutral perspectives. A typical role play would ask four students to resolve a dispute involving Jean, John, and two co-mediators. The dispute centers on John's belief that Jean has copied his math homework, turned in "her" paper, and received an A because he cannot find his recently completed homework assignment. Jean is upset that John has accused her of cheating. The two student mediators go through the process of helping Jean and John resolve their dispute.

Next, participants in training work on identifying positions versus interests of disputants. Exercises stress the importance of following the steps for conducting a mediation session (opening statements, identifying the conflict, making proposals, exploring options, reframing proposals, constructing a written agreement, and signing the agreement). Prospective mediators participate in four to five mock mediations and are critiqued by the training coordinator. Participation in these mock mediations provides trainees with invaluable feedback regarding their skills at structuring the session, asking questions to identify key issues, and reframing proposals to encourage creative problem solving (Burrell, Donohue, & Allen, 1990).

The process that student mediators learn is similar, regardless of their level (third through the twelfth grade). That is, the process steps involve:

1. Introducing mediators to disputants and asking if mediation is desired.
2. Gaining agreement to follow the ground rules (no interrupting, no name calling, etc.)
3. Asking each disputant for a description of the problem.
4. Paraphrasing each position.
5. Asking disputants what they could do to resolve their problem.
6. Finding out what disputants want from each other.
7. Restating respective positions.
8. Helping disputants to generate ideas toward possible solutions.
9. Asking disputants what is best for each party.
10. Restating.
11. Asking if the resolution is fair and can be carried out.
12. Finalizing the agreement and congratulating the participants (Brinkman, 1991; Burrell & Bankier, 1992).

To summarize, the content of the training program is adjusted to meet the school's goals and students' abilities and knowledge about dispute resolution processes. However, each school's training involves a minimum of 12 to 15 hours. The majority of schools that have implemented programs believe that "training should be ongoing and intensive" (Araki, 1990, p. 54). Program coordinators design a program that is adjusted to meet the audience level, training schedule, and mediation expertise for each school.

Unfortunately, the Milwaukee Public School system does not have a systemwide program coordinator. Rather, trainers are selected randomly and assigned to schools requesting training. Jobs of trainers from within the system include part-time teachers, administrators, and human resource personnel, with varying experience in mediation, ability to function as a trainer, and commitment to conflict resolution processes. Thus, training from school to school varies. Moreover, program evaluation is not uniform.

MEDIATION AT THE COLLEGE LEVEL

College-Based Mediation Models[1]

Young people operate at different levels of competence with regard to interpersonal conflict. As they age and develop mentally and emotionally, they come to understand and respond to conflict differently (Jones & Brinkman, forthcoming). Thus, any program intending to incorporate student peers as mediators must adapt its operation and mediator training to young people at that age level. Whereas the previous section examined mediation programs designed for elementary, middle, and high school students, this section presents a brief general overview of mediation designed for college-age students and then describes a specific campus mediation program at a state college in the Northeast.

According to Volpe and Witherspoon (1992), mediation in college is probably the best-known nonviolent alternative to adjudication (Folger & Shubert, 1986; Levitz, 1990). The intervention by a neutral peer trained in mediation offers the disputing students an opportunity to come together in a structured setting to talk about their differences and how they might resolve them constructively (hence the term *nonadversarial mediation*).

As in the community at large, college mediation is especially recommended in cases that involve an interpersonal relationship. When people must live near one another as in a neighborhood, residence hall, apartment complex, or trailer park; work together at a place of employment; or attend classes at a school or college setting, a breakdown in communication accompanied by harmful, negative emotions may make it difficult for disputing parties to continue living, studying, or working together in close

---

[1]The authors would like to thank Mrs. Barbara M. Geider, Vice President for Student Affairs, SUNY College at New Paltz, for her helpful suggestions on this part of the article.

proximity without escalating the conflict. In the college's classroom and residence hall environment, peer rejection and violence may be prevented or relationships repaired through mediation.

Normally, peer mediation in institutions of higher education is usually tied into the formal grievance, dispute resolution, and college/university judicial system. Folger and Shubert (1986), who conducted in-depth interviews at 20 institutions of higher education, found that disputes between students are likely to come to the attention of college staff in the Office of Vice President for Student Affairs, the Dean of Students, or the Director of Housing. The initial step in dispute resolution at all 20 institutions calls for informal resolution at the lowest level, that is, direct confrontation between disputing students. For students who are unable to settle their disputes without the intervention of a third party, three different models for incorporating mediation exist.

The required mediation model stipulates that disputing students mediate regardless of circumstances. Usually, if mediation fails to resolve the dispute, the matter is then turned over to the judicial system for a decision by someone who acts as judge or arbitrator.

The required adjudication model dictates that disputing students first formalize their dispute by submitting their differences to the campus judicial system. After they have entered the formal judicial system, the students may be encouraged to mediate as a step in the judicial process. As Levitz (1990) reported, campus disputes share with the court system the fact that cases are frequently settled prior to judgment through mediation.

The referral model promotes the idea of options, choice, and voluntary participation. It requires that disputing students first go through an intake process. This role is typically assigned to college staff in the Office of Vice President for Student Affairs. The staff member uses the intake process to explore the feasibility of mediation. The disputing students are then referred to either mediation or adjudication with the understanding that they may pursue the other option later.

Folger and Shubert (1986) also found that institutions typically manage student disputes through a centralized or decentralized operation, usually depending on the size of the institution. Smaller colleges and universities may lean toward more centralized programs, where student disputes are coordinated through a single office, usually that of the Vice President for Student Affairs, the Dean of Students, or Director of Housing. There are, however, numerous procedures to take into account the diversity of issues (e.g., academic and nonacademic). To simplify the process for students, many smaller institutions have assigned these multiple procedures to staff in a single office.

Larger institutions may lean in the opposite direction, toward more decentralized programs where no single office serves a gatekeeping function for all disputes. The administrative responsibility depends on the nature of the allegation (academic or nonacademic), where it originated (in the classroom, in a residence hall, or at a student activity), and where the student citing the dispute is enrolled (undergraduate, graduate, or professional school). In large institutions, where the sheer number of students would be burdensome, the disputes may be better handled if they are distributed over a larger domain.

The Mediation Program at the State University College at New Paltz, NY

Originally funded by the Office of Court Administration under New York State legislation, a mediation program was created in 1983 on the campus of the State University College at New Paltz. When funding permits, the Office of the Vice President for Student Affairs maintains a campus mediation institute or center, promotes the use of mediation as an alternative means of resolving conflicts, and participates in the training of campus mediators. In matters that overlap, the Vice President for Student Affairs works with the director of an off-campus community mediation center.

Goals of the Program.   Where appropriate, mediation is offered to the college's students as an alternative to campus adjudication. Essentially, its goals are (a) to serve the college as a resource for resolving disputes, (b) to prevent the escalation of disputes, (c) to help relieve the college judicial system, and (d) to teach students how to resolve their problems in a constructive manner.

Typical Cases.   Following the adjudication model, the campus judicial system refers some cases to the campus mediation program (Eaton, 1984). Those referred to mediation typically involve interpersonal conflicts—such as harassment, noise, prejudicial behavior, roommate conflicts, and romantic involvements—and intergroup conflicts. Because the residence hall environment is characterized by close living conditions, diversity of students, and difficulty in isolating oneself from others, it places stresses on interpersonal relationships, creating a need to effectively manage and resolve many different types of interpersonal conflicts (Sillars, 1980). For this reason, the staff in the Office of Residence Life at the college is actively involved in the campus mediation program.

Other cases referred to mediation involve interpersonal conflicts that exist as a result of formal judicial proceedings, in which, in the judgment of the administrative hearing officer, mediation services may be useful. Once a particular matter has been adjudicated, the disputing students may be brought together under the auspices of mediation to restore communication and repair damage done to their relationship.

Finally, remaining cases involve conflicts that stem from formal complaints alleging violation of regulations for which, in the judgment of the administrative hearing officer, informal mediation is an appropriate alternative. Even though these complaints involve the breaking of campus regulations, the nature of the case may involve a relationship or communication problem that needs to be resolved if the students are going to remain on campus.

The Campus Institute/Center.   The program is coordinated by a resident director of one of the residence halls, who is also trained as a mediator. She maintains a pool of trained mediators, some of whom are also students, student affairs staff, or faculty. Copies of signed agreements are maintained in her office.

The coordinator of the program is responsible for explaining the mediation process to the disputing students. If both parties agree to participate in mediation, a meeting is scheduled at a convenient time, mediators are asked to serve, and the process is monitored until a mutually satisfactory agreement is reached or until it becomes apparent that mediation is inappropriate for this particular dispute. Trained individuals are asked to serve in pairs as co-mediators.

The campus mediation center also conducts outreach programs within the residence halls, designed to inform students of its services, encourage them to seek mediation, and present educational programs regarding techniques for developing and maintaining healthy interpersonal relationships in general.

Training Campus Mediators   The training of campus mediators is similar to that offered at the community-based institute, except that it is conducted on campus by campus faculty and administrators. Because the campus program and the neighboring community-based program were originally funded through state legislation, the training of mediators is certified by the New York State Unified Court System's Office of Management Support (the Office of Court Administration) and supervised by a state-approved trainer. On the campus at New Paltz, the former Vice President for Student Affairs, who continues as an administrative officer at the college, is a state-approved trainer. He is assisted in the actual training by faculty from the communication department and the current Vice President for Student Affairs and her staff. This certification training program consists of 26 contact hours followed by an apprenticeship, and strives for a balance between conflict resolution theory and practice using practical exercises, including role playing. At present, students enrolled in the Interpersonal Conflict course taught by faculty from the communication department are invited to join with administrative staff from the residence halls to form a class of trainees. Although the interest among students, staff, and faculty in being trained is much greater, a decision has been made to limit the class to approximately 20 trainees.

The theoretical part of the training is conducted in a classroom setting and begins with a state-prepared videotape of three community mediation sessions that emphasize a number of key aspects of mediation. Lectures are presented on a variety of topics, including the nonviolent types of conflict resolution (adjudication, arbitration, conciliation, ombudsman intervention, and mediation), a definition of mediation, and a brief history of mediation in the United States and New York state. Mediation is then compared in greater detail to its primary alternative, adjudication, and different cultural perspectives on mediation are also described. Finally, theoretical sources of conflict, the rules theory approach to mediation, and the role of the mediator as a communicator (e.g., active listening, avoiding arousing defensiveness, helping orientation) are discussed. The theoretical material is covered in detail in Cahn (1992, pp. 40–71), which is an assigned reading.

The practical part of the training is conducted over a weekend in a workshop setting, and is based on materials contained in Aks (1984). After introducing the trainees to a description of the campus mediation program, the training begins with a Prisoner's Dilemma Simulation to emphasize the harm of competition and benefits of cooperation in resolving conflicts. Next, the trainees are introduced to the stages of successful mediation, namely, setting the stage, making an opening statement, identifying issues and fact finding, structuring the discussion, writing an agreement, and concluding the mediation. The training then takes each stage, one at a time, and combines replays of relevant portions of the state-approved videotape on mediation with practical exercises. Attention is also given to selection of a neutral site for mediation, effective arrangement of tables and chairs, and mediator communication techniques for maintaining neutrality and objectivity.

Throughout the weekend training, the focus is on the mediator's role and skill development. Essentially, trainees are taught how mediators take charge of the mediation, develop and extend resources of information, enforce rules for the session, encourage disputants to make constructive proposals, write satisfactory agreements, and fill out various forms required for data reporting and record keeping. Trainees are taught a variety of communication skills that facilitate the mediation and create an atmosphere for constructive resolution of the conflict (Burrell, Donohue, & Allen, 1990).

Toward the end of the training, a campus-prepared videotape of an entire mediation simulation is shown to illustrate a typical mediation involving college roommates. Then, trainees are assigned roles to play in fictional mediations, to be followed by critique and discussion. Every trainee plays the role of co-mediator at least once and the role of a disputant to experience what mediation is like from the disputants' point of view.

Typical Role Play. Instructions to trainers for setting up and conducting a simulated mediation were presented by Levitz (1990). Because mediation sessions are confidential, role plays normally involve fictitious situations but are similar to the types of cases that occur frequently in the community or on campus. A campus example might be as follows: A student by the name of Jim hired another student, Felecia, who lives in a nearby residence hall, to type his term paper. Jim paid Felecia in advance for the typing. When Jim went to pick up his paper on the agreed date, Felecia had only completed half of it. Jim was upset because the paper was due in a few hours. An argument ensued, and Jim demanded his money back. Felecia refused, and Jim became threatening. Felecia became frightened, and then called the campus police and pressed harassment charges against Jim, who countered by charging that Felecia had failed to meet her obligations. The case was referred by the campus police to the campus mediation center.

Trainers assign trainees roles as Jim and Felecia, take them from the classroom out into the hallway, and permit them to read about the above incident. Meanwhile, other trainees are assigned roles as co-mediators, who have no knowledge about the incident. They set up the classroom to facilitate the session and invite the disputants to enter, sit, and begin mediation. Role plays typically run for about an hour. Some resolve rather easily, while others become problematic. In each case, a discussion follows the session, whether it ends on its own or is terminated by a trainer.

Additional incidents may be invented by experienced mediators for the purposes of role playing, or taken from the literature on mediation on college campuses. In the latter situation, for example, Volpe and Witherspoon (1992) described a situation at an American college that involved an African-born international student who objected to the classroom behavior of an African-American student. After class, the two students got into a fight. Enough details of the incident were provided by Volpe and Witherspoon to enable trainees to role play the disputants during mediation. Presumably, during the mediation both trainees who role play the students have an opportunity to explain their culture and expectations until a mutual understanding is reached.

Post Training. At the completion of the training, trainees are invited by the campus mediation center to volunteer for an assignment to work with more experienced co-mediators in subsequent campus disputes. Some of the trainees may be invited to co-mediate in off-campus mediations conducted by the community-based program, or are offered advanced training for divorce/custody/visitation mediation in the county family court.[2]

CONCLUSIONS

It is important to understand that the goals of mediation training and/or conflict resolution programs are not designed to rid conflict from students' lives. Rather, these programs are aimed at giving students an opportunity to resolve conflicts in a nonviolent manner. In addition, those students who are trained as mediators gain valuable intervention skills and feel that they have contributed to improving their school environment. Integrating mediation programs into school curricula permits all students to contribute constructively and positively to the school's atmosphere.

In addition, school administrators have found that mediation programs empower students to resolve their own disputes. Dreyfuss (1990) argued that "traditional discipline works against the ethical development of children in school" (p. 25). In short, children become adversaries of school rules. Similarly, school administrators become adversaries who are trapped into a narrow set of options to deal with an increasingly diverse student population. School-based mediation is rich in its heroes, literature, and history. Through students' involvement as mediators and conflict managers, students will make choices. Through these choices, students will gain knowledge, attitudes, new experiences, and perspectives that develop creativity (Dreyfuss, 1990).

Mediation is not going to change the entire student population, nor does it mean that a student who is picked as a conflict manager/mediator and does a good job is never going to have a conflict again. What it does mean is that school systems are taking an important step toward solving one of their toughest problems, violence. To summarize, school systems who have instituted mediation programs are taking ". . . this problem and turning it into an opportunity, the opportunity to put the process of peacemaking into a workable, usable form in our schools. This will have a tremendous impact on how kids live their lives" (Bankier, 1992, p. 9).

Numerous school systems and colleges/universities across the United States have integrated into their curricula conflict resolution skills/training, whereby misconceptions about conflict are addressed and restructured. Students are taught that a conflict is what the disputants perceive it to be,

---

[2]For more information on how to set up a mediation program on a college campus, see Girard, Rifkin, and Townley (1985). Those who are interested may also wish to join the National Association of Mediators in Education (NAME), 425 Amity St., Amherst, MA 01002.

emerges out of life's everyday events, and reveals what disputants consider to be important and relevant to them. Students are also shown how the elements for resolution are found in the conflict itself. Schools that have implemented mediation programs report that utilization of the process is great, the ratio of resolution to disputes is high, and, most important, participants find the process useful and would recommend mediation to other students (Crary, 1992).

To conclude, there is viability for school-based mediation programs. Mediation increases communication, promotes understanding, and reduces hostility in the educational setting. Researchers have suggested that children who are rejected by their peers are more aggressive and disruptive (Coie, Dodge, & Kupersmidt, 1990), and are more likely to become delinquent or drop out of school as adolescents (Parker & Asher, 1987). Further inquiry is warranted into how "trained individual members of a society can function effectively within that society as agents of peaceful dispute resolution" (Crary, 1992, p. 251). It is our belief that students, educators, and the community at large can only benefit from the mediation process.

REFERENCES

Aks, R. G. (1984). *Mediator Training: A manual for principled problem solving.* Unpublished manuscript, Hudson Valley Institute for Conflict Resolution, State University College, New Paltz, NY.

Araki, C. T. (1990). Dispute management in the schools. *Mediation Quarterly, 8,* 51–62.

Bankier, P. (1992, March). *Perspectives on conflict resolution: School peer mediation.* Madison, WI: Wisconsin Educators for Social Responsibility.

Bluestein, J. (1988). *21st century discipline: Teaching students responsibility and self-control.* Albuquerque, NM: Edgell Communications, Inc.

Brinkman, H. (1991, June). *Conflict resolution training in the school environment.* Paper presented at the International Association for Conflict Management Conference, Den Dolder, The Netherlands.

Burrell, N. A., & Bankier, P. (1992, April). *Training students to mediate conflict: An evaluation of the Milwaukee peer-mediation program.* Paper presented at the 13th Annual Discourse Analysis Conference, Temple University, Philadelphia, PA.

Burrell, N., Donohue, W. A., & Allen, M. (1990). The impact of disputants' expectations on mediation: Testing an interventionist model. *Human Communication Research, 17,* 104–139.

Burrell, N., & Vogl, S. (1990). Turf-side conflict mediation for students. *Mediation Quarterly, 7,* 237–250.

Cahn, D. (1992). *Conflict in intimate relationships.* New York: Guilford.

Cheatham, A. (1988). *Directory of school mediation and conflict resolution programs.* Amherst, MA: National Association for Mediation in Education.

Cohn, D. A., Patterson, C. J., & Christopoulos, C. (1991). The family and children's peer relations. *Journal of Social and Personal Relationships, 8,* 315–3-.5.

Coie, J. D., Dodge, K. A., & Kupersmidt, J. (1990). Peer group behavior and social status. In S. R. Asher & J. D. Coie (Eds.) *Children's status in the peer group* (pp. 17–59). New York: Cambridge University Press.

Crary, D. R. (1992). Community benefits from mediation: A test of the "peace virus" hypothesis. *Mediation Quarterly, 9*, 241–252.

Dreyfuss, E. T. (1990, Spring). Learning ethics in school-based mediation programs. *Update on Law-Related Education,* 22–27.

Eaton, D. (1984). *Residence hall conflict resolution center: Pilot program.* Unpublished manuscript, Student Affairs Division, State University College, New Paltz, NY.

Folberg, J., & Taylor, A. (1984). *Mediation: A comprehensive guide to resolving conflicts without litigation.* San Francisco, CA: Jossey-Bass.

Folger, J. P., & Shubert, J. J. (1986). *Resolving student-initiated grievances in higher education: Dispute resolution procedures in a non-adversarial setting (Report No. 3).* Washington, DC: National Institute for Dispute Resolution.

Girard, K., Rifkin, J., & Townley, A. (1985). *Peaceful persuasion: A guide to creating mediation dispute resolution programs on college campuses.* Amherst, MA: The Mediation Project.

Hocker, J. L., & Wilmot, W. W. (1992). *Interpersonal conflict (3rd edition).* Dubuque, IA: Wm. C. Brown.

Jones, T., & Brinkman, H. (forthcoming). "Teach your children well": Suggestions for peer mediation programs in the schools. In J. Folger & T. Jones (Eds.), *Third parties and conflict: Communication research and perspectives.* Beverly Hills, CA: Sage.

Keltner, J. (1987). *Mediation.* Annandale, VA: Speech Communication Association.

Kemmis, D. (1993). Dispute resolution good training for citizenship. *Consensus, 16,* MIT-Harvard Public Disputes Program Newsletter.

Kreidler, W. J. (1984). *Creative conflict resolution.* Glenview, IL: Scott, Foresman.

Kreidler, W. J. (1990). *Elementary perspectives: Teaching concepts of peace and conflict.* Cambridge, MA: Educators for Social Responsibility.

Kressel, K., & Pruitt, D. (1985). Themes in the mediation of social conflict. *Social Issues, 41,* 170–198.

Levitz, C. M. (1990). Nonadversarial conflict resolution simulation in a school setting. *Social Education, 54,* 263–266.

Levy, J. (1989). Conflict resolution in elementary and secondary education. *Mediation Quarterly, 7,* 73–88.

Maxwell, J. P. (1989). Mediation in the schools: Self-regulation, self-esteem, and self-discipline. *Mediation Quarterly, 7,* 149–156.

Moore, C. W. (1986). *The mediation process.* San Francisco, CA: Jossey-Bass.

Parker, J. G., & Asher, S. R. (1987). Peer relations and later personal adjustment: Are low-accepted children "at risk"? *Psychological Bulletin, 102,* 357–389.

Putnam, L. L., & Poole, M. S. (1987). Conflict and negotiation. In F. M. Jablin, L. L. Putnam, K. H. Roberts, & L. W. Porter (Eds.), *Handbook of organizational communication: An interdisciplinary perspective.* Newbury Park, CA: Sage.

Sadalla, G., Henriquez, M., & Holmberg, M. (1987). *Conflict resolution: A secondary school curriculum.* San Francisco, CA: Community Board Program.

Sillars, A. L. (1980). Attributions and communication in roommate conflicts. *Communication Monographs, 47,* 180–200.

Volpe, M. R., & Witherspoon, R. (1992). Mediation and cultural diversity on college campuses. *Mediation Quarterly, 9,* 341–351.

5 Cognitive Behavioral Perspectives on Marital Conflict

Robert L. Weiss
Crystal Dehle
University of Oregon

Conflict is one of those highly serviceable words (like *stress*) whose meaning we take for granted because of word familiarity. *Marital conflict* has an even greater intuitive appeal, because the disagreeable aspects of marriages are widely purveyed in popular culture. Just how serviceable is the term *conflict*? Writing as we are from a cognitive-behavioral perspective, one depending largely on behavioral observational methodology, a precise, all-purpose definition of *conflict* is still lacking. Conflict is apparent in at least two different modes: process or outcome. With regard to outcome, anyone observing spouses doing battle (in a nonrole-play situation) would conclude that they are having a conflict (e.g., displaying overt mutual exchanges of intentionally hurtful behaviors). Conflict as process is less readily apparent to the observer; it must be inferred or synthesized from observations. On the basis of observed behaviors, conflict is said to exist. The rules of observation define conflict as process, because observers must learn to properly weight those behaviors indicative of conflict.

Conflict also has other formal meanings, as in the antagonism between two or more mutually desired yet exclusive goal states. Thus, the perceived risk of further loss can block an otherwise strong desire for X (e.g., in attaining X, I risk losing Y). Someone else's desire for Z, or at least their desire that I not attain X, can block one's desire to attain X. Conflict may be either intrapersonal or interpersonal.

Marital researchers have embraced both approaches. Either spouse can be judged the agent who blocks attainment of X. Marital conflict also may be inferred from coping tactics (e.g., based on observations of attack, withdrawal, side tracking, etc.). However, when used descriptively, marital conflict may confound the blocking of intention (as described above) with the doing of battle. That is, in observing the tactics of a battle, one infers that an intention was somehow blocked. Or, for couples who divorce, we naturally conclude that they had to have been in conflict, or why else did they divorce? In these cases conflict serves as an explanation for our observations, yet it is not always measured independently of those observations.

Other usages of marital conflict include: (a) differences in values, invalidating what one holds dear (e.g., whether children are a valued aspect of married life), and (b) violation of relationship rules (e.g., the marriage contract, trust, or commitment to support one another). Note that these conflicts can be defined either as the observation of arguing behaviors (what we see) or as the violation of expectations (what we must infer). As well, researchers often use conflict and marital adjustment (or satisfaction) interchangeably (low levels of marital adjustment is said to equal conflict).

In our view, it is easy (but ill advised) to speak of marital conflict without having a direct measure of conflict. For example, is the presence of negativity synonymous with conflict? If couples receive high scores for negative behavior, are they in or are they experiencing conflict? Worse, conflict also has a temporal dimension (e.g., the period before divorce is often described as one of high conflict). In this sense conflict may persist for a period of time.

These distinctions help frame the task before us, namely, to determine what cognitive-behavioral theory and research tell us about marital conflict. Our focus is primarily psychological, as opposed to other alternatives (e.g., communication models, family therapy, or sociology, among others). We will attempt to distinguish research on marital conflict in terms of both process and outcome. Is there an isomorphic representation between conflict and what our behavioral codes describe? In the heyday of behavioral marital therapy (BMT), David Olson asked, "Are frequencies all that count?" Do three instances of negative behavior tell us about this or that couple (i.e., the current distinction between "insider vs. outsider" observation). Admittedly, subjective experiences of upset may not always be captured by trained observers because inferring a couple's experiences from observed behavior is complicated. Almost by definition, the cognitive-behavioral approach encompasses both of these points of view, (e.g., within-person cognitive representations and what observers note as the spouses' actual behaviors). (For an additional consideration of models of marital conflict, the reader is referred to Cahn, 1992.)

In light of these nuances, this chapter asks whether the term *marital conflict* is serviceable. In a section entitled "Brief Overview of Observational Methodology," we review methods of behavioral observation that have spearheaded developments in the field. In "Three Models of Marital

Conflict," we discuss three prominent, current models of marital conflict that have spawned a large body of empirical research (e.g., Gottman's physiological affect, behavioral exchange, and attributions based models). This chapter does not purport to be a comprehensive review of empirical findings (cf. Weiss & Heyman, 1990a, 1990b). Rather, we show how one group of researchers has developed knowledge of marital conflict; ours is a guided tour of the theory and methods researchers have employed, using selected recent empirical work as examples. We illustrate how thinking about this problem has progressed, and suggest possible new lines of research.

BRIEF OVERVIEW OF OBSERVATIONAL METHODOLOGY

For convenience, we can divide behavioral observation approaches into two categories: those that rely heavily on some form of on-line direct observation of interactions vs. those that encode meta-communications generated by the spouses apart from their direct interaction. The first we shall refer to as behavioral observation and the second, collectively, as video-mediated recall.

Behavioral Observation

Direct observation typically involves a laboratory setting in which couple interactions are videotaped. Couples are usually instructed to attempt to resolve a problem or conflict within their relationship. Both amount of structure and setting can vary, ranging from being (individually) explicitly coached so as to heighten realistic reactions (Margolin, Burman, & John, 1989), to being given scenarios designed to elicit conflict about a standard situation (e.g., as with the revealed difference technique: Birchler, Weiss, & Vincent, 1975). Settings can be home or laboratory.

Outside observers are trained specifically in the use a coding system. (Examples of coding systems can be found in Markman & Notarious, 1987). The sensitivity or grain of these observations varies with the approach: so-called microanalytic approaches (e.g., Marital Interaction Coding System, or MICS: Weiss & Summers, 1983) are the most sensitive. A comprehensive set of behavior codes is used to describe each spouse's behavior (in speaker and listener roles) throughout the interaction. Microanalytic systems view the interaction as a continuous stream of events. They retain the natural order (sequence) of interaction behaviors by encoding basic units (e.g., "thought units"). For example, a thought unit is a self-contained utterance. A "speaker turn" represents one person's behavior bounded on either side by the other person's speaker or listener behavior (i.e., the floor switches from one speaker to the other speaker).

Coding units may be represented as a single stream of discrete alternating behaviors (e.g., H W H W . . .) or as a double stream of speaker-listener blocks:

H *H *H . . .
*W W W . . .

where the asterisk designates the speaker in each block).

Macrocoding systems require ratings (judgments) based on temporal samples (e.g., time slices ranging from a few minutes to the time of the entire session). A code or rating is used to describe each interval, by either summarizing the entire interval or highlighting the most salient behavior in that interval. Whenever two or more behaviors occur in the interval, a rating is assigned to the strongest behavior (e.g., choosing between negative and neutral).

The two approaches differ in degree of coder judgment. Rating systems usually define molar behaviors reflecting larger conceptual entities. Thus, for example, raters may be required to determine the degree of hostility displayed within an interval. Hostility is a judgment based on a set of criteria (meanings) that go beyond the occurrence of specific behaviors.

Finally, choice of observational system leads to different statistical treatment of the data and, therefore, addresses very different questions. The results of microcoding can be described either as base rate (total activity per session) or lag sequential analyses (e.g., within-session, serially dependent sequences).

Whenever the actual sequence of events is preserved, the interaction can be described as a pattern of antecedent-consequent pairs. These statistical occurrences of stimulus-response (S-R) pairs define new (synthesized) codes. Rarely would a microcoder directly apprehend such S-R pairs. For example, when husband "problem solves" (PS), his wife may turn her attention away, indicating that she is "not tracking" (NT); this pattern of H PS → W NT, if observed frequently, would describe a newly synthesized code, such as problem avoidance. Because we do not directly observe this code, it is said to be synthesized code.

Having reviewed these methodological basics, we now consider what behavioral observation approaches contribute to our main concern, which is marital conflict. First, microbehavioral coding systems record what might be thought of as "twitches." The utility of these behaviors (twitches) is determined by external validity (i.e., whether the codes label behaviors known to be relevant to conflict or problem solving). Rating systems begin with conceptually more complex units and ask whether these units differentiate couples. One such unit may be conflict itself; the issue is whether we can train raters to make the response *conflict* when a specific set of conditions is met. Raters will agree to the extent that they share a common understanding of these conditions. Thus, to rate *disgust*, an observer must have a cultural understanding of the term plus knowing which facial and verbal features qualify as disgust.

Marital conflict can be synthesized from individual behaviors (i.e., specific behaviors observed during an interaction) or defined by a rating system that allows us to apprehend conflict directly. It should be obvious from this methodological discussion that conflict is most often going to be a fairly high-level inference, based largely on the meaning of the codes or the rating categories. Furthermore, it is most likely that conflict will refer to tactics (e.g., withdrawal).

Video-Mediated Recall

A different approach to obtaining data relevant to marital conflict requires each partner to independently describe his or her thoughts and feelings that occurred during a previously experienced recorded marital interaction. (See Fletcher & Kininmonth, 1991, for a review of various related approaches.) In one format, video-mediated recall, spouses are shown consecutive short segments (e.g., consecutive 20 secs) of their previous interaction; after viewing each video segment, they speak freely into a cassette recorder expressing their thoughts and feelings at the time of the interaction. These verbal accounts of thoughts and feelings (mostly expressed as fragments) are then rated, according to rules ranging from a simple designation of positive/negative (Halford & Sanders, 1990) to rather complex judgments of focus, valence, and, collectively, content (Heyman, 1992).

This and related approaches involve retrospective cuing and assume that the thoughts and feelings recorded in this way not only were active during the initial interactions, but that they truly served as antecedents to subsequent behaviors (Halford & Sanders, 1990). As with all attributional explanations, the idea is that these cognitive representations precede some target behavior (i.e., that cognitions lead to behavior). The latter is especially important in establishing sequential patterns, as is discussed later.

Having reviewed some popular methods for observing marital interactions, we turn next to a consideration of how the various models contribute to our understanding of marital conflict.

THREE MODELS OF MARITAL CONFLICT

Among the various cognitive-behavioral approaches to marital interaction, three bear directly on marital conflict and have generated a host of empirical studies. Included are Gottman's physiological theorizing, versions of the behavioral exchange models proposed by Weiss and others, and the cognitive attributional models proposed by Fincham and colleagues.

Gottman's Physiological Affect Model

John Gottman and his colleagues have stressed the importance of behavioral observation in understanding marital conflict. His interest in combining both behavioral and physiological methodologies into a model of marital discord is noteworthy (e.g., Gottman, 1990; Gottman & Krokoff, 1989; Gottman & Levenson, 1986, 1992; Levenson & Gottman, 1985). His study of factors associated with changes in marital satisfaction over time, and factors that predict divorce, are particularly informative.

Gottman's strategy has been to relate certain interaction patterns or conflict styles (derived from observations of couples' interactions) to underlying physiological mechanisms. Starting with a simple typology, which describes couples as either conflict engagers or conflict avoiders, he has sought links to what he terms *diffuse physiological arousal* (DPA). In a general sense, DPA is equated with emotional arousal: How individuals learn to cope with this discomfort describes their conflict management style. Based on their earlier work, Levenson and Gottman (1985) showed that couples who reported low marital adjustment also showed considerable physiological linkage during marital conflict discussions (i.e., their autonomic nervous system activity ebbed and flowed in synchrony). Level of physiological arousal demonstrated during an eyes-open resting period (before engaging in a conflict discussion) predicted marital satisfaction three years later. Husbands low in marital adjustment showed higher levels of physiological response during conflict discussions than those of either their own wives or high marital adjustment husbands. (It is necessary to point out that as yet these findings have not been subjected to replication by other laboratories.)

In an attempt to further specify emotional arousal (DPA), Gottman and Krokoff (1989) designed an observational rating system that coded for specific emotions—the Specific Affect Coding System (SPAFF). This rating system defines five negative affects (i.e., anger, disgust/contempt, sadness, fear, and whining) and four positive affects (i.e., affection, humor, interest, and joy). According to their theory, some couples (the conflict avoiders) strengthen their avoidant styles whenever their escape (avoidance) results in a reduction of DPA. Thus, by first isolating those transition moments during an interaction when both husband's and wife's DPA index is reduced, it becomes possible to determine whether a contingency exists such that specific affects become associated with the reduction in DPA. Presumably, what is learned is a response that restores physiological calm.

Both Gottman and Levenson (1992) and Krokoff (1991) reported studies that expand somewhat on this physiological-affective model of marital conflict. Using divorce as the ultimate manifestation of marital conflict, the quest turned to isolating antecedent events that lead up to marital disillusion and dissolution. Gottman and Levenson (1992) introduced the concept of regulated and nonregulated couples. Couples were first classified as regulated or nonregulated based on the behavioral ratings of conflict discussions obtained at Time 1. Using a point graph system (Gottman, 1979), a cumulative plot of the difference between positive- and negative-coded speaker behaviors at each turn to talk is constructed for each spouse separately. An upward sloping graph indicates that, as the session progresses, the couple becomes more positive (i.e., positive minus negative yields a net positive score). Couples with a net positive score are defined as regulated. Whenever the continuous graph lines describe a negative slope, a net negative difference in speaker behaviors has occurred as the session progressed. The regression coefficients of the lines in each case are used to classify couples. The validity of this typology can be tested by asking whether a couple's status, as defined on the basis of their problem-solving interaction, relates meaningfully to other known manifestations of conflict and distress, most important, to whether they are divorced at Time 2.

In general, the results were very supportive of the interaction-derived typology. Not only were the nonregulated couples at greater risk for divorce (as measured at Time 2), but significant group differences were also found on two other observational rating systems (the MICS and SPAFF). For example, the nonregulated couples were higher than their regulated counterparts on MICS code categories Gottman and Levenson named "defensiveness," "conflict engagement," and "stubbornness," and lower on "listener withdrawal." (These same categories were initially defined in an earlier longitudinal study reported by Gottman & Krokoff, 1989). Results for the SPAFF were also consistent with expectations (e.g., nonregulated couples were more angry, more whining, less affectionate, less interested in their partners, etc.). The physiological data were less convincing, but suggested greater arousal in the nonregulated wives.

The second approach, reported by Krokoff (1991), also embodied a predictive (longitudinal) design to test whether conflict communication style (e.g., conflict "avoider" vs. "engager") moderates strong affects (e.g., anger and disgust/contempt, as measured by the SPAFF, described above). Of interest here was the attempt to assess whether differences in self-reported communication orientation moderate the association between expressed strong negative affect, on the one hand, and measures of marital satisfaction at Time 1, and changes in marital satisfaction from Time 1 to Time 2 (e.g., three years later), on the other hand.

In one respect, Krokoff's findings were consistent with others who also reported greater overall effects for wives. However, for conflict engagers, strong negative affect (mainly anger) was associated with both lower contemporaneous marital satisfaction and changes in marital satisfaction. For avoiders, the pattern was different: Wives' greater tendency to use disgust/contempt (in Time 1 problem-solving interactions) was associated with greater contemporaneous dissatisfaction but with greater improvement in satisfaction over time. (We will also address this paradoxical effect below.) Thus, it would appear that communication orientation, as defined here, moderates the association between expression of strong affects during problem-solving interactions and marital satisfaction. Note that Krokoff's dependent variables were not adequacy of conflict resolution tactics, but rather how a tendency to respond with anger or disgust/contempt to partner behaviors was predictive of either current satisfaction or changes in marital satisfaction. Nor does this study link (wives') responses to specific antecedent partner affects. In discussing the cognitive-behavior interface later in this chapter, we will show how negative-partner cognitions can serve as antecedents to continued negative cognitions. However, what Krokoff (also, Gottman & Krokoff, 1989) has shown is that not all negative affects are functionally the same.

It is important to note with regard to what has been viewed as the paradoxical effect of negative affect that insiders (the spouses themselves) and outsiders (trained observers) may not only have different definitions of negative behaviors, but so-called negative behaviors may not always function according to their a priori categorization (see Gottman & Krokoff, 1989). Thus, being expressive about one's dissatisfaction with some aspect of a marriage certainly would be expected to predict low marital satisfaction scores when both measures are taken at the same time. Yet it is altogether possible that this same expressivity may catalyze relationship change if, and only if, the expression of coded negativity does not immobilize the partner. Either the wife's verbal attacking behavior, or the husband's withdrawal, stubbornness, and whining, if persistent over time, may lead to decreased marital satisfaction. However, expression of concerns and response to expressed concerns may be done in a manner that is — over time — beneficial to the relationship. (For a more detailed analysis of this general issue from differing perspectives, the reader is referred to Weiss & Sher, 1991).

Behavioral Exchange Models

In one sense, the behavioral exchange approaches were the major impetus for the outpouring of theory and research that has characterized the area of marital conflict since the late 1960s (e.g., Jacobson & Margolin, 1979; Weiss, 1978; Weiss & Heyman, 1990a). The original, largely behavioristic models dealt with marital assessment, behavioral determinants of marital satisfaction, and therapy, by focusing on tactics: what spouses did that maintained marital grievances. Originally, notions of coercive control, the reliance on negative reinforcement as a means of quelling annoying demands, and reciprocity of negative affect were among the identified tactics that spouses utilized, even though these more often led to escalation rather than de-escalation of conflict. With minor exceptions, the so-called behavioral exchange models were actually hybrid conceptions that drew heavily on concepts from behavior modification, social psychology, social learning theory, cognitive, and, in some instances, systems theory approaches. Not surprisingly, much of this work was aimed at developing and evaluating effective interventions for distressed marriages. Weiss and Heyman (1990b) and Cahn (1992) have provided current reviews and interpretations of empirical developments in this area.

The early behavioral exchange models were performance based, in the sense that they highlighted what couples do rather than what they think. Much of what couples do was brought to light by means of behavioral observation that relied heavily on definitions of codes (e.g., Weiss, 1989). The search was guided by asking what conditions maintain desirable and undesirable interaction behaviors. Stimulus conditions (e.g., settings) could act to make certain behaviors more likely to occur than others. The consequences of behavior (reinforcing control) were thought to represent a major source of what controls behavior (Weiss, 1978). What soon became apparent from empirical studies was that marital distress is associated with increased predictability of partner behavior. Patterns of reciprocity and escalation of negative affect were noted from various statistical analyses of coded, problem-solving (i.e., conflict-resolving) attempts. Distressed couples showed a propensity toward a tit-for-tat exchange of aversive responses; whereas nondistressed couples seemed to be able to cycle out of negative exchanges (Gottman, 1979), distressed couples seemed to remain locked in a feedback loop (e.g., continued blaming, failure to build on positive suggestions for change, etc.). Furthermore, distressed couples also showed a greater tendency for cross-situational consistency in negative affect reciprocity (i.e., high correlations between negative affect reciprocity scores derived from different interaction contexts; Gottman, 1980). This might suggest the influence of a relationship trait, such as "negative reciprocity." Early evidence suggested that the marital distress factor is peculiar to the specific dyad; yet, when the same partners interacted with nonspouses, there was no evidence for a trait-like disturbance. That is, as individuals, distressed spouses were able to display more positive and less negative behaviors with nonspouses; apparently we reserve the so-called "negative interaction patterns" for our loved one.

How a given couple is likely to behave in a conflictual interaction is a function of clusters of proximal and distal variables. These represent varied contexts of influence: (a) those that precede the specific interaction (e.g., previous interaction outcomes with this partner, previous success with conflict-resolving tactics, sentiment, or efficacy expectations, to name a few), (b) the context provided by the interaction itself, and (c) the context of evaluation — how the interaction is subjectively evaluated (e.g., Bradbury & Fincham, 1991; Weiss, 1984). Thus, what a couple takes away from their interaction is filtered through a series of contexts. These filters may represent intraindividual variables (e.g., personality temperament), relational efficacy (e.g., beliefs in one's ability to succeed in the relationship), relationship sentiment (e.g., marital satisfaction), or relationship skillfulness (e.g., conflict-resolving skills), among others. The interaction process — how well the interaction progresses — is itself a context. I may believe in my ability to be fair, but display behaviors during an interaction that outside observers would rate as uncooperative (see, for example, Notarius, Bensen, Sloane, Vanzetti, & Hornyak, 1989). Finally, the evaluation I then make of the interaction is a resultant of variables defined in the prior two contexts. For example, the sentiment I feel for my spouse (the standing level of regard) interacts with what I do (behaviors displayed), which, in turn, influences whether I evaluate the interaction favorably ("We did good") or unfavorably ("We never get anywhere in these attempts"). The evaluation becomes part and parcel of a larger attributional network, in that spouses erect an explanatory theory of their interactions (see the sub-section on attributions, later in the chapter). We conclude this section with two illustrative studies that reflect promising lines of research on marital conflict.

Determinants of Interaction Satisfaction.   Haefner, Notarius, and Pellegrini (1991) studied both aspects of the contextual filters discussed previously by examining whether the determinants of immediate satisfaction with a problem-solving discussion differed for husbands and wives. They reasoned that husbands and wives would be affected by different aspects of the "behavioral stream," (i.e., the interaction itself) and that such differences would be moderated by marital distress. The main dependent variable was spouses' satisfaction with their just-completed interaction. The videotaped interactions were coded according to summary categories "organized around problem-solving and affective domains of marital and family communication" (p. 72). Specifically, these included two problem-solving categories — problem-solving facilitation and inhibition — and two affective categories — emotional-validation and invalidation. (Although these categories are by no means novel in this literature, they are built up, as it were, from individual behavior codes, as already discussed.)

The results, not surprisingly, indicate that husbands' satisfaction with the interaction was strongly related to their preexisting level of marital satisfaction as well as their wives' behavior: specifically, husbands were most satisfied when wives emitted high rates of problem-solving facilitation and emotional validation, and, conversely, lower rates of problem-solving inhibition and emotional invalidation. But even more interesting was the lack of significant associations between wives' satisfaction with the interaction and (a) their own marital satisfaction and (b) their husband's interaction behaviors. However, the interaction between these variables (i.e., pre-interaction satisfaction × husband's behavior) indicated that wives who reported high marital satisfaction were most reactive to husbands' problem-solving inhibiting behaviors; the maritally satisfied wives were most satisfied with the interaction when their husbands emitted fewer problem-solving inhibiting behaviors. Wives who reported low marital satisfaction were unaffected by husbands' problem-solving inhibitory behaviors. Haefner, Notarius, and Pellegrini suggested that this "sensitivity" (to husbands' negative interaction behaviors) on the part of maritally satisfied wives may prove to be the key in understanding the so-called paradoxical effect noted previously. When contrasted with the wives in less satisfied marriages, who were not responsive to their husbands' negative behavior, the satisfied wives may have used their dissatisfaction with the interactions as a stimulus to agitate for change, or at least reengage their husbands later on in hopes of resolving the conflict. "This couple may pay a price in immediate satisfaction for engaging in conflict, but they may win in the long run . . ." (Haefner, Notarius, & Pellegrini, 1991, p. 79).

Withdrawal and Marital Conflict.   Withdrawal, as a conflict-resolving tactic, is an all too familiar complaint of couples who seek marital therapy. Christensen, and his colleagues (e.g., Christensen & Heavey, 1990), developed a self-report measure of what they consider to be the ubiquitous "demand-withdrawal" pattern in marriage; one person seeks ever-more closeness while the other prefers distance. Others (e.g., Guthrie & Snyder, 1988) have studied the subjective meaning of different interaction patterns such as these through use of self-report and behavioral observation. The general conclusion from these studies is that wives view their own greater comfort in using "confrontational" behaviors as their (legitimate) attempt to get closer to their partner and as a means of resolving issues; husbands, unfortunately for constructive engagement, experience these attempts as threatening ("nagging") and certainly as unproductive. Clearly, these behavior patterns indicate opposing, strongly held meaning, which provides fertile ground for demand–withdrawal escalation sequences.

Withdrawal is both a behavior and a state (e.g., one withdraws and remains in a withdrawn state until one reengages). Using behavior codes to capture withdrawal is more difficult because the observer must infer that a given response indicates the onset of withdrawal, even though the behavior may be quite subtle and require greater familiarity with the couple than is possible in such research. Unfortunately, reliably coding "eyes glazed over" greatly pushes the limits of reasonable coding, although a spouse may "always know when he is withdrawing!" In an early study, Heyman and Weiss (1989) sought to compare observer coding of withdrawal with both spouses' encoding of withdrawal episodes. A target spouse (typically the husband) was asked to signal whenever the target judged that he or she was withdrawing as the couple watched a videotape of their prior conflict-resolving interaction. Both spouses (target and nontarget) independently made retrospective, on-line judgments. In addition, MICS coders coded the same videotaped interaction using a newly developed withdrawal (WI) code. As expected from insider–outsider observation studies, the nontarget spouse and the outside MICS coders showed good agreement, but neither was in substantial agreement with the target person's own designations of his or her withdrawal.

Initially, Gottman and Krokoff (1989) used a combination of individual MICS codes to create a withdrawal category, and found 3 years later that withdrawal was weakly related to concurrent dissatisfaction, but significantly related to change (deterioration) of marital satisfaction. Roberts and Krokoff (1990) coded the same videotaped interactions but with a different rating system (i.e., more like a rating than the multicode microsystems we have been discussing). Using both base rate frequency and sequential patterns, they found withdrawal sequences that differentiated distressed and nondistressed couples. Satisfied couples displayed a W:withdrawal → H:withdrawal pattern, whereas dissatisfied couples showed a H:withdrawal → W:hostility pattern. Schaap (1984) also found, with Dutch couples, increased levels of W:blame → H:acquiescence, which is quite like the all too familiar "Yes, dear. Anything you want." Finally, a study by Smith, Vivian, and O'Leary (1991) found that observation of premarital withdrawal predicted lower levels of marital satisfaction measured at 18 and 30 months postmarriage. However, the interaction of positivity and withdrawal were associated with gains in marital satisfaction measured at 30 months postmarriage.

In the first study of its kind known to us, using behavioral observation methodology to compare clinically depressed husbands with nondepressed husbands interacting with their wives, Perry (1993) found clear differences in base rate frequencies of withdrawal, as defined in the MICS-IV behavioral observation approach; depressed husbands, but not their wives, showed significantly higher rates of withdrawal than their nondepressed male counterparts. Unlike other studies discussed here (and those for depressed wives reported in the literature), Perry did not find evidence of sequential patterning; the wives of depressed husbands did show significantly less total (coded) behavior and significantly less facilitative behaviors. Thus, wives of depressed husbands were neither more negative nor withdrawn on a code-by-code basis, but their conflict-resolving interactions with their depressed husbands were certainly more constricted and lacking in affect than was found for wives of nondepressed husbands. (On average, Perry's samples had been married for upwards of 18 years; not surprisingly, overt evidence of conflict was not to be found.)

These innovative approaches to a phenomenon as complex as withdrawal behavior once again highlight the importance of context. Often, as we have already seen, it is the interaction of scores and not just single scores (of coded behaviors) that provide us with insights into the processes of conflict resolution. Like the self-report approaches, behavioral observation compels us to look at the functionality of the behavior if we are to discern patterns that can be related to conflict resolution. What is the effect on subsequent behaviors whenever spouse A withdraws? We see here also the manner in which such empirically derived patterns force us to define broader tactics (e.g., Withdrawal → Blame, or Withdrawal × Positivity combinations). In at least one case, with a depressed sample of husbands, we see how it may be necessary to align code categories themselves if we are to gain a fuller picture of how certain couples approach conflict resolution. In the next section, we consider the contribution of more explicitly cognitive approaches, those emphasizing the role of attributions.

Attribution-Based Approaches

"He's only affectionate toward me around other people." "We wouldn't fight if she didn't nag at me all the time." Understanding attributions like these is an important part of understanding couples in conflict. Attributions, in the context of dyadic relationships, refer to the explanations offered for events occurring within the relationship. This section discusses how attributions are linked with marital satisfaction, both concurrently and longitudinally. Although behavioral approaches were predominant in the early research on marital satisfaction, it is becoming increasingly apparent that cognitive processes, like attributions, may help inform us about processes underlying the covert behavioral differences between distressed and nondistressed couples. It is a well-established finding that distressed couples, as compared to nondistressed couples, display higher rates of negative behavior and are more likely to reciprocate negative behavior in problem-solving interactions. Can examination of distressed couples' attributions help explain the genesis and/or maintenance of negative reciprocity cycles? Are attributions a mediator in the behavioral exchanges of distressed couples?

Attribution Dimensions.   Research focusing on individual dimensions for the attributions made by spouses consistently indicates that distressed couples, as compared to nondistressed couples, explain their partners' positive and negative behaviors in a way that casts their partners in a negative light. In distressed couples, negative partner behaviors are attributed to global and stable causes internal to the partner, and are viewed as intentional, blameworthy, and selfishly motivated. Positive partner behaviors fare no better. They are attributed to situationally specific, unstable, and unintentional factors, rather than to the goodwill of the partner. Holtzworth-Munroe and Jacobson (1985) refer to attributions that minimize positive behavior and maximize negative behavior as distress-maintaining attributions. These are distinguished from relationship-enhancing attributions, which maximize the impact of positive behaviors while minimizing the impact of negative behaviors.

The individual indices described have been used to construct composite attribution indices, the most common of which are the causal- and responsibility-attribution indices. Causal attributions include judgments concerning the locus, stability, and globality of an event. Responsibility attributions include judgments of blame, intent, and selfish motivation. Much of the research examining the links between attributions and satisfaction and attributions and behavior have used the causal/responsibility indices, but Fincham and Bradbury (1992) caution that both individual and composite indices for attribution should be used until the data support the use of one method over the other.

Attributions and Satisfaction. Bradbury and Fincham's (1990) review of this research concluded that support for the attribution/satisfaction link has been found consistently in experimental, longitudinal, and clinical studies. Distressed couples concurrently report more distress maintaining attributions than relationship-enhancing attributions (Holtzworth-Munroe & Jacobson, 1985), they report more attributions for negative than for positive events (Camper, Jacobson, Holtzworth-Munroe, & Schmaling, 1988), and they report more causal and responsibility attributions than do nondistressed couples (Fincham & Bradbury, 1988). There is also some evidence suggesting a causal link between attributions and satisfaction. Fincham and Bradbury (1987) found that after controlling for Time 1 satisfaction, the wives' causal and responsibility attributions predicted their satisfaction one year later. Distressed wives tended to view the causes of negative behavior and marital problems as located in the husbands (i.e., the husbands' stable, global, blameworthy, intentional, and selfishly motivated behaviors). Interestingly, this predictive relationship was not significant for the husbands — their attributions at Time 1 did not predict their satisfaction at Time 2. A causal link is further suggested by the finding that marital satisfaction at Time 1 did not predict later attributions, nor was another cognitive variable (unrealistic relationship beliefs) useful in predicting Time

2 satisfaction. Caution is warranted, however, in inferring a casual link between attributions and satisfaction, because this is a correlational design and third variables cannot be completely ruled out.

Research examining the influence of one potential third variable — depression — suggests that the attribution/satisfaction link is not an artifact of depression. A series of studies by Fincham, Beach, and Bradbury (1989) on samples of clinic and community wives indicated that the attributions of community wives accounted for significant variance in marital satisfaction after controlling for the effect of depression. Moreover, no differences in attributions were found between clinically depressed, maritally distressed wives and nondepressed but distressed wives, but both groups differed from the nondepressed and nondistressed wives. Thus, the results of both studies indicate that the marital distress-attribution association is not an artifact of depression.

Attributions and Behavior. The final question to address is whether attributions are related to interactional behavior. This is a difficult question to study, because methodologies for eliciting ongoing attributions are often problematic. Couples do not often spontaneously report attributional thoughts, and there is some question as to whether the reactivity inherent in attributions elicited by direct probes (e.g., "Why do you think that happened?") makes them unrepresentative of the private attributions that go unreported. Some studies have utilized paper and pencil attributional measures (e.g. Relationship Attribution Measure, [RAM]; Fincham & Bradbury, 1992) for eliciting attributions about particular problem areas discussed in a problem-solving interaction, but links between specific attributions and specific behaviors are weakened as the attributions reported become more distant from the behavior they are believed to influence. Limitations notwithstanding, there are some preliminary findings suggesting that attributions are linked to interactional behavior.

In the only experimental study reported in this area, Fincham and Bradbury (1988) attempted to manipulate attributions for negative partner behavior in a sample of distressed and nondistressed couples. The manipulation was designed to provide some couples with an external explanation for the negative spousal evaluations written by one of the spouses about his or her partner. The results indicated that negative behavior toward the spouse was more likely in the distressed couples when there was no apparent external justification for the negative evaluation. In addition, rates of positive behavior also increased when the external justification was absent. No differences across conditions were found in the nondistressed couples.

Bradbury and Fincham (1988) correlated attributions with z scores obtained from sequential analyses of problem-solving behaviors and found that husbands were less likely to reciprocate their wives' positive behavior if the locus of the problem was believed to be internal to the wife, intentional, selfishly motivated, and blameworthy. Husbands were more likely to reciprocate negative behaviors when the wives' contribution to the problem was viewed as intentional. The wives were less likely to reciprocate positive behaviors if they believed their husbands' contribution to the problem was global, intentional, and selfishly motivated. The wives were more likely to reciprocate negative behaviors if they viewed their husbands as the locus for the problem, and attributed the husbands' behavior to stable, blameworthy, and selfishly motivated factors.

Fincham and Bradbury (1992) found that responsibility attributions mediated the relationship between causal attributions and anger expressed in an interaction. They also found that responsibility attributions were related to the amount of whining in an interaction. In summary, while there is no direct test of the influence of ongoing attributions on interactional behavior, there are data suggestive of a link between causal and responsibility attributions and negative behavior.

Attributional Style. Attributions, or attributional style, used in consistent ways across various marital situations have also been linked to marital satisfaction. Theories relating marital distress and attributional style developed from learned helplessness theories of depression, which suggested that there exists an attributional style correlation with depression. To empirically examine the importance of attributional style to marital satisfaction, Baucom, Sayers, and Duhe (1989) assessed patterns of attributions across various marital events using a newly constructed measure called the Dyadic Attribution Inventory (DAI). The attributional patterns measured in this study reflected subjects' composite ratings of events along dimensions of locus (i.e., me, partner, outside circumstances) and consistency (i.e., stability, globality). The results indicated that couples' use of a consistent attributional style correlated significantly with marital discord. More specifically, distressed couples seem to use consistent explanations for partner behavior (especially negative behavior), and they appear to use those explanations consistently across situations. Conversely, nondistressed couples show more flexibility in their attributional patterns, as indicated by higher levels of variability in the attributions made for positive and negative partner behavior.

The more rigid use of attributions by distressed couples is consistent with empirical findings on the communication patterns of distressed couples. Distressed couples show greater degrees of predictability in interactional behavior (i.e., greater reciprocity), indicating that they are more "locked in" to each other and less able to respond in the flexible way used by nondistressed couples. Thus, it appears that both the overt processes involved in conflict (i.e., behavior) and the covert processes (i.e., attributions) are characterized by rigidity and inflexibility.

Attributional style, as used within marital research, is also consistent with the notion of sentiment override proposed by Weiss (1984). Weiss hypothesized that spouses may develop a general sentiment about their partners that then influences how they perceive and encode their partners' behavior. It is a cognitive bias in perceiving the partners that would likely express itself in attributions made for partners' behavior. Work in our lab (Dehle, Weiss, Heyman, Leonard, & Roberts, 1993) has provided preliminary evidence of sentiment override in a sample of wives married to physically aggressive husbands.

Each of the 50 couples that participated in the study completed a 10-minute problem-solving interaction, followed by a video-mediated recall procedure designed to elicit the cognitions experienced during the interaction. Each spouse's behavior in the videotaped interaction was coded in two ways: the Marital Interaction Coding System (MICS); and the video mediated cognitive coding system (VICCS), which was used to code audiotapes of the wives' cognitions reported during the video-mediated recall procedure.

The results suggested that the wives of physically aggressive husbands, as compared to wives of nonaggressive husbands, could be distinguished by the patterning between antecedent and consequent cognitions. Specifically, if these wives reported a negative cognition (as per the video-mediated recall task), they were more likely to follow this with another negative cognition. Although for both groups of wives there were sequential links between a husband's negative behavior and a wife's subsequent negative cognition, what differentiated the two groups was the predictability of wives' subsequent negative cognitions given their preceding negative cognitions.

The findings suggest the influence of a negative cognitive set, or filter, in ongoing dyadic interactions involving aggressive couples. This filter, namely, sentiment override, has important implications for therapeutic interventions with aggressive couples. One common intervention focuses on teaching each partner to identify behavioral cues that signal the escalations of negativity that may potentially lead to violence. This skill, often called *tracking*, requires that both partners closely attend to both their own and their partner's behaviors. Our results suggest that women with aggressive husbands are not tracking behavior as much as they are attending to their overriding (negative) sentiment about their partner. Clinicians working with conflicted couples such as these should be aware of the influence of sentiment when teaching skills designed to produce behavioral change within a couple. If partner sentiment is not also targeted for change, it is likely that behavioral interventions will be less effective.

Although we did not examine the effect of negative cognitions on subsequent negative behavior, other research conducted by Halford and Sanders (1990) using maritally distressed couples indicated that the probability of negative behaviors was higher if preceded by negative cognitions. Collectively, these studies describe a process whereby negative behavior increases negative cognitions (i.e., attributions and sentiment), which, in turn, increase negative behavior and then lead to further escalation of distress. Thus, an overall picture linking on-line cognitive processes (like attributions) and behavior is beginning to emerge, but much work is left to be done. The value of such research for understanding couples in conflict will no doubt be immeasurable.

SUMMARY AND CONCLUSIONS

The aim of this chapter has been to examine the contribution of the cognitive-behavioral approach to marital conflict by first reviewing the construct itself, then the observational methodology that has become the hallmark of this approach, and finally various models within the larger area that have spawned much of the empirical work. Our approach has focused largely on the development of themes rather than reiterating empirical findings.

The more general behavioral approach to marital conflict today addresses three domains: affect, behavior, and cognition. The work of John Gottman and his colleagues has provided a window into marital conflict by studying aspects of emotional arousal that map onto specific patterns of problem-solving discussions. Like others, Gottman has also identified how patterns of expressed negative affect can predict divorce (the ultimate criterion of marital conflict). From among the considerable activity generated by behavior exchange models, two approaches seem especially promising: determinants of interactions that spouses find subjectively satisfying, and withdrawal as a conflict management technique. Finally, from the avowedly cognitive perspective, we considered recent work in attribution and marital conflict. The issues here center on how attributions (and cognitions, more broadly) determine the course of marital conflict. We were particularly concerned with how negative cognitions about spouse behavior may gain a limited functional autonomy, as in the sentiment override hypothesis.

Marital conflict is a broad area of theory and research, and there are many different persuasions involved. In this chapter, we have eschewed attempts to integrate the various points of view, focusing as we have on the so-called cognitive-behavioral approach. (Cahn, 1992, provides a very readable integrative exposition.) Nor have we delved into the large marital therapy literature. We have tried for the most part to focus on the basics of marital conflict from this psychological perspective.

What conclusions would we leave the reader to ponder? First, and foremost, this approach is comprehensive, representing affect, behavior, and cognition. Second, although there has been a tendency for work to proceed mainly within each of these areas, marital conflict is now being viewed in a more contextual fashion. That is, by studying both proximal and distal variable sets, we gain a much clearer sense of how to measure so-called pre-existing context variables (e.g., sentiment, expectations, etc.); the variables that in turn serve as filters affecting the quality of ongoing conflict-resolving interactions. The way couples evaluate their interactions then becomes part of the distal context for the next go around.

Whereas behavioral observation provides samples of what couples do, we cannot always be sure that what they say about their interactions operates in a truly antecedent fashion. Does asking a couple for their cognitions stimulate them to come up with explanations, or do these mini-theories actually propel actions? (Such direct inquires may also be a form of intervention, in that couples now know what to ask themselves.) Here, too, longitudinal studies help clarify the role of cognitive variables.

The emphasis on behavioral observation methodology has been particularly fruitful. Discerning very early on, through behavioral observation, those patterns of communication that are associated with marital distress (and, ultimately, divorce) is a major development in this field. The various forms of negativity (in contrast to positive exchanges) appear to warrant particular attention. The danger, of course, is in building a theory of marital intimacy based on distress: We also need to develop models based on constructive engagement. Nor should we assume that currently popular forms of conflict management apply throughout the marital life cycle. But having the wherewithal to track relationship changes seems to be the hallmark of the approaches reviewed here. Generating refutable hypotheses is still the recommended way to build our knowledge base in this, a complex field of sustained intimacy.

REFERENCES

Baucom, D. H., Sayers, S. L., & Duhe, A. (1989). Attributional style and attributional patterns among married couples. *Journal of Personality and Social Psychology, 56*, 596–607.

Birchler, G. R., Weiss, R. L., & Vincent, J. P. (1975). Multimethod analysis of social reinforcement exchange between maritally distressed and nondistressed spouse and stranger dyads. *Journal of Personality and Social Psychology, 31*, 349–360.

Bradbury, T. N., & Fincham, F. D. (1988). *The impact of attribution in marriage: Attributions and behavior exchange in marital interaction.* Paper presented at the 22nd Annual Convention of the Association for the Advancement of Behavior Therapy, New York.

Bradbury, T. N., & Fincham, F. D. (1990). Attributions in marriage: Review and critique. *Psychological Bulletin, 3*, 3–33.

Bradbury, T. N., & Fincham, F. D. (1991). A contextual model for advancing the study of marital interaction. In G. J. O. Fletcher & F. D. Fincham (Eds.), *Cognition in close relationships* (pp. 127–147). Hillsdale, NJ: Lawrence Erlbaum Associates.

Cahn, D. D. (1992). *Conflict in intimate relationships.* New York: Guilford.

Camper, P. M., Jacobson, N. S., Holtzworth-Munroe, A., & Schmaling, K. B. (1988). Causal attributions for interactional behaviors in married couples. *Cognitive Therapy and Research, 12,* 195–209.

Christensen, A., & Heavey, C. L. (1990). Gender and social structure in the demand/withdraw pattern of marital conflict. *Journal of Personality and Social Psychology, 39,* 73–81.

Dehle, C., Weiss, R. L., Heyman, R. E., Leonard, K., & Roberts, L. (1993). *Negative cognitions in victims of marital aggression: The sentiment override hypothesis.* Manuscript submitted for publication.

Fincham, F. D., Beach, S. R. H., & Bradbury, T. N. (1989). Marital distress, depression, and attributions: Is the marital distress-attribution association an artifact of depression? *Journal of Consulting and Clinical Psychology, 57,* 768–771.

Fincham, F. D., & Bradbury, T. N. (1987). The impact of attributions in marriage: A longitudinal analysis. *Journal of Personality and Social Psychology, 53,* 510–517.

Fincham, F. D., & Bradbury, T. N. (1988). The impact of attributions in marriage: An experimental analysis. *Journal of Social and Clinical Psychology, 7,* 147–162.

Fincham, F. D., & Bradbury, T. N. (1992). Assessing attributions in marriage: The relationship attribution measure. *Journal of Personality and Social Psychology, 62,* 457–468.

Fletcher, G. J. O., & Kininmonth, L. (1991). Interaction in close relationships and social cognition. In G. J. O. Fletcher & F. D. Fincham (Eds.), *Cognition in close relationships* (pp. 235–255). Hillsdale, NJ: Lawrence Erlbaum Associates.

Gottman, J. M. (1979). *Marital interaction: Empirical investigations.* New York: Academic.

Gottman, J. M. (1980). Consistency of nonverbal affect and affect reciprocity in marital interaction. *Journal of Consulting and Clinical Psychology, 48,* 711–717.

Gottman, J. M. (1990). How marriages change. In G. R. Patterson (Ed.), *Depression and aggression in family interaction* (pp. 75–101). Hillsdale, NJ: Lawrence Earlbaum Associates.

Gottman, J. M., & Krokoff, L. J. (1989). Marital interaction and satisfaction: A longitudinal view. *Journal of Consulting and Clinical Psychology, 57,* 47–52.

Gottman, J. M., & Levenson, R. W. (1986). Assessing the role of emotion in marriage. *Behavioral Assessment, 8,* 31–48.

Gottman, J. M., & Levenson, R. W. (1992). Marital processes predictive of later dissolution: Behavior, physiology, and health. *Journal of Personality and Social Psychology, 63,* 221–233.

Guthrie, D. M., & Snyder, C. W., (1988). Spouses' self-evaluation for situations involving emotional communication. In P. Noller & M. A. Fitzpatrick (Eds.), *Perspectives on marital interaction* (pp. 123–152). Philadelphia, PA: Multilingual Matters, Ltd.

Haefner, P. T., Notarius, C. I., & Pellegrini, D. S. (1991). Determinants of satisfaction with marital discussions: An exploration of husband-wife differences. *Behavioral Assessment, 13,* 67–82.

Halford, W. K., & Sanders, M. R. (1990). The relationship of cognition and behavior during marital interaction. *Journal of Social and Clinical Psychology, 9,* 489–510.

Heyman, R. E. (1992). *Cognitive and behavioral differences between physically abusive and non-abusive early married couples.* Unpublished doctoral dissertation, University of Oregon, Eugene.

Heyman, R. E., & Weiss, R. L. (1989, November). *Self-report and observational measures of withdrawal in marital interactions.* Paper presented at the 23rd Annual Convention of the Association for the Advancement of Behavior Therapy, Washington, DC.

Holtzworth-Munroe, A., & Jacobson, N. S. (1985). Causal attributions of married couples: When do they search for causes? What do they conclude when they do? *Journal of Personality and Social Psychology, 48*, 1398–1412.

Jacobson, N. S., & Margolin, G. (1979). *Marital therapy: Strategies based on social learning and behavior exchange principles.* New York: Brunner/Mazel.

Krokoff, L. (1991). Job distress is no laughing matter in marriage, or is it? *Journal of Social and Personal Relationships, 8*, 5–25.

Levenson, R. W., & Gottman, J. M. (1985). Physiological and affective predictors of change in relationship satisfaction. *Journal of Personality and Social Psychology, 49*, 85–94.

Margolin, G., Burman, B., & John, R. S. (1989). Home observations of marital couples reenacting naturalistic conflicts. *Behavioral Assessment, 11*, 101–118.

Markman, H. J., & Notarius, C. I. (1987). Coding marital and family interaction: Current status. In T. Jacob (Ed.), *Family interaction and psychopathology: Theories, methods, and findings* (pp. 329–390). New York: Plenum.

Notarius, C. I., Benson, P. R., & Sloane, D., Vanzetti, N. A., Hornyak, L. M. (1989). Exploring the interface between perception and behavior: An analysis of marital interaction in distressed and nondistressed couples. *Behavioral Assessment, 11*, 39–64.

Perry, B. A. (1993). *Marital problem-solving interactions of depressed males.* Unpublished doctoral dissertation, University of Oregon, Eugene.

Roberts, L. J., & Krokoff, L. J. (1990). A time-series analysis of withdrawal, hostility, and displeasure in satisfied and dissatisfied marriages. *Journal of Marriage and the Family, 52*, 95–105.

Schaap, C. (1984). A comparison of the interaction of distressed and nondistressed married couples in a laboratory situation: Literature survey, methodological issues, and an empirical investigation. In K. Hahlweg & N. S. Jacobson (Eds.), *Marital interaction: Analysis and modification* (pp. 133–158). New York: Guilford.

Smith, D. A., Vivian, D., & O'Leary, K. D. (1991). The misnomer proposition: A critical reappraisal of the longitudinal status of "negativity" in marital communication. *Behavioral Assessment, 13*, 7–24.

Weiss, R. L. (1978). The conceptualization of marriage from a behavioral perspective. In T. J. Paolino & B. S. McCrady (Eds.), *Marriage and marital therapy: Psychoanalytic, behavioral, and systems theory perspectives* (pp. 165–239). New York: Brunner/Mazel.

Weiss, R. L. (1984). Cognitive and behavioral measures of marital interaction. In K. Hahlweg & N. S. Jacobson (Eds.), *Marital interaction: Analysis and modification* (pp. 232–252). New York: Guilford.

Weiss, R. L. (1989). The circle of voyeurs: Observing the observers of marital and family interactions. *Behavioral Assessment, 11*, 135–147.

Weiss, R. L., & Heyman, R. E. (1990a). Marital distress. In A. Bellack & M. Hersen (Eds.), *International handbook of behavior modification* (pp. 475–501). New York: Plenum.

Weiss, R. L., & Heyman, R. E. (1990b). Observation of marital interaction. In F. D. Fincham & T. N. Bradbury (Eds.), *The psychology of marriage: Basic issues and applications* (pp. 87–117). New York: Guilford.

Weiss, R. L., & Sher, T. G. (1991). Negative communication in marital intraction: A misnomer? [Special Issue]. *Behavioral Assessment, 13*, (1).

Weiss, R. L., & Summers, K. J. (1983). Marital interaction coding system-III. In E. E. Filsinger (Ed.), *Marriage and family assessment: A sourcebook for family therapy* (pp. 65–84). Beverly Hills, CA: Sage.

6 Conflict Between Parents and Their Children

Lori N. Osborne
Frank D. Fincham
University of Illinois

Potential conflict exists when two parties have incompatible goals; actual conflict occurs when interaction reveals that these incompatible goals exist (Cahn, 1992). Because socialization requires parents to redirect child behavior so that it is situationally appropriate and conforms to cultural or subcultural norms, the immediate goals of parents and children are often at odds, resulting in the potential for conflict. Seen from this perspective, conflict is omnipresent in parent–child relationships, particularly those involving young children. Some observational studies estimate that children engage in behavior eliciting parental control as often as once every 15 minutes (Forehand, King, Peed, & Yoder, 1975). Furthermore, there are certain child behaviors that are widely recognized as aversive, and, therefore, conflict engendering (e.g., rule violation, aggressive or destructive behavior, whining or yelling, and ignoring parents; Hoffman, Fagot, Reid, & Patterson, 1987; Patterson, 1982). Because conflict experienced as part of the socialization process is likely to influence later conflict behavior and general child adjustment, it is important to examine parent–child conflict. However, no cohesive, identifiable literature has emerged on this topic, a circumstance that may reflect the belief that the imbalance of power between parents and preadolescent children precludes the expression of true conflict.[1] The present chapter, therefore, draws on several related sources in discussing conflict between parents and their preadolescent children.

Although no body of literature has focused on parent–child conflict per se, attention has been paid to different types of parenting style and parents'

---

[1]This chapter focuses primarily on studies of children below the age of 6 years.

efforts to socialize their children. In the first section of the chapter, styles of parenting are examined to see what they reveal about parent–child conflict. This analysis shows that different forms of parent–child conflict are associated with more or less adaptive forms of child adjustment, but the mechanisms relating modes of parent–child conflict to adjustment are unclear. The second section of the chapter, therefore, examines the processes that underlie parent–child conflict. These two sections serve as a springboard for the conceptual analysis of parent–child conflict that is offered in the third section. The chapter concludes with a summary of the main points.

PARENT STYLES AND PARENT-CHILD CONFLICT

Although parent–child conflict shares many features of conflict found in other close relationships, the imbalance of power between conflicting parties makes it unique. At the heart of parent–child conflict is the impact of parental power on children's development. Children require guidance in order to attain the skills necessary to function adaptively in society (Maccoby & Martin, 1983). At the same time, autonomy and self-reliance are paramount among the competencies a child needs to obtain. This tension between the child's need for autonomy and the exercise of parental control is central to parent–child conflict.

The exercise of parent power can take many forms, which may be more or less effective for promoting adaptive child behavior. Two major lines of research document modes of parent power assertion and child competencies associated with them. The first emerges from Baumrind's (1967; 1971a; for reviews, see Baumrind, 1989; Maccoby & Martin, 1983) studies of middle-class parents and their nursery school children; the second arises from Patterson's (1976; for reviews, see Patterson, 1982; Patterson, Reid, & Dishion, 1989) work with socially aggressive children. Each is examined in turn.

Parent Styles and Firm Control

Baumrind has maintained that rather than representing a threat to children's autonomy, parental power assertion is essential for the development of child competence. However, the extent to which parental power assertion benefits children depends on other aspects of the parent–child relationship. Baumrind's definition of parental power assertion (which she called *firm control*) included measures of conflict outcome; the parents' willingness to confront child misbehavior; willingness to persist in the face of child opposition; and open acknowledgment of parental power, rather than using guilt or other psychological control techniques. In her investigations of naturally occurring parenting styles, Baumrind has identified two types of parents who exercise firm control and one type who does not.

Parental style was initially identified by observing child behavior patterns in nursery school children and then examining the socialization efforts of the parents associated with different child behavior patterns (Baumrind, 1967). The child behavior patterns and corresponding parent styles are summarized in Table 6.1.

As shown in the table, both authoritative and authoritarian parents exercised firm control; however, they expressed very different attitudes about the purpose of this control. In addition, authoritative and authoritarian parents differed in aspects of parenting not directly related to parent–child conflict. Compared to authoritarian parents, authoritative parents were more warm and more likely to respond to child requests outside of conflict situations. Two particularly relevant differences in the present context were authoritative parents' high scores in maturity demands and parent–child communications. Maturity demands included the degree to which parents provided information and rationales both within and outside of conflict interactions, as well as the degree to which the parents

TABLE 6.1

Child Behavior Patterns		
Pattern I	*Pattern II*	*Pattern III*
Highly competent: Independent; willing to take on new experiences; seem content	Dysphoric: Seem discontent, withdrawn, and mistrustful	Immature: Lack independence and self-control

Parenting Styles		
Authoritative	*Authoritarian*	*Permissive*
Try to raise their children in a rational, issue-oriented manner. Place relatively few restrictions on child behavior; however, take a firm stand when parent and child opinions diverge	Value obedience as an end in itself. Try to maintain traditional relations; do not encourage expressions of self-will or autonomy. Value order and conformity	Do not exercise firm control. Originally conceived as parents who view their role not as control agents, but as resources. Empirically found to be disengaged from their children; insecure about their ability to control child behavior, and angry and frustrated over their lack of control

respected the child's decisions. Parent–child communication included the degree to which parents solicited child input and welcomed verbal give and take.

Although Baumrind conceptualized these indices as separate from firm control, they are likely to lead to very different modes of conflict. In conflict episodes, authoritative parents are more likely to explain the rationale for their point of view, to elicit the child's reasons for resisting, and to engage in a dialogue about the conflict. They would also be more likely to concede if the child offered good reasons for resisting, but would remain firm when they took a stand. In contrast, authoritarian parents would discourage child input, and would not provide rationales for their side of the conflict, but, rather, expect to be obeyed on the basis of parental authority alone.[2]

In subsequent studies that first identified parent types and then measured child competency, results were not as clear-cut (Baumrind, 1971a, 1991). Subcategories of parenting behavior were identified, and their relationship to child competency was not as neat as in Baumrind's (1967) study. However, the superior competency of children of authoritative parents remained a robust finding. Thus, Baumrind concluded that parents' exercise of power in conflict situations is not harmful, and in fact is beneficial, as long as it is balanced by demands for maturity, clear communication about reasons for control, and responsiveness to the child both within and outside conflict situations.

Firm Control and Socially Aggressive Children

A parenting style that does not easily fit into Baumrind's typology emerged from Patterson's work with socially aggressive children. This population is of particular interest because (a) families with such children often seek professional help because of intolerable levels of parent–child conflict, (b) observational studies reveal frequent bursts of aversive and angry parent–child interactions, and (c) social aggression in children is associated with a wide variety of child adjustment problems, including peer rejection and poor school performance (Gardner, 1992; Patterson, 1982; Reid & Patterson, 1989; Vuchinich, Bank, & Patterson, 1992).

Parents of socially aggressive children exhibit some features of firm control. For example, they are willing to confront child misbehavior. In

---

[2]It should be noted, however, that the conclusions drawn here about conflict episodes are tentative. This is because, as noted earlier, Baumrind's measures of maturity and communication draw from both conflict and nonconflict interactions. Thus, it is difficult to determine the contribution of conflict episodes to the composite measure. It seems safe to say, however, that factors both within and outside the conflict episode seem to moderate the impact of firm control.

fact, they are less likely than parents in normal populations to ignore the aversive behavior of their children. Their responses are more intense than those of parents in normal populations and include threats, sarcasm, or humiliation; statements that convey a negative attitude (e.g., "don't bug me"); and physical punishment. However, unlike either authoritative or authoritarian parenting, where a willingness to confront conflict was associated with ultimate child compliance, confrontations between parents and their socially aggressive children do not lead to compliance. Instead, they are often associated with an increase in child noncompliance (Patterson, 1982).

One way to conceptualize the relationship between socially aggressive children and their parents is a failure of firm control. Patterson has suggested that for these parents, threats and commands do not really function as control efforts, because parents rarely follow through on them. Still, the behaviors of these parents seem to represent high intensity demands for compliance that one would normally expect to elicit cooperation. Furthermore, these parental demands do sometimes escalate into physical punishment, albeit on an irregular and somewhat unpredictable basis (Patterson, 1982). It is, therefore, not clear whether the phenomenon to be explained is why parents of socially aggressive children fail to exercise firm control or why their children refuse to comply.

Firm Control or Willingness to Comply?

In the lines of research stimulated by Baumrind's and Patterson's pioneering work, the relative contribution of firm control and children's willingness to comply has been questioned. Lewis (1981) pointed out that Baumrind's measure of firm control includes an index of conflict outcome (whether or not the child actually complied). She suggested that the measure of firm control may actually represent children's willingness to comply, rather than parents' ability to take a firm stand in the face of child noncompliance. To support this contention, she cited Baumrind's subcategory of harmonious families. Baumrind (1971b) created this subcategory to identify families where the parents did not overtly exercise control, but still seemed to maintain control. In harmonious families, the children seemed to intuit their parents' desires, and to act accordingly. Daughters of harmonious parents exhibited similar competencies to children of authoritative parents. Thus, Lewis (1981) concluded that the competencies seen in children of authoritative parents are not associated with firm control, but rather represent families where children are predisposed to comply with their parents.

A parallel critique can be offered for parent–child conflict in families with socially aggressive children. It has been suggested that parents of socially aggressive children fail to exercise firm control (Patterson, 1982). However, a reasonable alternative explanation seems to be that socially aggressive children are particularly unwilling to comply with parental demands, thus precipitating frequent and intense episodes of parent–child conflict. This latter account also explains why parents of socially aggressive children engage in more efforts to control their children's behavior and yet experience lower rates of child compliance than do parents from nonclinical populations.

In summary, the exercise of firm control by authoritative parents may be more apparent than real because of a possible predisposition in their children to cooperate with parental demands. Parents of socially aggressive children seem to be unable to exercise firm control, a circumstance that may reflect their children's predisposition to resist compliance with parental demands. Given the association between authoritative parenting and child competence, and the high level of maladjustment in socially aggressive children, it is important to resolve this ambiguity.

Conflict Modes or Parenting Style?

Drawing inferences about parent–child conflict from research on parenting gives rise to a second interpretational problem. Specifically, Darling and Steinberg (1993) observed that "any parenting typology (including Baumrind's) captures a configuration of parenting practices, thus making it difficult to ascertain what aspect of parenting affects which developmental outcomes" (p. 491). Because modes or patterns of conflict covary with other aspects of parenting style, it is not clear whether differences in child adjustment result from different conflict modes or aspects of parenting style that are unrelated to conflict.

Comments

Several modes of parent–child conflict have been identified that are associated with varying levels of child adjustment. However, the exact significance of parent–child conflict for child adjustment is not clear. Two factors contribute to this ambiguity. First, the relative contribution of parent versus child behaviors to the form of conflict has been questioned, making it unclear what processes various forms of parent–child conflict represent. Second, it is not clear if different modes of parent–child conflict account for variations in child adjustment, of if other aspects of parenting style unrelated to conflict processes primarily affect child outcome. To address these issues, we examine research on the processes that underlie parent–child conflict.

CONFLICT PROCESSES

Recent work on processes that may underlie parent–child conflict focuses on factors that may promote or inhibit child compliance in conflict episodes. This work is examined here to determine the role of parent and child behaviors in different modes of conflict, and for what it reveals about how conflict modes might affect child adjustment. Three processes that potentially underlie parent–child conflict are discussed: inconsistency, power assertion, and responsiveness.

Inconsistency as a Precipitant of Parent–Child Conflict

Two major theories have been advanced to explain the origins of parent–child conflict in socially aggressive children. Each suggests that inconsistencies in parenting evoke parent–child conflict. However, inconsistency is conceived in different ways. The first of these theories was proposed by Patterson and involves negative reinforcement; the second, proposed by Wahler and Dumas, involves unpredictability.

Inconsistency and Negative Reinforcement

Patterson (1982; see also Reid & Patterson, 1989) defined *parental inconsistency* as the failure to follow through on initial commands or requests, and argued that such inconsistency gives rise to coercive parent–child conflicts through the process of negative reinforcement. He emphasized that almost all children engage in aversive behaviors and that it is the manner in which parents respond to such behavior that is critical for the future of parent–child conflict. If the parent responds by withdrawing a request, then each party's behavior is negatively reinforced. The child's aversive behavior is reinforced because it leads to the withdrawal of the parental demand; the parent's withdrawal of demands is reinforced because this leads to the termination of child aversive behavior. More generally stated, both the child's aversive behavior and the parent's withdrawal of their demands are negatively reinforced, because each of these actions terminate an aversive stimulus. As a result of this negative reinforcement, parent and child behaviors are likely to be repeated, resulting in escalating cycles of mutually coercive behavior. Thus, socially aggressive children ignore their parents' high-intensity bids for control, because they have learned from past experience that their parents will ultimately give in.

Although Patterson's (1982) clinical observations were consistent with this analysis, initial microanalyses of exchanges of discrete positive and aversive behaviors did not strongly support this viewpoint (for reviews, see

Gardner, 1992; Robinson, 1985). Gardner (1989, 1992) argued that this was because the final outcome, not the single behavior exchanges, produced negative reinforcement. She found that mothers of conduct disordered children were significantly more likely to back off from a command when their children engaged in angry conflict behaviors than were control mothers. The rates at which conflict occurred were directly correlated to the degree to which mothers ultimately succumbed to their children's conflictual behavior, suggesting that maternal relenting encouraged higher rates of child noncompliance.

Inconsistency and Unpredictability

In contrast to Patterson and Gardner, Wahler and Dumas (1986) conceptualized inconsistency as parental behavior that does not logically result from the behavior of the child. Instances would include mothers who respond negatively to both aversive and nonaversive behavior in their children or positively to both the child's negative and positive behavior. Wahler and Dumas (1986) hypothesized that as a result of inconsistent responding, the child is unable to predict the mother's responses from his or her own behavior. Citing a substantial body of research to document the inherently aversive nature of unpredictable experiences (e.g., Epstein & Roupenian, 1970), Wahler and Dumas (1986) suggested that children in this situation are motivated to behave in ways that will allow them to predict their mother's behavior. Specifically, they postulate that children of inconsistent mothers engage in extremely aversive behaviors in order to produce a predictable, albeit negative, maternal response, thus precipitating conflict episodes.

Investigations of this hypothesis focus on a specific population: mothers with few, or primarily aversive social supports, referred to as *insular* mothers (Dumas & Wahler, 1985; Wahler, Williams, & Cerezo, 1990). Dumas and Wahler (1985) found that noninsular mothers increased their rates of negative responding when their children engaged in aversive behaviors. In contrast, insular mothers increased their rates of negative parenting for any child behavior, both aversive and nonaversive. Furthermore, insular mothers responded consistently to their children's aversive behavior (by always responding negatively) and inconsistently to their children's nonaversive behavior. Thus, the mother's behavior was predictable for child negative, but not positive, behaviors. Consistent with Wahler's theory that children tend to engage in behaviors that provide maximum predictability, the rates of aversive behavior in children of insular mothers were three times higher than those of controls, resulting in higher rates of parent–child conflict.

In a second study, Wahler, Williams, and Cerezo (1990) compared the conditional probabilities that child aversive behaviors would occur given contingent maternal behavior versus noncontingent maternal behavior or behavior that fails to discriminate among different forms of child behavior. They found that child aversive behavior was least likely to occur after mothers' contingent behavior and most likely to occur immediately after mothers' noncontingent or indiscriminate behavior. Rates of child aversiveness also correlated with maternal indiscriminate behavior. Although intriguing, Wahler's conclusions must be considered tentative, because the first study relied on correlations and the second used measures of questionable reliability.

Inconsistency and Parent Styles

Inconsistency has been discussed as a distinctive feature of parents of socially aggressive children, and most of the studies on this topic focus on this population. It is worth noting, however, that inconsistency can be related to the parental styles described earlier. Specifically, Baumrind's descriptions imply that both authoritarian and authoritative parents are probably consistent, whereas permissive parents may be inconsistent (cf. Baumrind, 1967).

Comments

How can one reconcile the data relating to Patterson's and Wahler's hypotheses? One possibility is that both forms of inconsistency occur. Wahler, Williams, and Cerezo (1990) found mixed support for this hypothesis, and conjectured that unpredictability and negative reinforcement may work in tandem to produce escalating coercive cycles. An additional explanation is suggested by differences in the nonconflict behaviors of the samples studied (cf. Gardner, 1992). Patterson and Gardner both have described parents who are irritable and highly reactive to child behaviors. In contrast, Wahler, Williams, and Cerezo (1990) described depressed and disengaged mothers who, in nonconflict interactions with their children, are detached and affectless, and seem to be merely "going through the motions" (p. 405). Thus, negative reinforcement may be more salient in families where parents engage in many forceful attempts to alter child behavior, whereas Wahler's predictability hypothesis may pertain more in situations where there are a high number of child bids for parent attention. In support of this idea, both Gardner (1989, 1992) and Wahler, Williams, and Cerezo (1990) found strongest evidence of negative reinforcement effects in conflict interactions initiated by a maternal command rather than a child request.

Despite these differences, both theories of inconsistency seem to share a common feature: They highlight the child's need to control his or her environment as an important factor underlying parent–child conflict. The child's inability to predict parent behavior renders the child helpless vis-à-vis a major component of his or her environment. Aversive child behaviors that elicit predictably aversive parent responses can be seen as the child's attempt to gain mastery and control over this environment.

The negative reinforcement hypothesis by definition involves the child's attempt to be in control, and socially aggressive children faced with high-intensity power assertion from their parents (e.g., threats and insults) may be particularly motivated to achieve control. That is, the high-intensity control efforts of their parents may represent a greater threat to socially aggressive children's autonomy than do the control efforts of normal parents. This possibility is supported by a line of research suggesting that power assertion itself can lead to noncompliance and parent–child conflict.

Power Assertion as a Precipitant of Parent–Child Conflict

Although inconsistency has been identified as a possible precipitant of parent–child conflict, particularly in clinical populations, research focusing more on community samples suggests that power assertion per se produces noncompliance (Crockenberg, 1987; Crockenberg & Litman, 1990; Kuczynski, & Kochanska, 1990; Kuczynski, Kochanska, Radke-Yarrow, & Girnius-Brown, 1987). From this perspective, variations in parental power assertion produce variations in child compliance and, hence, differing degrees of parent–child conflict. At the same time, it is suggested that noncompliance is not a unitary construct, but rather can exist in more or less competent forms (Crockenberg & Litman, 1990; Kuczynski & Kochanska, 1990; Kuczynski, Kochanska, Radke-Yarrow, & Girnius-Brown, 1987). Children's willingness to comply, but also their ability to engage in more or less competent noncompliance, may be related to the level of power assertion that is employed (Crockenberg & Litman, 1990; Kuczynski & Kochanska, 1990; Kuczynski, Kochanska, Radke-Yarrow, & Girnius-Brown, 1987). Before addressing this question, it is necessary to first examine what is meant by competent noncompliance.

Noncompliance: All Bad?

A number of rationales have been provided for distinguishing forms of noncompliance in preschool children. Crockenberg and Litman (1990) suggested that noncompliance may function as an expression of autonomy. They distinguish defiance, where the child's primary purpose is to resist parental control, from simple refusal, which focuses on expressing the child's desires. Kuczynski and Kochanska (1987, Kuczynski, Kochanska,

Radke-Yarrow, & Girnius-Brown, 1990) further suggested that children's noncompliance should be evaluated as a social skill. Socially skilled strategies are both more sophisticated and less aversive to others. From this perspective, defiance is the least skillful social strategy, as it is unsophisticated and likely to be aversive to parents. Similarly, any strategy involving anger or whining is unskilled. Negotiation, which involves using explanations or attempts to compromise or bargain, represents a sophisticated and nonaversive strategy. Simple refusal and passive noncompliance are seen as occupying a middle ground, with simple refusal being seen as relatively more, and passive noncompliance as relatively less, skillful.

Various findings support the notion that these different forms of noncompliance represent differing levels of skill. More socially skilled forms of compliance increase as children grow older (Kuczynski & Kochanska, 1987; Kuczynski, Kochanska, Radke-Yarrow, & Girnius-Brown, 1990). Children who engaged in more competent noncompliance were more socially competent in nonconflict interactions (Kuczynski, Kochanska, Radke-Yarrow, & Girnius-Brown, 1990). Interestingly, only noncompetent forms of noncompliance were associated with problem behaviors (Kuczynski, Kochanska, Radke-Yarrow, & Girnius-Brown, 1990).

Different forms of noncompliance represent distinct and unrelated modes of interaction. Less skilled approaches tend to correlate with each other, as do more skilled strategies, but less skillful strategies are uncorrelated with more skillful ones (Kuczynski & Kochanska, 1987). In an investigation of simple refusal and defiance in two different settings, Crockenberg and Litman (1990) demonstrated that the two approaches loaded on different factors. Longitudinal research tracking compliance from 2 to 5 years old shows that specific noncompliance behaviors change over time; however, children exhibiting noncompliance deemed more skillful at one age used more skillful strategies at a later age; similarly, less skilled strategies used early on correlated with less skilled strategies employed later (Kuczynski, Kochanska, Radke-Yarrow, & Girnius-Brown, 1990).

Although the distinction between more or less competent forms of noncompliance is supported by existing research, the data do not clarify whether modes of noncompliance are properties of the child or properties of the conflict interaction. It has been suggested that noncompliance strategies emerge as reactions to particular forms of maternal control strategies (Crockenberg, 1987; Crockenberg & Litman, 1990; Kuczynski, & Kochanska, 1990; Kuczynski, Kochanska, Radke-Yarrow, & Girnius-Brown, 1987). Specifically, it has been argued that greater power assertiveness is related to both increased noncompliance and to less competent forms of noncompliance. The concept of power assertiveness is, therefore, discussed next.

Forms of Parental Power Assertion

Parental power assertion has been examined in relation to child peer rejection (e.g., Pullatz, 1987), cognitive competence (e.g., Hess & McDevitt, 1984), and maladaptive social cognition (e.g., Hart, Ladd, & Burleson, 1990). Of particular interest are researchers who, in contrast to Baumrind, have suggested that parental power assertion provokes noncompliance (e.g., Crockenberg, 1987; Crockenberg & Litman, 1990; Kuczynski & Kochanska, 1990; Kuczynski, Kochanska, Radke-Yarrow, & Girnius-Brown, 1987).

It should be noted that various conceptions of power assertion have been used. One distinction made is between direct commands (e.g., "Put the napkin on the table") and indirect commands that are stated as a suggestion or a polite request (e.g., "Could you please put the napkin on the table?") or directives that include parental bargaining or negotiation (Crockenberg, 1987; Crockenberg & Litman, 1990; Kuczynski & Kochanska, 1990; Kuczynski, Kochanska, Radke-Yarrow, & Girnius-Brown, 1987). Direct commands have also been contrasted to reasoning (i.e., providing an explanation or justification for the requested action; Crockenberg & Litman, 1990; Hart, Ladd, & Burleson, 1990; Hess & McDevitt, 1984; Kuczynski & Kochanska, 1990; Kuczynski, Kochanska, Radke-Yarrow, & Girnius-Brown, 1987). In the first case, direct commands are seen as relatively power assertive because they do not leave much room for discussion; in the second case, they are seen to be assertive because they do not attempt to persuade the child of the justice of the command.

Although additional forms of power assertion exist (e.g., physical enforcement, such as grabbing the child's arms and physically removing him or her; Kuczynski, Kochanska, Radke-Yarrow, & Girnius-Brown, 1990), the affect accompanying the power assertion may be more important than the form it takes. Of particular note is the construct of "negative control" (Crockenberg & Litman, 1990), which requires the expression of anger or annoyance combined with intrusive behaviors, such as criticism, shouting, slapping, spanking, and physical constraint. The defining feature of this construct seems to be the level of implied hostility. Just as noncompliance can focus primarily on disobedience or the expression of child desires, it might be equally important to differentiate power assertion whose primarily purpose is to shape child behavior from power assertion whose primary purpose is to express anger and hostility.

Correlates of Power Assertion

The hypothesis that greater power assertion provokes both incompetent forms of noncompliance, and that moderate power assertion provokes both compliance and competent noncompliance, has been tested by examining correlations between forms of power assertion and forms of compliance.

Competent Versus Incompetent Noncompliance. In general, studies support the notion that high power assertion produces less competent noncompliance, and that low power assertion is associated with more competent noncompliance. Negative control, direct commands, and physical enforcement are all associated with defiance (Crockenberg, 1987; Crockenberg & Litman, 1990; Kuczynski & Kochanska, 1990; Kuczynski, Kochanska, Radke-Yarrow, & Girnius-Brown, 1987); reasoning and indirect commands are associated with negotiation (Kuczynski & Kochanska, 1990; Kuczynski, Kochanska, Radke-Yarrow, & Girnius-Brown, 1987). Self-assertion is more likely than defiance or compliance in association with guidance (Crockenberg & Litman, 1990).

To some extent, the results of these studies follow logically from the terms defined. For example, Crockenberg and Litman's (1990) construct of *guidance* can involve suggestions formulated as questions (e.g., "Wouldn't you rather put the toy away?") that invite the child to express his or her reasons for resisting the suggestion and, thereby, elicit behavior that has already been defined as competent noncompliance. Still, it is noteworthy that these moderate attempts at power assertion initiate a dialogue and decrease the likelihood of direct defiance.

Compliance. The relation of power assertion to compliance is less clear. Although the more extreme versions of power assertion seem to be reliably associated with defiance, direct commands are associated with both defiance and compliance (Crockenberg & Litman, 1990; Kuczynski, Kochanska, Radke-Yarrow, & Girnius-Brown, 1990). One ambiguity is that most studies have not examined whether a mixture of strategies was employed. In the one study where this was done, the mixture of direct commands and guidance proved to be the most effective method of obtaining compliance (Crockenberg & Litman, 1990). Notably, negative control combined with guidance, while less effective than mere control or control plus guidance, was more effective than negative control alone. Thus, while guidance alone correlates with competent noncompliance, guidance in combination with more assertive control may produce compliance.

Noncompliance. As noted earlier, power assertion that functions primarily to express parents' hostility may have particular effects. Crockenberg (1987) examined this hypothesis using parent behaviors from the construct of negative control described earlier, and conducted analyses that controlled child irritability. She found that angry and punitive mothers produced children who were angry, noncompliant, and tended to withdraw from parent–child interactions (the effect of negative control was, however, stronger for irritable infants). Negative control continued to predict child noncompliance and anger when child withdrawal was controlled. Thus, hostile power assertion seems to be especially associated with child noncompliance and angry child behavior.

Power Assertion and Parenting Styles

Although the association of parental power assertion with less competent forms of noncompliance seems to contradict Baumrind's endorsement of firm control, this may not be the case. In fact, the strategy associated with the highest level of compliance — guidance plus direct control — bears a remarkably close resemblance to Baumrind's description of authoritative parenting. In both cases, there is a combination of a well-defined stand, along with a willingness to discuss, justify, and consider child input. However, studies of power assertion do suggest that authoritative parents' high scores on firm control resulted, in part, from the use of control strategies that were most likely to induce compliance, rather than from mere persistence in control efforts.

Studies of power assertion might also explain Baumrind's (e.g., Baumrind, 1967) somewhat puzzling finding that authoritarian parents, who place a high value on obtaining compliance, received lower scores than authoritative parents in her measure of firm control. Authoritarian parents, by definition, use power assertive methods, particularly direct commands without justification; these methods are associated with child noncompliance. Thus, it is likely that parent–child conflict in authoritarian families resulted in fewer positive outcomes than in authoritative families.

Finally, data on negative control seems to speak directly to conflict in families with socially aggressive children. Patterson's (1982) descriptions of irritable parents who threaten, insult, and sometimes physically punish their children recalled descriptions of negative control. This seems to indicate that in addition to inconsistency, these hostile behaviors may provoke noncompliance.

Comments

Underlying descriptions of power assertion and more or less competent forms of compliance seems to be the issue of child autonomy. Autonomy can be seen as a skill that requires less power assertive control techniques in order to develop. There are also indications that children will resist threats to autonomy, and that the likelihood of their resistance increases in tandem with the escalation of parental power assertion. Furthermore, children seem to be more likely to comply in interactions that appear to offer compliance as a choice, thus preserving their sense of autonomy.

Power assertion that preserves autonomy seems to contribute to child compliance, but this explanation of the origins of conflict is incomplete. It seems unlikely that choices are available in every instance of child compliance, and there is evidence of child compliance in response to relatively power assertive techniques (e.g., direct commands; Crockenberg & Litman, 1990). This suggests that child compliance and, hence, the avoidance of parent–child conflict may also have their origins in interactions that do not involve conflict. One process that has been hypothesized to perform this function is parental responsiveness. Therefore, we now turn to discuss this topic.

Responsiveness as a Precipitant of Child Compliance

Although many investigations of parent–child conflict focus on conflictual interaction, it has been suggested that the roots of compliance may lie in nonconflictual aspects of the parent–child relationship. Specifically, parental responsiveness to children in nonconflict situations may produce greater compliance in other situations, thus reducing the frequency and intensity of parent–child conflict (Martin, 1981; Parpal & Maccoby, 1985; Westerman, 1990). Responsiveness has been variously defined, and several examples are discussed before examining underlying similarities.

Early evidence for this hypothesis comes from studies on the relationship of attachment to child compliance (for a review, see Honig, 1985). These studies show that securely attached children are significantly more compliant than insecurely attached children. Furthermore, the hallmark of mothers of securely attached children was their ability to adjust their responses to child behavioral cues, particularly in regards to distress signals. This implied a connection between maternal responsiveness and child compliance.

The connection between parental responsiveness in nonconflict situations and child compliance in potential conflict episodes was experimentally tested by Parpal and Maccoby (1985). Here, *responsiveness* was defined as maternal cooperation with child-initiated interactions, along with the absence of maternal attempts to shape the interaction. Mothers were trained to engage in a "responsive play" session, in which the child would direct the interaction. Only responsive behaviors, such as following the child's suggestions and imitating the child's play behavior, were allowed. The responsive play session was followed by a control session, in which mothers issued a series of direct commands (e.g., "Put the toy in the box"). Two control groups were employed: mothers who ignored their children while filling out questionnaires, and mothers who engaged in free play with their children. Children who participated in the responsive play session were significantly more compliant to direct commands than children in the free play or ignore conditions. This effect was most pronounced for between group comparisons of children who had previously been rated as "difficult."

Parpal and Maccoby's (1985) experimental evidence was supported by differences in responsiveness between parent–child dyads with or without a history of general noncompliance. Summarizing a series of studies of school-aged children, Robinson (1985) reported that parents of noncompliant children, when instructed to follow their children's lead in free play, seem to be unable to do so. Instead, they tend to issue commands, criticize, and otherwise direct the interaction.

Consistent with this idea, Westerman (1990) compared structured interactions of mothers and children with and without a history of noncompliance. Mothers were asked to aid their children in a block-matching test. Westerman found a particular form of responsiveness was used by mothers of compliant children that was absent in the interactions of the conflicted dyads. The mothers of compliant children adjusted their level of guidance in response to the level of their children's performance: Their instructions were more specific when their children were doing poorly and less specific when their children were doing well. Westerman suggested that this behavior represented a more general tendency for mothers of compliant children to identify children's needs and adjust their levels of response accordingly. He further suggested that responses that were appropriate to the child's performance level functioned as guidance, whereas instructions that were too specific, given the child's performance, represented intrusiveness.

Responsiveness and Parenting Styles

It seems clear that the parenting styles described above involve very different levels of parental responsiveness. Baumrind (1967) specifically stated that authoritative parents are significantly more responsive than either authoritarian or permissive parents. Wahler, Williams, and Cerezo (1990) described insular mothers as unresponsive and Patterson's (1982) descriptions seem incompatible with responsive parenting.

Comments

What seems to unite studies on parental responsiveness is the way that responsive interactions, however defined, support the child's striving for autonomy and control. In Parpal and Maccoby's (1985) responsive play session, children exercised autonomy and self-directedness. In Westerman's (1990) structured interaction, mothers shaped children's behavior only to the extent that it would allow the children to continue to experience mastery of the task. A similar process can be seen to underlie responsiveness in infancy: Mothers of securely attached infants respond in a way that allows infants to experience a sense of self-regulation, rather than distress (Maccoby & Martin, 1983).

Taken together, these studies suggest that the child's experience of autonomy in nonconflict parent–child interactions makes the child more willing to submit to limits on autonomy in potential conflict situations. Children who have been responded to by their parents may perceive themselves as sharing goals with their parents (Maccoby & Martin, 1983). Children with this perception may experience instances of parental control as less threatening to their overall autonomy, and may be more willing to comply.

Concluding Comments

This section began with the question of what processes underlie parent–child conflict. The question was motivated by ambiguities regarding parent–child conflict in families of highly competent children (children of authoritative parents). It was unclear if conflict in these families was primarily characterized by parents who maintained a firm stance during parent–child disputes, or whether the essential features in these families was that the children were more disposed to comply with parents' directives. A second question revolved around the relation of parental control attempts in the context of extremely conflicted parent–child interactions. While these parents seemed to employ relatively power assertive attempts at child control, these attempts were not successful. We are now prepared to draw some tentative conclusions.

TOWARD A MORE COMPLETE UNDERSTANDING OF PARENT–CHILD CONFLICT

In this section, we integrate many of the observations offered earlier in an attempt to provide a more complete understanding of parent–child conflict.

Similarities in Conflict Processes

Several processes were posited to underlie parent–child conflict: parental inconsistency or unpredictability, power assertiveness, and responsiveness. First, the interdependency of these concepts should be noted. Responsiveness and inconsistency could almost be viewed as two instantiations of the same phenomenon. Inconsistent parenting is inherently unresponsive; both processes reflect the extent to which parent behavior is predicated on child actions. Commonalities are also evident in power assertion and responsive ness. Power assertion that includes suggestions, explanations, and a willingness to engage in dialogue can be seen as responsiveness within a conflict situation. Although power assertion and inconsistency are conceptually distinct, they appear to be empirically related, in that both occur in families with socially aggressive children.

Most important, the conflict processes examined all seem to involve children's need for autonomy and a sense of mastery. Any form of parental power assertion can be seen to represent some threat to child autonomy. However, parents who are generally responsive to child needs may create in the child a perception of shared parent–child goals (Maccoby & Martin, 1983). This perception of shared goals renders parent control attempts less threatening to the child's overall sense of autonomy. Power assertion can also be modified to be responsive to child autonomy through the use of suggestions and explanations. This strategy may produce child compliance, but also may evoke child noncompliance whose primary function is to communicate rather than to oppose. More power assertive parenting methods represent a direct threat to child autonomy, and evoke child resistance. This is particularly true of hostile parent behaviors, which can be seen to be inherently threatening. Hostile power assertive strategies may produce particularly high power attempts on the child's part to maintain autonomy, such as angry and defiant noncompliance.

Aversive child reactions elicited by extreme power assertion may have particular effects in maintaining parent–child conflict. For example, aversive child resistance may increase the likelihood that parents will back down during a conflict episode. Thus, the child may learn that aversive conflict is the most effective method of ultimately maintaining autonomy.

In contrast, unpredictable parenting represents an indirect threat to child autonomy and sense of mastery, in that it robs children of the ability to influence and interpret their parents' behaviors. There is reason to believe that children in this situation will elicit conflict in order to achieve predictability and control.

Conflict Processes and Parenting Styles

The implications of conflict processes for understanding parenting style should be clear. It has been suggested that conflict modes result from the degree to which parents were willing to exercise power, or firm control, in conflict episodes (Baumrind, 1967; Patterson, 1982). However, the parent styles in which successful parental power assertion was thought to occur also entail processes that have been shown to promote child compliance. Conversely, parenting styles involving a supposed failure of parental power assertion entail processes that promote child noncompliance.

Specifically, Baumrind's (1967; 1971a) description of authoritative parenting included every process thought to promote child compliance: responsiveness in nonconflict interactions, consistency, and mixed power assertive methods that combine direct commands with suggestions and explanations. It seems likely, therefore, that parent–child conflict in authoritative families is influenced as much by children's willingness to comply as to parents' willingness to take a stand.

Authoritarian parents (Baumrind 1967; 1971a) engage in a mixture of conflict-promoting and conflict-inhibiting behaviors. They use relatively high levels of power assertion and are unresponsive; however, they do appear to be consistent. While they seem to experience more noncompliance than do authoritative parents, they do not seem to experience the pervasive conflict associated with socially aggressive children.

Parents of socially aggressive children exhibit every behavior associated with child noncompliance. They have been variously characterized as inconsistent, unresponsive, and highly power assertive (Dumas & Wahler, 1985; Gardner, 1992; Patterson, 1982; Wahler, Williams, & Cerezo, 1990). This implies that the frequent and intense conflict seen in these families is precipitated by socially aggressive children's unwillingness to comply with parental demands.

Taken together, these findings suggest that children's willingness to comply with parents' demands is essential in shaping the mode of parent-child conflict. Does this mean that Baumrind's emphasis on firm control is misguided? We would suggest that it is not. However, the importance of parental control must be examined in the context of the effect of conflict modes on child adjustment. This is discussed next.

Conflict Modes and Child Adjustment

Earlier, we were unable to determine to what extent conflict modes, rather than other aspects of parenting style, influence child adjustment. Although undoubtedly both conflictual and nonconflictual aspects of parenting affect child outcome, the discussion of conflict processes previously detailed suggests ways that conflict processes might uniquely contribute to child adjustment. Specifically, conflict processes associated with adaptive child functioning seem to promote child autonomy, whereas conflict processes associated with child maladjustment seem to inhibit the development of autonomy.

Children's experience of autonomy might relate to their adjustment in a variety of ways. Most obviously, the ability to function independently can be seen to be a necessary skill. Furthermore, as the discussion of competent noncompliance suggested, autonomous functioning in conflict episodes may allow children to develop sophisticated social skills, such as bargaining and negotiation. Finally, the experience of mastery and control inherent in autonomous functioning could contribute to children's perception of their own competence and, thus, to their self-esteem and their willingness to approach new challenges.

To fully understand the relations among conflict modes, child autonomy, and child outcome, a distinction needs to be made between actual autonomy, in which the child functions independently, and perceived autonomy, in which the child has a sense of mastery and control. Although actual autonomy implies an absence of parental control, perceived autonomy may require parental assistance. Thus, for example, in Westerman's (1990) exploration of responsiveness, mothers did not refrain from control, but rather used control that would promote their child's sense of mastery. Similarly, the sense of control over their environment that children may derive from predictable, consistent parenting does not result from lack of parental control, but rather from parental control that proceeds logically from child behavior (Wahler & Dumas, 1986). Thus, although children's subjective experience of autonomy and mastery may result, in part, from being allowed to function independently, this experience may depend to an even greater extent on the exercise of parent control.

From this perspective, both intrusiveness and neglect can similarly function as threats to autonomy that engender conflict and jeopardize child adjustment. This point of view recalls the parenting style that least involves attempts at parental control: permissive parenting. Permissive parents were disengaged and unresponsive, but also angry about their lack of control. Their children lacked two qualities that seem to be associated with autonomy: independence and self-control (Baumrind, 1967). It seems possible that these adjustment problems resulted from lack of parental control and the concomitant failure to promote children's experience of autonomy.

Taken together, these findings seem to partially affirm Baumrind's assertion that firm control is essential for child adjustment. However, it seems that the central feature of this control is not its high level of power assertion, but rather the degree to which it is responsive, contingent, and moderately power assertive, thus promoting child autonomy.

Precipitants of Parent Behavior

It might be objected that the conclusions outlined earlier set an impossible task for parents. Parents are asked to walk a thin line between engaging in too much and too little control. How can this be achieved?

A comprehensive answer is not possible here. Instead, we briefly describe three very different lines of research that reach similar conclusions about the importance of parent perceptions in reaching this goal. Earlier, it was suggested that parent behaviors that promote incompetent noncompliance, thus fostering maladaptive parent–child conflict, all represent threats to child autonomy. The three lines of research detailed below suggest that conflict-promoting parent behaviors occur when parents fail to identify children's attempts to engage in autonomous behavior. Children's most basic attempt at autonomous functioning can be seen to be the effort to express their own personal goals and desires. Thus, the ability to promote child autonomy, both within and outside conflict episodes, is predicated on parents' ability to identify and interpret the goals suggested by their children's behavior. The following research suggest that modes of conflict depend on whether parents are able to engage in such interpretations.

The first line of evidence comes from Wahler's work with insular mothers. Wahler (1990; Wahler & Dumas, 1989) suggested that stress might affect these mothers' abilities to accurately perceive their children's behavior, thus allowing their judgments to be based on broad attributional biases unrelated to child actions. Wahler (& Dumas, 1989; Wahler & Hahn, 1984) observed that mothers seeking help for conflictual relations with their children produced impoverished descriptions of their children's behavior. Although these mothers could produce global judgments about how their children behaved (e.g., "He was bad"), they were often unable to produce detailed or specific descriptions of what the child had done. Furthermore, clinical evidence suggests that global descriptions of child behavior may resemble descriptions of aversive behavior that mothers recently experienced in nonchild interactions (Wahler, 1990). Wahler (1990; Wahler & Dumas, 1989) suggested that instead of perceiving child behaviors accurately, indiscriminate mothers filter child observations through a "response set" based on stressful interactions with people other than their children. Although Wahler's theory of diminished perception is still in the formulative stage, initial empirical investigations lend support to this hypothesis (Dumas, 1986; Wahler & Sansbury, 1990).

A second line of evidence comes from a prospective, longitudinal study of mothers at risk for maltreating their children (Pianta, Egeland, & Erickson, 1989). High-risk mothers who did not abuse their children were characterized, in part, by the sophistication of their conception of the parent–child relationship, and the degree to which they recognized the potential for reciprocity in relationships between mothers and small children. Mothers who perceived young children as able to express needs were less likely to maltreat their children. This was in contrast to mothers who viewed their children as passive and unable to communicate needs and desires (Cohler, Weiss, & Grunebaum, 1970). Thus, extremely power assertive modes of parenting correlated with parents' inability to recognize children's expressions of needs and desires.

Finally, work by Dekovic, Gerris, and Janssens (1991) suggested that parenting behaviors are related to the level of sophistication of parent's conceptualization of the parent–child relationship. Based on work by Newberger (1980), they specified four levels of conceptual sophistication, each of which seems to represent an increasing awareness of the child's individuality:

Level 1: Egoistic (self-orientation). Parents view the child only as the child affects their own experiences and needs.

Level 2: Conventional (norms) orientation. Beliefs about childrearing are based on conventional rules describing normative parent–child relations.

Level 3: Individualistic (child) orientation. Reasoning about the parent–child relationship includes the child's point of view, a conception of the child as an individual, and the idea of mutual exchange.

Level 4: Process (systems) orientation. Parents view themselves and their children as part of a mutually influencing system.

Dekovic, Gerris, and Janssens (1991) found that low levels of conceptualization correlated with parental use of power assertion, restrictiveness, and directive (as opposed to responsive) parenting. Higher levels of conceptualization corresponded with the use of induction and suggestions, rather than commands, and with responsiveness to the child. Although Dekovic, Gerris, and Janssens (1991) did not refer to parents' ability to perceive and interpret child behavior, it is clear that a less sophisticated conceptualization fosters observations of child behavior that are affected by parents' moods or by conventional ideas about child behavior, rather than by a recognition of the child's individual goals and desires. In contrast, a more sophisticated conceptualization, which entails a recognition of children's individuality, would promote recognition of children's striving for autonomy.

Taken together, these works strongly suggest that parents' ability to correctly identify their children's individual goals and to place these goals in the broader context of the child's overall development is a major component of parenting that promotes adaptive parent–child conflict.

CONCLUSION

Parents' attempts to control their children's behavior, and the resulting potential for conflict, are normative and pervasive aspects of the relationship between parents and their children. Different modes of parent–child conflict seem to be related to more or less adaptive child outcome. A critical feature that seems to determine the impact of parent–child conflict on child adjustment is whether both conflictual and nonconflictual parent-child interactions promote child autonomy. Whether or not this occurs seems to depend, in part, on parents' ability to recognize their children's expressions of goals and desires. This last observation is particularly important, because parents' ability to interpret their children's behavior can probably be fostered in parenting skills therapy (Wahler, 1990). Future work should, therefore, concentrate on explicating clinical methods that help develop this ability.

REFERENCES

Baumrind, D. (1967). Child care practices anteceding three patterns of preschool behavior. *Genetic Psychology Monographs, 75*, 43–88.

Baumrind, D. (1971a). Current patterns of parental authority. *Developmental Psychology Monograph, 4*, 1–103.

Baumrind, D. (1971b). Harmonious parents and their preschool children. *Developmental Psychology, 4*, 99–102.

Baumrind, D. (1989). Rearing competent children. In W. Damon (Ed.), *Child development today and tomorrow*. San Francisco; CA: Jossey-Bass.

Baumrind, D. (1991) The influence of parenting on adolescent competence and substance abuse. *Journal of Early Adolescence, 11*, 56–95.

Cahn, D. D. (1992). *Conflict in intimate relationships*. New York: Guilford.

Cohler, B., Weiss, J., & Grunebaum, H. (1970). Child-care attitude and emotional disturbance among mothers of young children. *Genetic Psychology Monographs, 82*, 3–47.

Crockenberg, S. (1987). Predictors and correlates of anger toward and punitive control of toddlers by adolescent mothers. *Child Development, 58*, 964–975.

Crockenberg, S., & Litman, C. (1990). Autonomy as competence in 2-year-olds: Maternal correlates of child defiance, compliance, and self-assertion. *Developmental Psychology, 26*, 961–971.

Darling, N., & Steinberg, L. (1993). Parenting style as context: An integrative model. *Psychological Bulletin, 113*, 487–496.

Dekovic, M., Gerris, J. R. M., & Janssens, J. M. A. M. (1991). Parental cognitions, parental behavior, and the child's understanding of the parent–child relationship. *Merrill-Palmer Quarterly, 37*, 523–541.

Dumas, J. E. (1986). Indirect influence of maternal social contacts on mother–child interactions: A setting event analysis. *Journal of Abnormal Child Psychology, 14*, 205–216.

Dumas, J. E., & Wahler, R. G. (1985). Indiscriminate mothering as a contextual factor in aggressive-oppositional child behavior: "Damned if you do and damned if you don't." *Journal of Abnormal Child Psychology, 13*, 1–17.

Epstein, S., & Roupenian, A. (1970). Heart rate and skin conductance during experimentally induced anxiety: The effect of uncertainty about receiving a noxious stimulus. *Journal of Personality and Social Psychology, 16*, 20–28.

Forehand, R., King, H. E., Peed, S., & Yoder, P. (1975). Mother–child interactions: Comparison of a non-compliant clinic group and a non-clinic group. *Behaviour Research and Therapy, 13*, 79–84.

Gardner, F. E. M. (1989). Inconsistent parenting: Is there evidence for a link with children's conduct problems? *Journal of Abnormal Child Psychology, 17*, 223–233.

Gardner, F. E. M. (1992). Parent-child interaction and conduct disorder. *Educational Psychology Review, 4*, 135–163.

Hart, C. H., Ladd, G. W., & Burleson, B. R. (1990). Children's expectations of the outcomes of social strategies: Relations with sociometric status and maternal disciplinary styles. *Child Development, 61,* 127–137.

Hess, R. D., & McDevitt, T. M. (1984). Some cognitive consequences of maternal intervention techniques: A longitudinal study. *Child Development, 55,* 2017–2030.

Hoffman, D. A., Fagot, B. I., Reid, J. B., & Patterson, G. F. (1987). Parents rate the family interaction coding system comparisons of problem and nonproblem boys using parent-derived behavior composites. *Behavioral Assessment, 9,* 131–140.

Honig, A. S. (1985). Compliance, control, and discipline. *Young Children, 40,* 50–58.

Kuczynski, L., & Kochanska, G. (1990). Development of children's noncompliance strategies from toddlerhood to age 5. *Developmental Psychology, 26,* 398–408.

Kuczynski, L., Kochanska, G., Radke-Yarrow, M., & Girnius-Brown, O. (1987). A developmental interpretation of young children's non-compliance. *Developmental Psychology, 23,* 799–806.

Lewis, C. C. (1981). The effects of parental firm control: A reinterpretation of findings. *Psychological Bulletin, 90,* 547–563.

Maccoby, E. E., & Martin, J. A. (1983). Socialization in the context of the family: Parent-child interaction. In E. M. Hetherington (Ed.), *Handbook of child psychology: Vol. 4. Socialization, personality, and social development* (4th ed., pp. 1–101). New York: Wiley.

Martin, J. A. (1981). A longitudinal study of the consequences of early mother–infant interaction: A microanalytic approach. *Monographs of the Society for Research in Child Development, 46,* 1–58.

Newberger, C. M. (1980). The cognitive structure of parenthood: Designing a descriptive measure. In R. L. Selman & R. Yando (Eds.), *Clinical-developmental psychology: New directions for child development* (pp. 45–67). San Francisco; CA: Jossey-Bass.

Parpal, M., & Maccoby, E. E. (1985). Maternal responsiveness and subsequent child compliance. *Child Development, 56,* 1326–1334.

Patterson, G. R. (1976). The aggressive child: Victim and architect of a coercive system. In E. J. Mash, L. A. Hamerlynck, & L. C. Handy (Eds.), *Behavior modification and families: 1. Theory and research* (pp. 267–316). New York: Brunner/Mazel.

Patterson, G. R. (1982). *A social learning approach to family intervention: III. Coercive family process.* Eugene, OR: Castalia.

Patterson, G. R., Reid, J. B., & Dishion, T. J. (1989). *A social learning approach to family interaction: IV. Antisocial boys.* Eugene, OR: Castalia.

Pianta, R., Egeland, B., & Erickson, M. F. (1989). The antecedents of maltreatment: Results of the mother–child interaction research project. In D. Cicchetti & V. Carlson (Eds.), *Child maltreatment: Theory and research on the causes and consequences of child abuse and neglect* (pp. 203–253). Cambridge; England: Cambridge University Press.

Pullatz, M. (1987). Maternal behavior and children's sociometric status. *Child Development, 58,* 324–340.

Reid, J. B., & Patterson, G. R. (1989). The development of antisocial behavior patterns in childhood and adolescence. *European Journal of Personality, 3,* 107–119.

Robinson, E. A. (1985). Coercion theory revisited: Toward a new theoretical perspective on the etiology of conduct disorders. *Clinical Psychology Review, 5,* 597–625.

Vuchinich, S., Bank, L., & Patterson, G. R. (1992). Parenting, peers, and the stability of antisocial behavior in preadolescent boys. *Developmental Psychology, 28,* 510–521.

Wahler, R. G. (1990). Some perceptual functions of social networks in coercive mother–child interactions. *Journal of Social and Clinical Psychology, 9,* 43–53.

Wahler, R. G., & Dumas, J. E. (1986). Maintenance factors in coercive mother–child interactions: The compliance and predictability hypothesis. *Journal of Applied Behavior Analysis, 18,* 13–22.

Wahler, R. G., & Dumas, J. E. (1989). Attentional problems in dysfunctional mother–child interactions: An interbehavioral model. *Psychological Bulletin, 105,* 116–130.

Wahler, R. G., & Hahn, D. M. (1984). The communication patterns of troubled mothers: In search of a keystone in the generalization of parenting skills. *Education and Treatment of Children, 7,* 77–87.

Wahler, R. G., & Sansbury, L. E. (1990). The monitoring skills of troubled mothers: Their problems in defining child deviance. *Journal of Abnormal Child Psychology, 18,* 577–589.

Wahler, R. G., Williams, A. J., & Cerezo, A. (1990). The compliance and predictability hypotheses: Sequential and correlational analyses of coercive mother–child interactions. *Behavioral Assessment, 12,* 391–407.

Westerman, M. A. (1990). Coordination of maternal directives with preschoolers' behavior in compliance-problem and healthy dyads. *Developmental Psychology, 26,* 621–630.

7 The Sandwich Generation: Conflicts Between Adult Children and Their Aging Parents

James Halpern
Suny College at New Paltz

> Ms. Miller makes a daily trip to a nursing home in Brooklyn to do her duty by her 90-year-old mother, who has no idea who she is. The trip usually reminds her of many things. Sad things. During the [1980s], the number of people 85 and over rose 32.6%. As a result there are generational divides. . . . Children find themselves tending their parents. For Richard Brotman and his mother, Dinah, it means dancing together and occasionally quarreling. (Bennet, 1992, p. 37)

Because Americans are living longer than ever before, life cycles, marital stages, and social changes are playing an increasingly important role in intergenerational interaction and conflict (Cahn, 1990), especially between the elderly and their adult children. The research makes clear that adult children have not abandoned, nor do they avoid, their elderly parents. Although anecdotes and clinical studies point to the existence of interpersonal conflict between aging parents and their adult children, there have been few empirical studies. Researchers seem almost reluctant to explore the underside of the elderly parent–adult child relationship, leaving many unanswered questions. The research does suggest that some of the findings on conflict between aging parents and their adult children are similar to the findings on conflict in other situations: (a) Generational differences are a source of conflict, (b) adult daughters are more likely than adult sons to be caught between the demands of work and caregiving and to be stressed and in conflict with their parents, and (c) the closer people are and the more time they spend together, the greater the potential for conflict.

143

Some of the research does address the unique aspects of this relationship. Conflict appears to be related to the difficulty families have in adapting to the role reversal or the threat of role reversal that can occur when a parent loses independence. There are a great many variables that need to be sorted out in order to understand conflict in this relationship. In some extended families the adult child is dependent, while in others the elderly parent is the dependent one. Interpersonal conflict is likely to look very different depending on whether the aging parent is independent or physically impaired or disabled, or mentally deteriorating, or financially dependent, or in a nursing home. Research findings in one situation cannot be generalized to another. However, the existing literature does not adequately sort out these different situations and how they affect interpersonal conflict. There is need for both qualitative and quantitative research, especially since the demographics make clear that the opportunities for greater contact and conflict will continue to increase.

THE FAMILY LIFE CYCLE

Elizabeth Carter and Monica McGoldrick (1989) suggested that there is a predictable series of concerns, issues, themes, and conflicts that individuals experience as a result of their place in the family life cycle. Each stage of family development presents new challenges and requires that the family redefine members' roles and relationships to accomplish specific tasks. The family life-cycle hypothesis suggests that families most often seek therapy because they are unable to make the transition from one stage to the next (Carter & McGoldrick, 1989; Haley, 1980; Minuchin, 1974). Families with adults in midlife (aged 40 to 65) must focus on their own midlife marital and career issues often while they are having to adjust to changing relationships with their children in order to take into account the adolescents' growing autonomy. At the same time, they also have to adjust to their own parents' diminishing independence and deteriorating health.

Family therapists (Bowen, 1978; Carter & McGoldrick, 1989; Minuchin, 1974) have suggested that conflict in families becomes less manageable if the combination of horizontal (current) and vertical (historical) stressors overwhelms the families' coping abilities and strengths. The potential for conflict appears to increase as the stress of career, marriage, and the care of children and the elderly fall on a generation of middle-aged adults (particularly women) who have been labeled the "keystone," "matron," "caught," "women in the middle," and the "sandwich" generation (Lang & Brody, 1983).

CHANGING DEMOGRAPHICS

America is aging. Pifer and Bronte (1986) suggested that the changing population trends will have consequences rivaling

the conquest and subsequent closing of the frontier, the successive waves of European immigration, the development of our great cities, the post-World War II baby boom, the civil rights and women's movements, the massive influx of women into the paid labor force, the revolution in sexual mores, and the decay of many of our urban centers. (p. 3)

Since 1960, the number of elderly people (people over age 65) has almost doubled. There were 17 million in 1960, and there are projected to be 51.1 million by 2020 (Taeuber, 1989). In the last 80 years, life expectancy in the United States has increased from 47 to 75 years (U.S. Senate Special Committee on Aging, 1985–1986). The most rapid growth in population has been and will continue to be the 85 and over group. Today, there are more older people (the ratio of elderly to nonelderly is approximately 1 to 5), and they are living longer.

As people age, women tend to outlive their husbands. Men tend to marry younger women (Taeuber, 1989). Men are more likely to die suddenly or quickly from lethal diseases, whereas women are more likely to suffer from chronic disabling diseases. For these reasons, older women are more likely than men to look to their children, other relatives, and/or formal support systems for help (Manton, 1989).

At the same time that there are more elderly who are living longer, and more elderly women without the support of a husband, other changes are occurring in the American family. Families are becoming more "verticalized," with more relationships that cross intergenerational lines and fewer sibling relationships or other age-peer relations within a single generation (Cantor, 1991). Adult children who are called on to provide care for their elderly parents have significantly fewer siblings to call on for support if it is needed. In 1931, almost six out of ten mothers had four or more children; by 1981, fewer than three out of ten had that many, and the majority of today's elderly parents have only one or two children (Halpern, 1987). Married couples for the first time have more parents than children. According to Cantor (1991), the typical family by the year 2020 will consist of at least four generations.

Adult children are often called on to care for their parents because of the parents' physical, emotional, and financial problems. Although the majority of older Americans are self-sufficient and wish to remain so as long as possible, there is a significant minority who need assistance in order to remain out of nursing homes. Some estimates suggest that between one fourth and one third of the noninstitutionalized elderly need some assistance with the activities of daily living (Brody, 1981; Shanas, 1979). Cantor (1991) pointed out that the elderly's need for care will increase exponentially:

> Based on the size of the aged population and greater life expectancy at advanced ages, it is projected that by the year 2000 the number of chronically disabled community-based elderly will grow by 31% to 7.16 million persons, as contrasted with only a 19.7% increase among the nondisabled. By 2060, when all members of the baby boom generation will be 85 and over, there will be a 17.9% growth, as compared with a growth of 12.6% among nondisabled older persons. (p. 339)

The care for the disabled elderly is provided, for the most part, by spouses and adult children.

HAVE ADULT CHILDREN ABANDONED THEIR ELDERLY PARENTS?

One way to deal with the potential conflicts brought on by the stress of providing care to elderly parents is to avoid them. Cahn (1992) pointed out that nonconfrontation can include many types of behavior, but one of the most powerful is avoidance. Shanas (1979) discussed the prevalence of the "alienation hypothesis," in which many adult children live far from their elderly parents and rarely see them. Thus, families may not be an important source of support for old people, and there may be little overt conflict between the generations due to avoidance or lack of contact. However, a variety of surveys (Cicirelli, 1981) indicates that older people are in regular face-to-face contact with their children, and even when they live at great distances, they still maintain regular communication. The White House Conference on Aging (1981) reported that more than three quarters of older Americans meet with one of their adult children each week. Thus, there appear to be many opportunities for overt conflict between generations.

There has been and continues to be a pervasive myth that adult children nowadays do not relate to or care about their elderly parents as responsively as they did in previous generations (Brody, 1985). Times have changed and intergenerational relationships have been affected, but "the good old days" never existed. Kent (1965) described the myth of the idyllic three-generation household of previous times as the "illusion of things past." In the majority of nonindustrial agricultural societies, elderly parents had considerable power over their children. Children who did not show filial responsibility would not inherit property rights. Adult children in previous generations, therefore, had a significant financial incentive to respect their elderly mothers and fathers. The status of the elderly in America and other industrialized societies is relatively low and, as society becomes more complex and modern, their status continues to decrease (Cohn, 1982).

Yet, the available evidence suggests that adult children continue to follow the biblical injunction to honor their mothers and fathers, although they are not always sure exactly what is owed or how much help to offer (Callahan, 1985). These children are not likely to live with their parents or provide financial assistance (only about 1% of the elderly population depend on their children for financial support), but they do provide the majority of the emotional and practical help, when needed (Cantor, 1983). Brody (1985), in reviewing the research, concluded that families provide a majority of the practical and virtually all of the emotional help for the disabled elderly. They provide 80% to 90% of medically related and personal care, in addition to help with the household tasks, shopping, and transportation. When an elderly person is institutionalized, it is because the family's caregiving capacities have been stretched to the limit by the parent's chronic physical or mental impairment. "After prolonged and strenuous efforts to care for their parents, adult children reached the limit of endurance (Brody, 1985, p. 20)." The research of the previous decades shows that adult children are the primary caregivers to their widowed mothers and fathers, and, where spouses are alive, children are the secondary caregivers (Cantor, 1991). Stone and Kemper (1989) analyzed the 1984 National Long-Term Care Survey, and found that most adult children who serve as caregivers are between the ages of 45 and 54. The same survey showed 2.7 million adult children providing care to a disabled elderly parent. The research is clear that where spouses are available, they (and not the children) provide most of the care (Cantor, 1983; Johnson & Catalano, 1983; Poulshock & Deimling, 1984; Shanas, 1979).

The notion that children took better care of their parents in previous generations has been proven false (Cantor, 1983; Mancini & Blieszner, 1989; Stoller, 1983;). Yet, 60% of today's caregiving daughters felt guilty about not doing enough for their parents, and 75% believed that children do not take care of their elderly parents as well as they did in "the good old days." Brody (1985) suggested that the debunked myth that the elderly were better cared for in previous generations is perpetuated because it is actually a confused or distorted memory. Because the care provided by adult children to their parents cannot match the recollections of the care they themselves received as children, "the good old days" may really be the memories that adult children have of the time in which their parents cared for them.

RESEARCH ON CONFLICT

The research is clear that elderly parents and children not only see each other and communicate regularly, but they also engage in a mutual system of exchange and support (Bengston & Roberts, 1991; Brubaker, 1990; Cheal, 1983). Houser and Berkman (1984) interviewed 400 elderly women in Los Angeles county and found that what was most important to the elderly was not how often they saw their children, but the quality of the relationship. They said they wanted emotional support from their children. Fortunately, many older parents do receive emotional support and intimacy in their relations with their adult children (Walker & Thompson, 1983). In addition to exchanging intimacy and emotional support, there is also an exchange of practical assistance (Lee & Ellithorpe, 1982).

What is wrong with this picture? Don't elderly parents and their children fight and argue? It is astounding that anecdotes abound on conflicts between the elderly and their children, and yet the research literature is minimal. In reviewing all of the research themes on aging parent and adult child relationships, Mancini and Blieszner (1989) concluded:

> few researchers have looked at the negative aspects of the older parent–adult child relationship. . . . Thus, the literature on older parents and their adult children paints a picture wherein cohesion is pervasive and conflict practically is nonexistent. (p. 284–285).

For the most part, discussion of conflict between the generations is not based on large samples or empirical data, but on clinical case studies (Bergman, 1983; Halpern, 1988). Mancini and Bleiszner (1989) suggested that selective reporting is widespread, and that the elderly are hesitant to reveal the negative or conflictual aspects of their relationships with their children. Researchers seem reluctant to explore conflict between the generations unless and until it becomes violent or abusive (Kosberg, 1988).

CONFLICT AS A FUNCTION OF LIVING ARRANGEMENTS AND DEPENDENCY

Research on conflict between the generations needs to be understood with regards to dependency and living arrangements. As for living arrangements, conflict is likely to look different if it takes place over the phone, because parent and child live far from each other, as opposed to if they live together as an extended family.

The White House Conference on Aging (1981) reported that of the four out of five older Americans who have children, almost three quarters of them live within half an hour of the nearest child, and that most older Americans live fewer than 10 minutes away from an adult child.

Physical proximity does not offer any clues as to the extent or even direction of dependency in the relationship. The elderly and their adult children may live in the same household, as 18% do, but in the vast majority of these intergenerational households the elderly are offering support to their adult children or there is an exchange of support (Aquilino, 1990). Only in a minority of cases do elderly parents and adult children live together with the elderly parent receiving care from his or her child. Conflict between the generations is likely to look different if there is dependency in the relationship and if the adult children are caregivers or receivers. The extent and length of the dependency is also likely to have a direct impact on the nature of the conflict.

Parents who need limited assistance may live close by, far away from, or with their adult children. Parents who need assistance with the tasks of daily living could similarly live far from, close by, or with an adult child, or could live in a facility, such as a nursing home. Studies of conflict need to differentiate between these very different aging parent–adult child situations. Findings on interpersonal conflict in one situation may not generalize to the others.

WHEN A CHILD RETURNS TO THE "EMPTY NEST"

According to Borland (1982), couples today are less likely to have children late in life compared with couples in previous generations. This means that couples today have a much longer life together without children living at home. The lengthened period of the empty nest appears to have advantages and disadvantages (Borland, 1982; Harkins, 1978). On the one hand, parents lose the major role of nurturers to their children, but on the other, they gain the freedom to pursue their own interests. It is often assumed that when adult children live with an elderly parent, the adult child is the caregiver. However, elderly parents are more likely to offer help to their children than to receive it (Mancini & Blieszner, 1989). There are many middle-aged children of the elderly with their own children who are not "sandwiched" but live with their parents for their own or for mutual support. Economic problems, a rise in unemployment, and high divorce rates have contributed to the need to economize and share expenses as some children return to the "empty nest" (Shehan, Berado, & Berado, 1984).

There are benefits of such multigenerational households, but research by Clemens and Axelson (1985) indicated that the potential for conflict is great. As much as elderly parents want to help their children, they are troubled by having more people in the household, which often results in less privacy, overcrowding, clashes of lifestyles, increased expenses, and disruption of some plans and activities. Suitor and Pillemer's (1987) findings of low levels of conflict between elderly parents and resident children contradicted those of Clemens and Axelson (1985). These researchers believed that their finding of a lack of conflict was due to the fact these relationships are often a matter of choice—with a lack of conflict a likely precondition for such an arrangement. They also found that conflict in an elderly couple relationship is relatively unaffected by an adult child sharing a residence, but that where conflict between parent and adult child exists, it contributes to stress and conflict in the elderly parents' marriage. A more recent study of intergenerational conflict in home with children and parents sharing responsibilities (Aquilino & Supple, 1991) indicated relatively low levels of conflict, with only 16% reporting heated arguments that included shouting. These researchers not only examined conflict directly, but also looked at gender differences. They found that fathers were more concerned with the frequency of disagreements, while mothers were more affected by how the disagreements were handled. For fathers, the most important determinant of satisfaction with the relationship was the frequency of enjoyable activities together, while for mothers the most important determinant was just being together.

ROLE CONFUSION AS A CAUSE OF CONFLICT

Most of what is known about conflicts between aging parents and their caregiving adult children is implied in the research literature, as opposed to direct findings. As Mancini and Blieszner (1989) pointed out, there is clearly "the need for studies on conflict" (p. 275). One potential source of conflict is that the clear-cut roles that exist when a parent cares for a child do not exist when a child cares for or helps a parent. Although there is variability and flexibility, there is some consensus that when children are young, parents are expected to provide physical, social, and emotional support. Children are expected to respect and listen to their parents, learn social skills, and do well in school. As parents become less independent or self-sufficient, there may be more confusion and stress concerning who is responsible for what. One study that illustrates this possibility was done by Fisher (1985), who explored families where a medical crisis resulted in an adult child planning to care for a parent. The children believed that a major shift in roles had taken place and that they were better able to make decisions regarding the welfare of their parents than the parents could for themselves. The parents did not share this view, however, and felt pressured into allowing some decision making by the adult child in order to receive the emotional support they needed. The adult children not only felt more protective of the parent, but also concerned and worried about the parent's future and their own burden of caregiving, and frustrated that the parent did not share their view of the change in roles. This case study analysis lends support to the position taken by family therapists (Haley, 1978; Hoffman, 1981; Minuchin, 1974) that when there is confusion in the family hierarchy (who is in charge of whom), there is likely to be stress, symptoms, and/or conflict. These therapists maintain that clarity in roles, and their acceptance, reduce conflict.

THE SANDWICH GENERATION: THE DEMANDS OF WORK AND PARENT CARE

Researchers (Baumhover, 1983; Dobson & Dobson, 1985) have referred to middle-aged adults raising children and caring for aging parents as the "sandwich generation." For these people, the formidable tasks involved with simultaneous childrearing and parent care is immense. Elaine Brody (1981) referred to women in their middle years, in the middle of older and younger generations, and in the middle of competing demands as "women in the middle." Litvin (1992) found that over one half of her sample of adult children caring for an aging parent had at least one child still living at home. However, the 1984 Long-Term Care Study (Stone & Kemper, 1989) indicates that only about 7% of women in the United States with children under the age of 15 were faced with the potential responsibilities of caring for their parents as well as their children. As caregiving seems to be the responsibility of older children (middle-aged) offering care to their elderly parents, there seems to be less likelihood that child care and parent care overlap (Boyd & Treas, 1989; Cantor, 1991; Scharlach & Boyd, 1989). Middle-aged adults are more likely to be sandwiched by the competing responsibilities of work and parent care.

The results of the 1984 Long-Term Care Study indicate that half of the adult children and spouses of the disabled elderly are working full time. There are currently 1.5 million employed caregivers who are not merely helping out a disabled elderly relative, but assisting them with the activities of daily living (Stone & Kemper, 1989). Most of these employed primary caregivers are women.

If the only major changes in American families were that people were living longer, there were more older people, and there were fewer adult children to share the responsibilities of parent care than in previous generations, the situation would be serious but perhaps manageable. The problem is that the responsibility for parent care is not equally distributed among the adult children. Women, the traditional caregivers in our society, are now in the work force in unprecedented numbers, yet they continue to provide most of the care to the elderly. Cantor (1980) found that of the children who were the major caregivers to their elderly parents, 75% were women, whereas other relatives, friends, and neighbors providing assistance were nearly all women. Stone and Kemper (1989) found that women working full time are four times more likely to be primary caregivers than are men working full time. Stoller (1983) found that whereas being employed decreased the average level of sons' assistance by more than 20 hours a month, daughters who were employed provided no less assistance than did those who were not employed.

Furthermore it was found that there was no lessening of care given to the elderly from daughters who had young children. Stoller concluded that these women simply give up their leisure time. "Less attention has been focused on the coping strategies of these middle-aged women, who increasingly must juggle competing role demands of employed worker, mother, and caregiving daughter" (p. 857).

Horowitz (1985) also found that sons were less likely to be primary caregivers to an elderly parent, and usually did so when there were no available female siblings. Daughters were also found to provide more personal and practical care, such as grooming and feeding, than did sons. Although daughters-in-law are not likely to be primary caregivers (Stoller, 1983), sons are more likely than daughters to lean on their spouse for support and assistance in caring for an aging parent (Horowitz, 1985).

The discussion of working women with parent-care responsibilities requires one final caveat. The competing demands of work, child care, midlife, home care, and parent care may appear to be obvious causes of stress and conflict, but there is evidence suggesting that work can actually be a source of respite and social interaction that enhances the self-efficacy and self-esteem of caregivers. Thus, the relationship between work and caregiving is complex and important (Scharlach & Boyd, 1989).

In addition to the gender of the adult child, marital status also predicts the likelihood and level of parent-care responsibility. Caregiving responsibilities fall disproportionately on adult children who are not married. Stoller (1983) interviewed 753 noninstitutionalized elderly persons and their informal helpers, and found that sons and daughters provided assistance in response to the older person's level of need, and that adult children who were married offered significantly less help than those who were not married.

THE STRESS OF CAREGIVING AND CONFLICT

Adult children seem to be fairly accurate at predicting their parents' concerns, particularly when parents are healthy (Cicirelli, 1981; Halpern &

Schroder, 1990). It is somewhat surprising that with regard to gender of parent and child, daughters were the least accurate predictors of their mothers' health and emotional needs. This finding and others suggest that a moderate level of involvement, as opposed to an overclose or distant relationship, is predictive of accurate understanding (Halpern & Schroder, 1990). It may be that when a parent becomes less independent or disabled that the stress or burden of parent care undermines empathy and sets the stage for emotional turmoil and interpersonal conflict.

Cantor (1983) showed that helping an aging parent can be extremely burdensome for family members, and that there is often a lack of mutual understanding. Adult children with parent-care responsibilities report enormous stresses and many interpersonal conflicts, particularly when aging parent and adult child share a household. The nature of the new parent-child relationship appears to contribute to interpersonal conflict when a child, as opposed to a friend or neighbor, cares for an aging parent. In Cantor's study, 92% of caregiving friends and neighbors reported that they got along well with the elderly individual, whereas only 53% of the adult child caregivers reported that they got along with their aging parent. Although adult children are likely to be caregivers to their aging parents, Cantor (1983) found that "only 48% of the children felt that they understood their sick parent well and only 28% felt that they were understood in return" (p. 599). Cantor believed that a source of conflict between aging parents and their adult children was that they were of different generations. Only 20% of the children maintained that they shared similar views on life with their parents. All groups of caregivers (spouses, friends, neighbors, and adult children) were worried about the health of the dependent person, but adult children seemed especially worried about obtaining help. When an adult child is called on to help a parent with emotional and practical support, much is lost:

> free time for oneself and opportunities to socialize with friends, take vacations, have leisure time pursuits, and run one's own house. The major adjustment in all cases was personally restrictive—giving up something to provide the time to care for or socialize with the homebound or older person. (Cantor, 1983, p. 600)

The sacrifices that adult children make when caring for an aging parent may be related to why there are problems and conflicts in the relationship.

Arling (1976) surveyed 409 elderly widows and found that contact with family members, especially children, did little to elevate the morale of the elderly parent, whereas contact with friends and neighbors reduced loneliness and worry. Arling concluded that friends and neighbors relate to the elderly person with common interests and lifestyles, while the children often have dissimilar concerns and interests. Furthermore, the family bond in old age is often characterized by role reversal, dependency, and formal obligation, whereas friendships are voluntary, reciprocal, and characterized by equality.

Poulshock and Deimling (1984) pointed out that the perception of "burden" has been used to refer to a variety of experiences related to caregiving, but that this burden has been measured differently in different studies. They therefore examined the factors that contribute to the perception of burden in caregiving. Of the 614 families that were studied, one half of the caregivers were spouses and the other half were adult children (83% daughters, 9% sons, and 8% daughters-in-law). The degree of the elderly person's impairment was clearly related to the experience of burden by the caregiver. Cognitive incapacity and the need for assistance with the activities of daily living (bathing, dressing, going to the toilet, incontinence, and eating) were closely related to the experience of burden. Although the researchers found that disruptive behaviors, including striking family members, swearing, and disrupting meals, were also found to contribute heavily to the experience of burden, it is still not known which impairments, if any, are linked to interpersonal conflict.

Parent care has rarely been studied over time. Children who assist parents for a day or a week may do so cheerfully, but the stress and conflict that arises in longer term and more demanding dependency may make both parent and adult child unhappy. An important longitudinal study was done by Johnson and Catalano (1983), who contacted the family members of individuals over 65 who had recently been discharged from a hospital. Interviews with relatives took place two to four weeks after the discharge, and then again eight months later. Consistent with other findings, they discovered that the majority of primary caregivers were spouses and children. They also found that over time, if the patients continued to be dependent on others, their mood declined and they felt more dissatisfied with their caregivers. The caregivers reported more stress and strain, and that the relationship became characterized by conflict.

The researchers found that the conflict caused by long-term dependency was most likely to be adapted to by "distancing or intensifying techniques." Approximately one third of the sample, most of whom were adult children, reacted to the greater demands from the parent and the parent's increasing dissatisfaction by establishing a greater physical distance between themselves and their parent or by reducing the frequency of contact. Adult daughters, who were found to be particularly susceptible to guilt and resentment, were likely to attempt to remain physically close while trying to establish a greater psychological distance. Johnson and Catalano suggested that this was accomplished by attempting to include other family members in the daily care of the parent. In direct contrast to the distancing techniques, some caregivers reacted to the increased dependency of the patient by intensifying the relationship. These ties could become so enmeshed that the pair withdrew from their other social relationships. Although this arrangement can lead to burnout in the caregiver, for some adult children the total commitment to the parent becomes a substitute for a failed marriage or miserable job situation.

Adult children seem to be less predisposed to this strategy and the potential for engulfment than are the spouses of the disabled elderly. The findings of Johnson and Catalano (1983) were supported by the more recent research by Skaff and Pearlin (1992). These researchers attempted to delineate the conditions under which adults caring for a relative with Alzheimer's disease experience role engulfment and loss of self. They found that spouses were more likely to experience a loss of self than were adult children, that women were more likely to experience a loss of self than were men, and that younger caregivers of both groups felt a greater burden and constriction of self than did older caregivers.

In reviewing the research on the effects of stress on both caregiving and care receiving, Litvin (1992) concluded that "significant questions concerning aspects of conflict in intergenerational relationships must be addressed in order to enhance the lives of both the elderly and their primary caregivers and to assure the continuation of a family support system" (p. 69). Litvin was one of the first researchers to directly study intergenerational conflict. She gathered data from 117 pairs of caregivers and receivers, using two structured questionnaires administered individually by personal in-depth interviews. Litvin examined four potential areas of conflict between the generations: disagreement over what is considered important in life, disagreement over concerns about the care receiver's welfare, feelings of stress in the relationship, and the extent to which the caregiver is seen as fulfilling the care receiver's needs. The results suggest that for both aging parent and adult child caregiver, a negative future outlook concerning the well-being of the elderly parent is strongly associated with higher levels of interpersonal conflict. For elderly parents, such conflict was associated with a current state of unhappiness and the view that there was a change in the quality of their relationship with their child. For adult children, interpersonal conflict was associated with their view that the parent participated significantly less with family and friends. Interpersonal conflict was found to be related to the children viewing their parent as in better health and more involved in social activities than did the parent. The parent's reaction to loss was found to be misunderstood by the adult child, who mistakenly viewed the parent's responses as manipulations. If the child sees the parent as relating less to the family, the child experiences increased tension. As the elderly parent participates less with others and focuses more on the primary caregiver who does not fulfill the expectations of increased support, more interpersonal conflict will be perceived by the parent.

Litvin's (1992) finding suggests that "overinvolvement" of a dependent parent and caregiving child is related to increased interpersonal conflict. This was supported by the fact that caregivers are less likely to experience a loss of self if they play roles other than caregiving (Skaff & Pearlin, 1992) and that contact with friends seems to protect against loss of self (Norris, Stephens, & Kinney, 1990; Skaff & Pearlin, 1992). Although there is little research that focuses directly on intergenerational conflict, there is even less that addresses the issues of conflict resolution. The implications of recent studies (Halpern, 1988; Litvin, 1992; Matthews & Rosner, 1988; Skaff & Pearlin, 1992) do suggest that a wider support network for both caregiver and care receiver is likely to reduce stress and interpersonal conflict. Such a hypothesis needs to be tested directly, however.

DIRECTIONS FOR FUTURE RESEARCH

In spite of the large numbers of research studies that have been done on aging parent–adult child relationships, it is astonishing that there is so little research on the form and content of conflict in extended families. There are almost all questions and few answers. Research has been done on conflict in different marital life cycles within a "systems-interactionist paradigm" (Cahn, 1992), but no one has applied the paradigm to conflict in extended families. It is not known for sure what the elderly and their children argue or fight about, but it can be assumed to include decision making, the raising of grandchildren/children, and money. It is not known if conflict between the generations is similar to conflict within couples generally or has a different character with different issues. Clear data about the behaviors that elderly parents and their children find objectionable do not exist. Tape recordings similar to those that have been conducted with married couples within the systems-interactionist perspective could be used to identify and specify problematic behaviors to determine the behaviors that partners find objectionable. What the elderly and their children are in conflict about, how they resolve issues, and how conflict affects their relationships needs to be explored.

There has been a lack of qualitative research on elderly parent–adult child relationships. Cahn (1992) suggested that conflict studied within a "cognitive-exchange paradigm" emphasizes perceptions and cognitions. From such a perspective, future researchers could use well-structured interviews in order to explore the underside of the adult child–elderly parent relationship. These interviews should take into account the variable of social desirability—the need to present socially desirable behaviors and attitudes independent of reality (Crowne & Marlowe, 1960) to get a direct look at the phenomenon of intergenerational conflict.

In addition to the two perspectives and research paradigms on conflict already described (systems-interactionist and cognitive-exchange), Cahn (1992) described a third: "rules-interventionist," which examines how a dispute between two people is affected by a third, neutral party. As the potential for conflict between elderly parents and their adult children is likely to increase, there is clearly a need for research on the impact of a third person—facilitator, helper, mediator, or therapist—on the elderly parent-adult child relationship. It is not known if some therapists or mediators are more effective than others, or even if therapy is effective at all in addressing the conflicts between aging parents and their children. It is not known if certain potential conflict situations (nursing home placement, financial conflicts, etc.) are more likely than others to be helped by the interventions of a third person.

The degree of the elderly parent's impairment is not directly translated into the experience of burden (Poulshock & Deimling, 1984). Similarly, it is not known if there are direct correlations between the degree of impairment, stress, and conflict. Interpersonal conflict is only one possible reaction to stress. Individuals under stress can develop physical symptoms or psychological symptoms—depression, for example—or experience no problems at all if they cope effectively with stress (Friedman & DiMatteo, 1982). It is not known if one type of impairment or one type of living situation is more likely to lead to depression whereas another is likely to lead to interpersonal conflict. Also neglected by researchers is the variable of predisposition to conflict, as well as the effects of the earlier relationship. Unresolved differences and conflicts between parents and children could lay dormant during the years of mutual independence, and reemerge when the relationship is intensified due to the stress of parent care (Bowen, 1978). To date, there have been no studies that test this hypothesis.

There have been no longitudinal studies like the one conducted by Johnson and Catalano (1983), discussed previously, that focus specifically on interpersonal conflict. Cahn (1992) reported that partners in couple relationships may experience conflict differently and behave differently as their dissatisfaction grows over time. A longitudinal study on elderly parent–adult child conflicts might examine the way in which the dynamics change over time.

In conclusion, one final observation should be made, which highlights the difficulty of doing research on conflict in personal relationships. As much as there is a need for intensive study of conflict in the elderly parent–adult child dyad, there is also a need to study conflict in the larger family system. Conflict between two family members most often effects and is affected by other family members. As already discussed, much research suggests that when there is a primary caregiver to an aging parent and that caregiver is an adult child, it is most often a daughter (Brody, 1985; Cantor, 1991; Lang & Brody, 1983; Stoller, 1983). More recently, however, Matthews and Rosner (1988) found that when a child cares for an aging parent, most of the siblings in the family are more or less active participants.

Bowen (1978) suggested that two-person relationships are unstable and that the most stable relationships occur in threes. The third person in a triangular relationship including an elderly parent and adult child may be the spouse of the parent, the spouse of the child, a sibling of the parent, a sibling of the child, a grandchild, or a friend or neighbor of either parent or adult child. For example, conflict between an aging mother and daughter may be related to how this daughter relates to her siblings or her husband. If she fights with her husband she may look to her mother for comfort and have a greater need to keep that relationship harmonious. If a child is having problems at school, a husband and wife may blame the child's difficulty on an aging live-in parent who demands their time or assistance. Scapegoating an aging parent could obviously increase conflict among certain members of the extended family and reduce conflict between others. Family systems theorists (Bowen, 1978; Carter & McGoldrick, 1989; Hoffman, 1981) suggest that to better understand conflict in a dyadic relationship, the context needs to be expanded to include all members of the family.

REFERENCES

Aquilino, W. S. (1990). The likelihood of parent–adult coresidence: Effects of family structure and parental characteristics. *Journal of Marriage and the Family*, *52*, 405–419.

Aquilino, W. S., & Supple D. R. (1991). Parent–child relations and parent's satisfaction with living arrangements when adult children live at home. *Journal of Marriage and the Family*, *53*, 13–27.

Arling, G. (1976). The elderly widow and her family, neighbors and friends. *Journal of Marriage and the Family*, *38*, 757–768.

Baumhover, L. (1983, August 28). Children, parents, "sandwich" middleage. *Stillwater News Press*, p.1c.

Bengston, V. L., & Roberts, R. E. L. (1991). Intergenerational solidarity in aging families: An example of formal theory construction. *Journal of Marriage and the Family*, *53*, 856–870.

Bennet, J. (1992, October 4). When elderly care for their elders. *New York Times*, pp. 37, 40.

Bergman, J. (1983). Prescribing family criticism as a paradoxical intervention. *Family Process*, *23*, 517–522.

Borland, D. (1982). A cohort analysis approach to the empty-nest syndrome among three ethnic groups of women: A theoretical position. *Journal of Marriage and the Family*, *44*, 117–129.

Bowen, M. (1978). *Family therapy in clinical practice*. New York: Jason Aronson.

Boyd, S. L., & Treas, J. (1989). Family care of the frail elderly: A new look at "women in the middle." *Women's Studies Quarterly*, *17*, 66–74.

Boyd, S. L., & Treas, J. (1989). Family care of the frail elderly: A new look at "women in the middle." *Women's Studies Quarterly, 17*, 66–74.

Brody, E. (1981). Women in the middle and family help to older people. *The Gerontologist, 21*, 471– 480.

Brody, E. (1985). Parent care as a normative stress. *The Gerontologist, 5*, 19–29.

Brubaker, T. H. (1990). Families in later life: A burgeoning research area. *Journal of Marriage and the Family, 52*, 959–981.

Cahn, D. D. (1990). Intimates in conflict: A research review. In D. D. Cahn (Ed.), *Intimates in conflict: A communication perspective* (pp. 1–22). Hillsdale, NJ: Lawrence Erlbaum Associates.

Cahn, D. D. (1992). *Conflict in intimate relationships*. New York: Guilford.

Callahan, D. (1985). What do children owe elderly parents? *The Hastings Center Report*, 32–37.

Cantor, M. H. (1980). The informal support system: Its relevance in the lives of the elderly. In E. Borgatta & N. McClusky (Eds.), *Aging and society* (pp. 131–144). Beverly Hills, CA: Sage.

Cantor, M. H. (1983). Strain among caregivers: A study of experiences in the United States. *The Gerontologist, 23*, 597–604.

Cantor, M. H. (1991). Family and community: Changing roles in an aging society. *The Gerontologist, 31*, 337–346.

Carter, E., & McGoldrick, M. (1989). *The changing family life cycle: A framework for family therapy* (rev. ed.). Needham Heights, MA: Allyn & Bacon.

Cheal, D. (1983). Intergenerational family transfers. *Journal of Marriage and the Family, 45*, 805–813.

Cicirelli, V. (1981). *Helping elderly parents: The role of adult children*. Boston: Auburn House.

Clemens, A. W., & Axelson, L. J. (1985). The not-so-empty nest: The return of the fledgling adult. *Family Relations, 34*, 259–264.

Cohn, R. M. (1982). Economic development and status change of the aged. *American Journal of Sociology, 87*, 1150–1161.

Crowne, D. P., & Marlowe, D. (1960). A new scale of social desirability independent of psychopathology. *Journal of Consulting Psychology, 14*, 349–354.

Dobson, J. E., & Dobson, R. L. (1985). The sandwich generation: Dealing with aging parents. *Journal of Counseling and Development, 63*, 572–574.

Fisher, L. R. (1985). Elderly parents and the caregiving role: An asymmetrical transition. In W. A. Peterson & J. Quadragno (Eds.), *Social Bonds in Later Life* (pp. 105–114). Beverly Hills, CA: Sage.

Friedman, M. R., & DiMatteo, M. R. (1982). *Interpersonal issues in health care*. New York: Academic.

Haley, J. (1978). *Problem-solving therapy: New strategies for effective family therapy*. New York: Harper Colophon.

Haley, J. (1980). *Leaving home: The therapy of disturbed young people*. New York: McGraw-Hill.

Halpern, J. (1987). *Helping your aging parents: A practical guide for adult children*. New York: McGraw-Hill.

Halpern, J. (1988, July/August). The reluctant caretaker: A son reaches out to his distant mother. *Family Therapy Networker*, 43–46.

Halpern, J., & Schroder, M. A. (1990, August). *Perceptions of the needs of elderly parents by adult children*. Paper presented at the 99th Annual Convention of the American Psychological Association, San Francisco, CA.

Harkins, E. (1978). Effects of empty nest transition on self-report of psychological and physical well-being. *Journal of Marriage and the Family, 40*, 549–556.

Hoffman, L. (1981). *Foundations of family therapy*. New York: Basic.

Horowitz, A. (1985). Sons and daughters as caregivers to older parents: Differences in role performance and consequences. *The Gerontologist, 25*, 612–617.

Houser, B., & Berkman, S. (1984). Aging parent/mature child relationships. *Journal of Marriage and the Family, 46*, 295–299.

Johnson, C. L., & Catalano, D. J. (1983). A longitudinal study of family supports to impaired elderly. *The Gerontologist, 23*, 612–618.

Kent, D. P. (1965). Aging—fact or fancy. *The Gerontologist, 5*, 2.

Kosberg, J. (1988). Preventing elder abuse: Identification of high-risk factors prior to placement decisions. *The Gerontologist, 28*, 43–50.

Lang, A., & Brody, E. (1983). Characteristics of middle-aged daughters and help to their elderly mothers. *Journal of Marriage and the Family, 45*, 193–202.

Lee, G., & Ellithorpe, E. (1982). Intergenerational exchange and subjective well-being among the elderly. *Journal of Marriage and the Family, 44*, 217–224.

Litvin, S. J. (1992). Status transitions and future outlook as determinants of conflict: The caregiver's and care receiver's perspective. *The Gerontologist, 32*, 68–76.

Mancini, J. A., & Blieszner, R. (1989). Aging parents and adult children. *Journal of Marriage and the Family, 51*, 275– 290.

Manton, K. G. (1989). Disability policy: Restoring socioeconomic independence. *The Milbank Quarterly, 67* (2).

Matthews, S. H., & Rosner, T. T. (1988). Shared filial responsibility: The family as the primary caregiver. *Journal of Marriage and the Family, 50*, 185–195.

Minuchin, S. (1974). *Families and family therapy*. Cambridge, MA: Harvard University Press.

Norris, V. K., Stephens, M. A., & Kinney, J. M. (1990). The impact of family interactions on recovery from a stroke: Help or hindrance? *The Gerontologist, 30*, 535–542.

Pifer, A., & Bronte, L. (Eds.). (1986). *Our aging society: Paradox and promise*. New York: Norton.

Poulshock, S. W., & Deimling, G. T. (1984). Families caring for elders in residence: Issues in the measurement of burden. *Journal of Gerontology, 39*, 230–239.

Scharlach, A. E., & Boyd, S. L. (1989) Caregiving and employment: Results of an employee survey. *The Gerontologist, 29*, 382–387.

Shanas, E. (1979). Social myth as hypothesis: The case of family relations of old people. *The Gerontologist, 19*, 3–9.

Shehan, C., Berado, D., & Berado, F. (1984). The empty nest is filling again. *Parenting Studies, 1*, 67–73.

Skaff, M. M., & Pearlin, L. I. (1992). Caregiving: Role engulfment and the loss of self. *The Gerontologist, 32*, 656–664.

Stoller, E. (1983). Parental caregiving by adult children. *Journal of Marriage and the Family, 45*, 851–858.

Stone, R. I., & Kemper, P. (1989). Spouses and children of disabled elders: How large a constituency for long-term reform? *The Milbank Quarterly, 67*, 485–506.

Suitor, J. K., & Pillemer, K. (1987). The presence of adult children: A source of stress for elderly couples' marriages? *Journal of Marriage and the Family, 49*, 717–725.

Taeuber, C. M. (1989). *Diversity: The dramatic reality in the issues facing the White House Conference in aging and beyond*. Oakland, NJ: Scott, Foresman.

U.S. Senate Special Committee on Aging. (1985–1986). *Aging America: Trends and Projections*. Washington, DC: American Association of Retired Persons.

Walker, A., & Thompson, L. (1983). Intimacy and intergenerational aid and contact among mothers and daughters. *Journal of Marriage and the Family, 45*, 841–849.

White House Conference on Aging. (1981). *Chartbook on aging in America*. Washington, DC: U.S. Government Printing Office.

II Approaches to Interpersonal Conflicts

8 A Communication Approach to Everyday Argument

William L. Benoit
University of Missouri, Columbia

Dudley D. Cahn
SUNY College at New Paltz

Billig (1987) encouraged scholars to consider the study of argument as an inspiration for contemporary social science. Walton (1992) explained that argumentation is "a kind of practical reasoning" useful in everyday conversation (p. 2). Because of the key role played by argument in everyday life and its worth as a scholarly subject, this chapter reviews communication research on argument as a form of interpersonal conflict.

Everyday argument merits scholarly attention because it is a more socially acceptable way of managing disagreement than some other options. Cody, McLaughlin, and Schneider (1981) found that reasoning was associated with other prosocial strategies such as altruism, negotiation, and disclaimers, and directly opposite the antisocial "threat" strategies. Thus, argument can resolve disagreements without resorting to unreasonable/violent methods.

This essay reviews in three sections the literature on argument in the communication discipline. First, after we take the position that communication is best understood as a goal-directed activity, we identify three primary goals of.communication. We go on to argue that the dimensions underlying these goals are also useful for describing three broad kinds of message effects. This analysis should be useful in understanding research on argument. Second, we briefly review the communication literature on the nature of argument. Finally, we analyze this research as it bears on the three primary dimensions of communication.

COMMUNICATION APPROACH: MESSAGE GOALS
AND EFFECTS

The claim that communication is a goal-directed activity pervades the literature on communication theory (see, e.g., Craig, 1986; Kellerman, 1992; Tracy, 1991). Admittedly, the claim requires qualifications: Communicators may not always accurately report their goals; goals may not always be clear either to the communicators themselves or to those observing their behavior; or communicators may have multiple goals and hidden agendas. However, it is reasonable to consider communication behavior, generally, as intentional. Furthermore, we do not devote the same amount of attention to all activities: Some aspects of communication proceed via automatic rather than controlled processing (see, e.g., Hample, 1992). When we suggest that communication is goal driven, we do not mean to imply detailed planning of every aspect of each message we produce.

This immediately raises the question of what sorts of goals guide message behavior. This question is complicated by the fact that goals can be conceptualized at several levels (Craig, 1986). However, we have found most informative the work of Clark and Delia (1979), who wrote that there are three primary goals of communication: instrumental, relational, and identity. Instrumental goals concern solving problems or accomplishing tasks, relational goals concern creating and preserving a positive relationship between interactants, and identity goals concern establishing or maintaining a desired image of the communicator with others. These goals are not equally salient in all interactions. Nevertheless, these are all potential goals in communication, at least one is actually a goal in every interaction, and two or three will function as actual goals for a communicator in some interactions. Moreover, these goals, at times, overlap. While distinguishing between relationship and identity concerns themselves, Hample and Dallinger (1992) argued that, in this study, these goals merged for participants into a single person-centered concern. Thus, these goals may not always appear discretely in everyday discourse or in communication research.

One useful way of conceptualizing the communication discipline is particularly relevant for the study of everyday argument. Some writers seem to be primarily concerned with message production. They tend to be interested in understanding questions related to encoding messages, like why certain types of people, or people in certain situations, tend to create certain kinds of messages. Taking a different perspective, other writers are more interested in the decoding of messages, or how people are likely to respond to messages. These researchers tend to focus on the effects of messages in receivers. We refer to these perspectives as *production* and *reception*, respectively. We do not claim, however, that every scholar or each piece of communication research fits exclusively and neatly into either production or reception.

This distinction has implications for the three fundamental goals of communication. When Clark and Delia (1979) explained that communicators pursue goals through communication, this seemed to concern message production. Messages are produced to solve problems, develop positive relationships, and/or impress others, and the messages may serve as clues to the communicator's goals.

However, communication can also be conceptualized as a process that has diverse outcomes on receivers of messages, affecting task completion or problem solving, relationships, and identity—whether intended or not. For example, several scholars have declared that every message has both content and relational aspects (see, e.g., Watzlawik, Beavin, & Jackson, 1967). So the instrumental, relationship, and identity goals of messages can also be seen as possible effects of messages.

Furthermore, messages can backfire. For example, a woman may try to enhance her identity to impress a man, but he may think that she sounds stupid. Moreover, a message may have effects on other goals not currently salient to the communicator. For example, a husband may direct his wife to take out the trash, but this demand could negatively affect their relationship, because she doesn't think he should order her around.

In sum, communicators use messages as means to achieve three potential goals in communication: instrumental, relationship, and identity. In a given situation one, two, or all three of these possible goals may be important to the communicator, and the goals that are salient guide creation of the message. Concomitantly, a message has potential effects in three areas: instrumental, relationship, and identity. A message is more likely to have effects in areas considered salient by the receiver. Thus, we refer to these three areas—instrumental, relationship, and identity—as *dimensions* of communication, because they can function both as goals that shape message production in communicators and as message effects in receivers (whether intended by the communicator or not).

With this brief introduction to the nature of the communication discipline and this understanding of the three primary dimensions of communication, we can turn to a discussion of an important species of communication: argument as a form of interpersonal conflict. The next section describes current thinking in the communication discipline on the nature of everyday argument.

THE NATURE OF EVERYDAY ARGUMENT

What is argument? Researchers' definitions of argument depend on the perspective they take and the research methodology they employ (Allen,

Burrell, & Mineo, 1987). We discuss functional, structural, and process orientations to everyday argument.

Functional Conception of Argument

A functional view focuses on purposes, goals, and objectives. What is the function served by argument? Hample (1983) saw argument as goal directed, as a means of accomplishing one's wants, or as a tool for improving the environment of the arguers.

Each of the three general goals of communication (instrumental, relationship, and identity) function as goals of argument. Benoit (1989) suggested that arguments function to negotiate the "face" of participants (i.e., identity). Furthermore, some theorists have maintained that argument functions to establish the rules operating in a relationship (see, e.g., Benoit, 1989). They have suggested that argument is viewed as a communicative act with multiple goals (see also Hample, 1983; Wenzel, 1985). Given the fact that argument is a form of communication, one should not be surprised that it pursues the same three general goals of communication.

As in the literature on communication, it is again possible to view instrumental, relational, and identify concerns as dimensions because researchers examine them as both goals and effects, whether intended or not. Most of the research on argument concerns instrumental effects, but Trapp (1990) included among possible consequences of argument "relational dissolution or reinforcement" and "self-concept damage or reinforcement" (p. 49). These sound like synonyms for relationship and identity effects. Therefore, we extend the functional view of argument by explicitly applying the three goals of communication in general to argument and by viewing the three concerns as dimensions that include both goals and effects.

Structural Conception of Argument

A structural view focuses on the sequential relationships between acts and interactants (Benoit & Benoit, 1989). The structural view may be applied to two different ways in which the word *argument* is used by both relational partners and communication researchers. According to O'Keefe (1977), $argument_1$ refers to "a kind of utterance or a sort of communicative act," whereas $argument_2$ is a "particular kind of interaction" (p. 121). Thus, an $argument_1$ can be considered to be a product that an arguer makes, as in "the lawyer made an argument." On the other hand, an $argument_2$ is an event or episode, a form of interaction in which people disagree. Here, we might say that "Joe and Linda had an argument on their front porch." Thus, arguers make $argument_1$s and interactants have $argument_2$s. Because some writers use the same word (*argument*) to refer to two quite different things (a kind of communicative act and a type of interaction), we must be careful to avoid creating confusion. Matters can become increasingly complex when argument$_2$s contain argument$_1$s.

Regarding the structure of argument$_1$s, Reinard (1991) defined them as "claims supported by reasons" (p. 6). Toulmin (1958) asserted that an argument consists of a claim (conclusion), data (evidence), and warrant (an assumption, often unstated, that justifies the conclusion on the basis of the data). Thus, argument$_1$s include a claim, supported by evidence, reasons, and/or warrants.

Aristotle (1984) described two general forms of reasoning: deductive and inductive. Deductive arguments begin with accepted generalizations and derive conclusions from them (e.g., All humans are mortal. Socrates is a human. Therefore, Socrates is mortal). Induction, on the other hand, examines particular instances of a class of objects, observes a regular characteristic, and concludes that this characteristic is probably true of all members of the class (e.g., Every swan thus far examined is white. Therefore, all swans are probably white). For a review of traditional concepts of argument, see Benoit (1992).

Although experts on making argument$_1$s attempt to identify formal structures as rules of logic, there is evidence that everyday reasoning is greatly varied and highly dependent on the social context in which it is employed. Willbrand and Rieke (1991) found that everyday reasoning did not adhere to a single set of rules of logic as traditionally described.

Canary, Brossmann, and Seibold (1987) viewed the structure of argument$_1$s as simple, compound, eroded, and convergent. A simple structure involves statements that support each other. Here an assertion, or claim, is developed through elaboration (evidence that supports the claim), amplification (explanation of its relevance to the argument), or justification (provision of a rationale for the claim). Second, as the name suggests, a compound structure is more complex, and occurs when one of the parts of a simple argument is expanded, when one argument is embedded within another argument, or when two points are made using the same form. Third, eroded arguments are statements that lack development, perhaps due to interruptions or to the communicator's inability to articulate support. Fourth, convergent structures occur when one interactant bolsters his or her own argument by using points advanced by another interactant. Other structural analyses examine children's arguments (Benoit, 1983b; Haslett, 1983; Meyer, 1992), discuss the recurring nature of argument (Trapp & Hoff, 1985), or investigate part of the structure, like c `enings and closing of arguments (Benoit & Benoit, 1990).

A structural view examines statement-response sequences. Jackson and Jacobs (1980) defined *argument$_2$* as disagreement-relevant communicative acts. They maintained that interactants have a preference for agreement (see also Pomerantz, 1984), and arguments provide a means for rectifying disagreement when it arises. Jackson and Jacobs (1980) indicated that arguments are organized around an adjacency pair (adjacency pairs are utterances that occur together, like question and answer, or request and response). Any adjacency pair can be elaborated through a presequence (utterances made before the adjacency pair itself), within a turn at talk, with an insertion sequence (like a question seeking clarification within a request-response adjacency pair), or through a postsequence (which elaborates the adjacency pair after it has occurred).

A structural approach emphasizes the incompatibility of the statements made by two or more interactants. Some scholars argue that everyday arguments (argument$_2$s) can be construed as interactional events or communicative acts that occur between (at least) two people. These interactions are characterized by overt disagreement, which stems from goals that are perceived to be incompatible (see, e.g., O'Keefe & Benoit, 1982). Trapp (1986) also included unresolved disagreement as an essential element of everyday argument (but also see Jackson, Jacobs, Burrell, & Allen, 1986).

Some of the structural features of arguments relate to the interactants' perspective and their emotional displays. Benoit (1983a) suggested that interactants must perceive that the issue at stake is worth the time and effort required in arguing. In addition, people report that arguments are frequently signaled by a negative tone of voice and higher volume, the assertion of irrational beliefs, manifestation of emotional reactions, uncompromising point of view, and potentially negative effects on the relationship between interactants (Benoit, 1982). Similarly, Martin and Scheerhorn (1985) described argument as a hostility-laden event with sharply contrasting opinions, loud voices, intense emotion, anger, and frustration. This work suggests that arguments have a constellation of identifiable features (generally, intense disagreement).

Finally, the structural perspective includes a description of rules that govern arguments. Benoit (1981) maintained that everyday argument (argument$_2$s) should be viewed as a collaborative activity through which interactants balance competitive and cooperative actions. Because arguments involve disagreements, threats to face, and winning or losing, the competitive nature of argument$_2$ should be readily apparent. However, participants must enact a certain level of cooperation for an argument to occur. Benoit (1981) explained that "Interactants observe the rules of turn-taking, they collaborate in the development of coherent discourse . . . and they collaborate in defining the rules by which arguments are evaluated" (p. 625). Hence, interactants must cooperate and share rules of arguing in order to compete in their everyday arguments.

Process Conception of Argument

A process view considers the changes that occur over time. The nature of argument (argument$_2$) can be described by examining its process, that is, the changes that occur as arguments move through initiation event, opening, elaboration, and closing. We now examine each stage of argument$_2$ separately.

Initiation of Argument   Witteman (1992) identified six initiators of conflict: rebuff, illegitimate demand, criticism, noncumulative annoyance, cumulative annoyance, and mutual cumulative annoyance. The presence of any one of these initiators may be necessary (but not sufficient) for starting an argument, because some people choose to ignore the initiator or react in some way other than arguing.

Alberts (1989a) identified different types of complaints in couples' communication: behavioral (partner's actions/inactions), personal characteristics (partner's personality, attitudes, emotional nature, or belief system), performance (how partner performed an action), complaining (partner's complaining), and personal appearance (physical looks). We view these complaints as an elaboration of Witteman's category of "criticism." We believe that in more intimate relationships, Alberts's list suggests that criticism or complaining is one of the more common initiators of argument.

Trapp and Hoff (1985) indicated that the decision to confront another may take some time, and Newell and Stutman (1983) described seven factors that influence the decision to confront: the nature of the relationship, perceived urgency, perceived responsibility to confront, perceptions of the partner, resources, appropriateness of time or place, and perceived outcome.

Argument Openings   Once the decision to confront another is made, the argument must be opened. Jackson and Jacobs (1980) suggested that an argument opens when a dispreferred response is produced or a preferred response is withheld. Similarly, in an analysis of children's arguments, Benoit (1985) reported that expressing an unwillingness or inability to engage in a proposed activity (i.e., refusing to comply with a request) accounts for most arguments. Thus, one viewpoint on the opening of arguments suggests that arguments stem from adjacency pairs, which are sets of related utterances (like question–answer; request–response). When the first part of an adjacency pair does not elicit the expected or preferred response, this may provoke a sequence of events recognized as an argument.

Benoit and Benoit (1990) found that utterances that prompt arguments include insults, accusations, commands, and refusals of requests. They observed that these all include explicit or implicit disagreements and threats to face. This is not an alternative to the position that arguments are adjacency pairs with a dispreferred response; rather, these are complimentary positions. For example, the reason why dispreferred second pair parts tend to create arguments may be the fact that they threaten the other's face.

McCorkle (1980) suggested that the beginning of an argument includes the statement phase, which contains an assertion or a claim, and a challenge by the interactional partner, which indicates an unwillingness to accept the claim advanced in the statement phase. When the advocates take apparently incompatible positions (in the statement and the challenge), an argument may develop.

However, McCorkle's primary concern is with what occurs next, which determines whether an argument ensues. Here, the interactant who proposed a claim may respond to the challenge or offer a transcending claim. This may prevent an argument from developing (or shift the dispute from the initial claim). However, when a claim and a challenge are not followed by a transcendent claim, an argument exists.

Elaboration of Argument   After the opening, arguments may be elaborated by repeating a claim-denial sequence or by developing reasons. The nature of this elaboration is negotiable. In children's discourse, a winner of a round of elaboration may be the interactant who can talk the loudest, produce the most rude comeback, produce evidence, provide reasons, or intimidate his or her partner (Benoit, 1985). The nature of the elaboration (mitigated-aggravated) is predicted by prior utterances (Benoit, 1985). Arguments may heat up (becoming aggravated, switching to relationship issues) or cool down (becoming mitigated, moving toward resolution) (Trapp & Hoff, 1985).

When reason giving is involved in the elaboration (e.g., when one makes a request), the assumption behind such an elaboration constitutes what counts as a recognizable reason for producing a dispreferred response (Jacobs & Jackson, 1981). When a request is made and the other person refuses, an argument may develop about the request (e.g., over the rights of the refuser to refuse, or the reasonableness of the refusal). However, making a request assumes, for example, that the other person has the ability to comply with the request (this is called a *felicity condition*). If the other person refers to a felicity condition during the elaboration of the argument ("I would take you to the mall but my car won't start"), this may be seen by the requester as a sufficient reason for refusing to comply with the request, and the argument may close at this point.

Closing of Argument.   Trapp and Hoff (1985) indicated that serial arguments are resolved when one party capitulates, both compromise, or they reach consensus. Benoit and Benoit (1990) found that interactants reported that arguments terminated in four ways—physical or psychological disengagement, agreement, apology, and restoration of the relationship—three of which address the disagreement and repair one's image or face.

Taken as a whole, these definitions reflect the diversity of the communication discipline, and offer a broad approach to argument by directing attention to argument's functions, structures, and process. The following section discusses how argumentation research addresses the three dimensions of argument.

ARGUMENT RESEARCH AND THE THREE DIMENSIONS OF ARGUMENT

Our purpose here is not to exhaustively review the literature, which would be difficult because much of the relevant scholarship does not identify itself as argument research. Instead, this review points scholars toward useful lines of communication research.

Data suggest that the instrumental, relationship, and identity dimensions function in interpersonal situations. Newton and Burgoon (1990) demonstrated the utility of these three goals in categorizing utterances of married/cohabiting couples. Carrocci (1985) described a conflict situation and asked participants to take the role of one roommate and write a response to the other's last statement. Carrocci separated responses into two categories: conflict over content and conflict over "relationship." However, the latter included identity concerns as well as relationship concerns. Carrocci discovered that the participants focused predominately on content issues.

The Instrumental Dimension of Argument

The first dimension of argument is instrumental, task oriented, or problem solving. For example, Zietlow and Sillars (1988) reported the following potential problem areas addressed by argument: housing; irritability; criticism of the partner; leisure time activities; household duties; and lack of communication, affection, or money.

Apart from work that addresses the nature of argument, most writing on the instrumental dimension of argument concerns how to improve one's skill in making argument$_1$s. Rieke and Sillars (1993), for example, justified their chapter on evidence with the observation that "most decision makers are influenced by evidence" (p. 110). Although effectiveness is not the only concern of these authors, it is an important one.

Beisecker (1970) content analyzed problem-solving discussions. He found that the greater the perceived issue-conflict and the more difficult it was to reach agreement, the more likely participants were to use issue-oriented strategies, particularly idea-rejection (disapproving of another's idea) and con-modification (altering an idea by rejecting and/or adding new elements).

Newton and Burgoon (1990) asked married/cohabiting couples to "enact" a typical disagreement. They found that one of the most common strategies was "content validation" (e.g., agreeing or problem solving). During the discussion, partners were less likely to use the verbal strategy of content-invalidation (e.g., disagreeing or exaggerating). Partners also tended to reciprocate one another's use of content validation or content invalidation.

Reinard (1991) suggested "Perhaps on no other area of argumentation has so much attention been focused as on the persuasive function of evidence" (p. 105). Research has found that arguments supported by strong evidence are more effective than those employing weak evidence (Brilhart, 1970). New evidence is frequently more persuasive than familiar information (Hample, 1978).

Research has also focused on reasoning, considering specifically the strength of argument$_1$s. Strong arguments (as rated by the participants) are more persuasive than weaker arguments (Benoit, 1987). Thus, research on message reception indicates positive relationships between argument strength and effectiveness.

The relationship between argument$_1$ and argument$_2$ emerges here. It is hoped that a particularly powerful argument$_1$ may convince others, so as to avoid argument$_2$s. Thus, argumentation textbooks focus on acquiring skill in making argument$_1$s, so that one can avoid argument$_2$s or win the argument$_2$s in which one becomes involved.

Few studies seem to have investigated the question of how people think everyday arguments are won. Benoit and Benoit (1989) asked participants in their study to remember two arguments they had had (one they won and one they lost) and to write a brief essay explaining why they won or lost the arguments. Six reasons appeared in the data: fairness, avoid conflict, argument$_1$ (including evidence, reason giving, and time to prepare), promise, *fait accompli*, and avoid harm to other. Benoit (1981) identified five rules for winning rounds of arguments among children: progression (the arguer who produces the most intense instance of the claim under dispute wins), equivalence (the person who produces the last instance of the claim wins), documentation (the disputant who produces acceptable evidence for the claim wins), reason giving (the advocate who provides an acceptable reason for the claim wins), and intimidation (an arguer whose interactional partner agrees or remains silent wins).

Many questions remain unanswered, such as to what extent argument$_1$s, occur in arguments$_2$s, at what point do people abandon argument$_1$s in favor of less reasonable tactics, to what extent are people expected to use argument₁s when having an argument₂, and how effective are argument₁s that do occur in argument₂s. Much of the research on the effectiveness of argument₁s has been conducted in public speaking situations rather than interpersonal ones, and we simply do not know the extent to which this work can be generalized.

The Relational Dimension of Argument

The second dimension concerns the establishment, maintenance, and repair of relationships. There are two ways in which the relational dimension emerges in an argument. First, relational issues may be the focus of an argument. For example, couples may argue about the depth of or commitment to their relationship. Second, and possibly more common, arguments over instrumental concerns may have unintended effects on the relationship (e.g., an argument over a task could lead to relationship dissatisfaction).

Several scholars discuss arguments that explicitly concern relationships. Here, "an individual's goals involve defining the relationship in a particular way, and arguments erupt when the partner's acts impede that goal or are expressions of competing goals" (Benoit, 1989, p. 430). Thus, at times, arguments address relationship issues. Given the analysis that suggests that communication is a goal-directed activity, that one goal of communication concerns relationships with others, and that argument is a form of communication, the claim that people argue over relationship concerns is reasonable.

At least one study shows how relationship goals influence message production. Canary, Cunningham, and Cody (1988) found that integrative tactics were used more than distributive or avoidance when the interactant's goal in message production was to change the nature of a relationship.

Others have researched indirect effects of argument on relationships using both survey (questionnaire) and subject diaries to discover what people believe about their arguing practices (Benoit & Benoit, 1987). This research indicates that people in general believe that some of their arguments do have effects on their relationships. Many arguments in the diary data (72%) did not affect the relationship, but in the remainder the effects on the relationship were mixed (some positive, some negative).

Before examining research on indirect effects of arguments on interpersonal relationships, it is important to realize that relationships are of different types. While the number of types varies with different researchers and may be viewed as a number of themes that vary from one type of interpersonal relationship to another, communication researchers have focused on three relational themes: affect, control, and longevity.

Some studies examine affect, or the emotional effect of argument, by comparing the argumentation behavior of relationally satisfied partners with those who are dissatisfied. Usually, it is assumed that arguing has contributed in some way to the partners' reported satisfaction or dissatisfaction with their relationship.

After participants rated their marital satisfaction, Canary, Brossmann, Sillars, and LoVette (1987) found that satisfied couples produced different argument sequences than did dissatisfied couples.

> Satisfied couples had a greater proportion of developed argument structures over undeveloped arguables than did dissatisfied couples. Of the argument structures, satisfied couples engaged in a greater proportion of simple structures, and tended to enact a greater proportion of convergent arguments. (p. 479)

Similarly, Canary, Weger, and Stafford (1991) discovered that relationship dissatisfaction was associated with reciprocation of diverging sequences (i.e., disagreement statements), while Canary and Sillars (1992) reported that relationship satisfaction was associated with convergent arguments (i.e., agreement statements).

Other studies pay less attention to what is said than how it is said to show the emotional impact of argument on relationship satisfaction-dissatisfaction. This line of research becomes especially important in everyday argument when one considers that marital and engaged couples claim that their partners appear more rational when they avoid getting angry and raising their voices (Honeycutt, Woods, & Fontenot, 1993).

Based on the claim that verbal communicative acts are key determinants of marital satisfaction, Ting-Toomey (1983) coded verbal disagreements and focused on three types of verbal behavior: integrative (confirming, coaxing, compromising, and agreeing); disintegrative (confronting, complaining, defending, and disagreeing); and descriptive (socioemotional description and questions, task-oriented descriptions and questions). Ideally, partners who value their relationship should argue in a way that contributes to integration of the relationship and avoid statements that lead to disintegration, but, unfortunately, the latter course is the more common. According to Ting-Toomey, marital partners typically begin a conflict in a manner directly attacking one another with criticism and negatively loaded statements, followed by attempts to justify oneself and blame the other.

In a similar manner, Alberts (1988) found that the verbal communication of nondistressed couples complained more about their partner's behavior, made more agreement responses, and expressed more positive affect than did that of distressed couples. Distressed couples complained more about their partner's personality characteristics, offered more countercomplaints, and expressed more negative affect than did nondistressed couples. Interestingly, the two groups of couples did not differ in the number of complaints made, but rather in the way they were made.

In addition, Alberts (1989b) found that adjusted couples are twice as likely to engage in types of complaint behavior designated effective as maladjusted couples. Less effective complaint behavior occurred more often in maladjusted than adjusted couples. Additionally, Newton and Burgoon (1990) found that use of supportive strategies in a disagreement was directly related to the partner's satisfaction, while use of accusation was negatively correlated with the partner's satisfaction.

Some studies have examined the issues of control, power, and dominance. Roloff and Cloven (1990) found that people who feel less powerful than their partners avoid arguments with them. Therefore, to create conditions conducive to argument$_2$s, both partners must perceive that they have mutual control. Meanwhile, Canary, Weger, and Stafford (1991) found that control mutuality (i.e., who influences whom in the relationship) was associated positively with convergent statements (e.g., agreement) and the extent to which points were developed (e.g., elaboration, amplification, and justification).

Finally, relationship longevity may also influence the production of arguments. Canary and Weger (1989) found that the longer the relationship, the more partners structured arguments as convergence sequences (i.e., agreement statements). Similarly, Canary, Weger, and Stafford (1991) again discovered that converging arguments were linked positively to the length of the relationship.

Thus, argument may alter relationships directly when relationship issues are discussed, and may produce unintended effects when instrumental or identity goals are being pursued. Although communication researchers have related everyday arguments to affect, control, and relationship longevity, argument's effect on other relationship characteristics needs to be examined (e.g., emotional and physical intimacy, trust, commitment, and attitudinal similarity).

The Identity Dimension of Argument

The third dimension of communication and argument concerns identity management. As with the relational dimension, the identity dimension emerges in an argument in two ways. First, identity issues may be the focus of an argument. Second, and possibly more commonly, arguments over instrumental concerns may have unintended effects on the identities of the arguers.

Some arguments directly address the face of arguers. Given the claim that an argument can be seen as an expansion of an adjacency pair after a dispreferred second pair part, how is face saved? There are a variety of types of repair strategies, one of which is the use of accounts defined as linguistic devices that function to change the potential pejorative meanings of one's actions and to repair one's identity (Buttny, 1990). For example, accounts are often given as reasons for not complying with a request, rejecting offers, and having an inability to answer questions. In all such cases, accounts function to transform what might initially be seen as reproachable behavior to an action seen as justifiable or understandable.

However, failure events may be viewed as sources of argument in interpersonal conflict, the reproach as an expression of dissimilarity or disagreement, and the account as a second part of an adjacency pair (e.g., complaint-account, blame-account). According to McLaughlin, Cody, and Rosenstein (1983), account sequences consist minimally of three turns: a reproach, an account, and an evaluation. The first turn (reproach) calls attention to something that is wrong, and the second (account) serves to mitigate the argument. The third turn (evaluation) honors, rejects, or ignores the offender's account. Buttny (1990) provided an intensive micro-analysis of one couple's use of blames, criticism, and accounts in marital therapy. Couple therapy is often characterized by recurring instances of partner criticism or blame. Repeated blaming suggests the salience or importance of an underlying issue over which partners disagree. Buttny suggested that recurring blames and criticism may give rise to accounts as a way to defend against the implied change.

Although the above lines of research on accounts examine how arguments address the face of arguers, other scholars address the unintended effects of arguments on face or identity. Here, message variables relevant to argument have been shown to increase perceived credibility (enhance identity) as well as attitude change. For example, use of evidence has been found to increase an arguer's credibility (McCroskey, 1967, 1970) as well as persuasiveness (see Benoit, 1991, for a discussion).

Moreover, some writers have argued that argument can be usefully viewed as a response to threats to one's image, face, or identity. Benoit and Benoit (1990), in their discussion of argument openings, suggested that aggravating utterances, which potentially threaten the face of interactants, consistently signal the beginning of an argument. Thus, argument can be viewed as a reaction to threats to one's preferred identity. Consistent with this analysis, Benoit and Benoit also found that three of the four ways arguments closed tended to repair face. Research on the role of argument in identity development led O'Keefe and Shepherd (1989) to claim that identity effects are best viewed as "by-products" of interactions.

Canary, Cunningham, and Cody (1988) reported that distributive strategies were used more when defending oneself (identity management). In addition, Canary and Spitzberg (1989) showed that communicators are perceived to be most competent when using the integrative strategy and its associated conflict tactics, whereas their use of avoidance and distributive strategies were negatively linked to perceptions of their competence. Finally, Canary and Spitzberg (1990) separated perceptions of self from perceptions of other to show that people perceived themselves as more competent and appropriate than partners judge them to be. They were most similar to one another for distributive tactics (behaviors) than avoidance, and then integration. Our explanation for this finding is that arguers may be more focused on their instrumental goal pursuits than on other outcomes, but partners are more sensitive to the impact of conflict tactics on their impressions of the partner as a person.

Thus, argument may alter identity directly when identity issues are the subject of discussion, and may produce unintended effects when other nonidentity goals (instrumental or relationship) are being pursued. Specifically, the research shows that accounts play a role in argument to save face, and that arguments, themselves, may enhance or harm one's identity characteristics such as credibility, persuasiveness, and competence.

Interrelationship of the Three Dimensions

Some research addresses the interrelationships among the three dimensions of communication and argument. Some theorists place the instrumental function in the foreground. Dillard, Segrin, and Harden (1989) suggested that primary or influence goals (instrumental) induce attempts to persuade or influence another person, while secondary goals (including relational and identity concerns) modify the message. Similarly, O'Keefe and Shepherd (1989) argued that "identity communication is subordinated to some other task" (p. 376). Thus, it appears that while there are three key potential goals (instrumental, relationship, and identity), some researchers view the instrumental dimension as most important.

Although we would agree that the instrumental goals are often (perhaps even usually) the foremost of arguers' concerns, the work on accounts cited previously demonstrates clearly that identity concerns are often key features of messages. Furthermore, an interesting anecdotal example occurred in Benoit and Benoit's (1989) data. One female participant wanted her male partner to tell her something. Eventually he did as she requested, but nonetheless she reported that she lost the argument because her partner became angry. Here, the relational consequences of the argument were more salient to her than the instrumental effect. Thus, we maintain that while instrumental concerns may be primary in general, relational and identity concerns occasionally predominate.

Because few studies interrelate the three dimensions, and others emphasize the importance of a single dimension, it is important to remain cognizant of the potential importance of all three dimensions. It appears that the three dimensions are interrelated and vary in importance depending on the social context in which they occur.

In conclusion, because argument is such a complex social phenomenon, the diversity of scholarship characteristic of the communication discipline enriches our understanding of an important form of interpersonal conflict. Because it is a more "civil" and nonaggressive approach to resolving conflicts in interpersonal relationships, it deserves more attention as a research topic. There is every reason to believe that researchers in other disciplines could answer Billig's call for more study of argument and further developments in theory and research by adding their expertise or by bringing additional methods and perspectives to bear on this worthwhile and important subject.

REFERENCES

Alberts, J. K. (1988). An analysis of couples' conversational complaints. *Communication Monographs, 55,* 184–197.

Alberts, J. K. (1989a). A descriptive taxonomy of couples' complaint interactions. *Southern Communication Journal, 54,* 125–143.

Alberts, J. K. (1989b). Perceived effectiveness of couples' conversational complaints. *Communication Studies, 40,* 280–291.

Allen, M., Burrell, N., & Mineo, P. (1987). Evaluating definitions of argument: Expert and naive. In F. H. van Eemeren, R. Grootendorst, J. A. Blair, & C. A. Willard (Eds.), *Argumentation: Perspectives and approaches: Proceedings of the conference on argumentation 1986* (pp. 93–102). Dordrecht; The Netherlands: Foris.

Aristotle (1984). *Rhetoric.* (W. R. Roberts, Trans.). In J. Barnes (Ed.), *The complete works of Aristotle: The Revised Oxford translation* (Vol. 2, pp. 2152–2269). Bollingen Series LXXI. Princeton: Princeton University Press.

Beisecker, T. (1970). Verbal persuasive strategies in mixed-motive interactions. *Quarterly Journal of Speech, 56,* 149–160.

Benoit, P. J. (1981). The use of argument by preschool children: The emergent production of rules for winning arguments. In G. Ziegelmueller & J. Rhodes (Eds.), *Dimensions of argument* (pp. 643–662). Annandale, VA: Speech Communication Association.

Benoit, P. J. (1982). *The naive social actor's concept of argument.* Paper presented at the meeting of the Speech Communication Association, Louisville, KY.

Benoit, P. J. (1983a). Characteristics of arguing from a social actor's perspective. In D. Zarefsky, M. O. Sillars, & J. Rhodes (Eds.), *Argument in transition* (pp. 544–559). Annandale, VA: Speech Communication Association.

Benoit, P. J. (1983b). Extended arguments in children's discourse. *Journal of the American Forensic Association, 20,* 72–89.

Benoit, P. J. (1985). Strategies for threatening face: Mitigating and aggravating bids and rejections. In J. R. Cox, M. O. Sillars, & G. B. Walker (Eds.), *Argument and social practice* (pp. 604–618). Annandale, VA: Speech Communication Association.

Benoit, P. J. (1989). Relationship arguments: An interactionist elaboration of speech acts. *Argumentation, 3,* 423–437.

Benoit, P. J., & Benoit, W. L. (1990). To argue or not to argue: How real people get into and out of interpersonal arguments. In R. Trapp & J. Schuetz (Eds.), *Perspectives on argument: Essays in honor of Wayne Brockriede* (pp. 55–72). Prospect Heights, IL: Waveland.

Benoit, W. L. (1987). Argumentation and credibility appeals in persuasion. *Southern Speech Communication Journal, 52,* 181–197.

Benoit, W. L. (1991). A cognitive response analysis of source credibility. In B. Dervin & M. J. Voigt (Eds.), *Progress in communication sciences* (Vol. 10, pp. 1–19). Norwood, NJ: Ablex.

Benoit, W. L. (1992). Traditional conceptions of argument. In W. L. Benoit, D. Hample, & P. J. Benoit (Eds.), *Readings in argumentation* (pp. 49–67). Berlin, Germany: Foris.

Benoit, W. L., & Benoit, P. J. (1987). Everyday argument practices of naive social actors. In J. W. Wenzel (Ed.), *Argumentation and critical practices* (pp. 465–473). Annandale, VA: Speech Communication Association.

Benoit, W. L., & Benoit, P. J. (1989). Accounts of failures and claims of successes in arguments. In B. E. Gronbeck (Ed.), *Spheres of argument* (pp. 551–557). Annandale, VA: Speech Communication Association.

Billig, M. (1987). *Arguing and thinking: A rhetorical approach to social psychology.* Cambridge, England: Cambridge University Press.

Brilhart, B. L. (1970). Relationships of speaker-message perception to perceptual field dependence. *Journal of Communication, 20,* 153–166.

Buttny, R. (1990). Blame-account sequences in therapy: The negotiation of relational meanings. *Semiotica, 78,* 219–247.

Canary, D. J., Brossman, B. G., & Seibold, D. R. (1987). Argument structures in decision-making groups. *Southern Speech Communication Journal, 53,* 18–37.

Canary, D. J., Brossmann, B. G., Sillars, A. L., & LoVette, S. (1987). Married couples' argument structures and sequences: A comparison of satisfied and dissatisfied dyads. In J. W. Wenzel (Ed.), *Argument and critical practices* (pp. 475–483). Annandale, VA: Speech Communication Association.

Canary, D. J., Cunningham, E. M., & Cody, M. J. (1988). Goal types, gender, and locus of control in managing interpersonal conflict. *Communication Research, 15,* 426–446.

Canary, D., & Sillars, A. (1992). Argument in satisfied and dissatisfied married couples. In W. L. Benoit, D. Hample, & P. J. Benoit (Eds.), *Readings in argumentation* (pp. 737–764). Dordrecht, The Netherlands: Foris.

Canary, D. J., & Spitzberg, B. H. (1989). A model of the perceived competence of conflict strategies. *Human Communication Research, 15,* 630–649.

Canary, D. J., & Spitzberg, B. H. (1990). Attribution biases and associations between conflict strategies and competence outcomes. *Communication Monographs, 57,* 139–151.

Canary, D. J., & Weger, H. (1989). The relationship of interpersonal argument to control mutuality: An observational analysis of romantic couples' conversations. In B. E. Gronbeck (Ed.), *Spheres of argument* (pp. 592–598). Annandale, VA: Speech Communication Association.

Canary, D. J., Weger, H., & Stafford, L. (1991). Couples' argument sequences and their associations with relational characteristics. *Western Journal of Speech Communication, 55,* 159–179.

Carrocci, N. M. (1985). Perceiving and responding to interpersonal conflict. *Central States Speech Journal, 36,* 215–228.

Clark, R. A., & Delia, J. G. (1979). Topoi and rhetorical competence. *Quarterly Journal of Speech, 65,* 187–206.

Cody, M. J., McLaughlin, M. L., & Schneider, M. J. (1981). The impact of relational consequences and intimacy on the selection of interpersonal persuasion tactics: A reanalysis. *Communication Quarterly, 29,* 91–106.

Craig, R. T. (1986). Goals in discourse. In D. G. Ellis & W. A. Donohue (Eds.), *Contemporary issues in language and discourse processes* (pp. 257–273). Hillsdale, NJ: Lawrence Erlbaum Associates.

Dillard, J. P., Segrin, C., & Harden, J. M. (1989). Primary and secondary goals in the production of interpersonal influence messages. *Communication Monographs, 56,* 19–38.

Hample, D. (1978). Predicting immediate belief change and adherence to argument claims. *Communication Monographs, 45,* 219–228.

Hample, D. (1983). The functions of argument. In D. Zarefsky, M. O. Sillars, & J. Rhodes (Eds.), *Argument in transition* (pp. 560–575). Annandale, VA: Speech Communication Association.

Hample, D. (1992). Writing mindlessly. *Communication Monographs, 59,* 315–323.

Hample, D., & Dallinger, J. (1992). The use of multiple goals in cognitive editing of arguments. *Argumentation and Advocacy, 28,* 109–122.

Haslett, B. (1983). Preschoolers' communicative strategies in gaining compliance from peers: A developmental study. *Quarterly Journal of Speech, 69,* 84–99.

Honeycutt, J. M., Woods, B. L., & Fontenot, K. (1993). The endorsement of communication conflict rules as a function of engagement, marriage, and marital ideology. *Journal of Social and Personal Relationships, 10,* 285–304.

Jackson, S., & Jacobs, S. (1980). Structure of conversational argument: Pragmatic bases for the enthymeme. *Quarterly Journal of Speech, 66,* 251–265.

Jackson, S., Jacobs, S., Burrell, N., & Allen, M. (1986). Characterizing ordinary argument: Substantive and methodological issues. *Journal of the American Forensic Association, 23,* 42–57.

Jacobs, S., & Jackson, S. (1981). Argument as a natural category: The routine grounds for arguing in conversation. *Western Journal of Speech Communication, 45,* 118–133.

Kellermann, K. (1992). Communication: Inherently strategic and primarily automatic. *Communication Monographs, 59,* 288–300.

Martin, R. W., & Scheerhorn, D. R. (1985). What are conversational arguments? Toward a natural language user's perspective. In J. R. Cox, M. O. Sillars, & G. B. Walker (Eds.), *Argument and social practice* (pp. 705–722). Annandale, VA: Speech Communication Association.

McCorkle, S. (1980). The transcending claim as a strategy of pseudo-argument. *Journal of the American Forensic Association, 17,* 11–17.

McCroskey, J. C. (1967). The effects of evidence in persuasive communication. *Western Speech, 31,* 189–199.

McCroskey, J. C. (1970). The effects of evidence as an inhibitor of counterpersuasion. *Speech Monographs, 37,* 188–194.

McLaughlin, M. L., Cody, M. J., & Rosenstein, N. E. (1983). Account sequences in conversations between strangers. *Communication Monographs, 50,* 102–125.

Meyer, J. (1992). The collaborative development of power in children's arguments. *Argumentation and Advocacy, 29,* 77–88.

Newell, S. E., & Stutman, R. K. (1983). Interpersonal disagreement: The study of social confrontation. In D. Zarefsky, M. O. Sillars, & J. Rhodes (Eds.), *Argument in transition* (pp. 725–739). Annandale, VA: Speech Communication Association.

Newton, D. A., & Burgoon, J. K. (1990). Nonverbal conflict behaviors: Functions, strategies, and tactics. In D. D. Cahn (Ed.), *Intimates in conflict* (pp. 77–104). Hillsdale, NJ: Lawrence Erlbaum Associates.

O'Keefe, B. J., & Benoit, P. J. (1982). Children's arguments. In J. R. Cox & C. A. Willard (Eds.), *Advances in argumentation theory and research* (pp. 154–183). Carbondale, IL: Southern Illinois University Press.

O'Keefe, B. J., & Shepherd, G. J. (1989). The communication of identity during face-to-face persuasive interactions: Effects of perceiver's construct differentiation and target's message strategies. *Communication Research, 16,* 375–404.

O'Keefe, D. J. (1977). Two concepts of argument. *Journal of the American Forensic Association, 13,* 121–128.

Pomerantz, A. (1984). Agreeing and disagreeing with assessments: Some features of preferred/dispreferred turn shapes. In J. Atkinson & J. Heritage (Eds.), *Structure of social action* (pp.

57–101). Cambridge, England: Cambridge University Press.

Reinard, J. C. (1991). *Foundations of argument: Effective communication for critical thinking*. Dubuque, IA: Brown.

Rieke, R. D., & Sillars, M. O. (1993). *Argumentation and critical decision making* (3rd ed.). New York: HarperCollins.

Roloff, M. E., & Cloven, D. H. (1990). The chilling effect in interpersonal relationships: The reluctance to speak one's mind. In D. D. Cahn (Ed.), *Intimates in conflict: A communication perspective* (pp. 49–76). Hillsdale, NJ: Lawrence Erlbaum Associates.

Ting-Toomey, S. (1983). An analysis of verbal communication patterns in high and low marital adjustment groups. *Human Communication Research, 9,* 306–319.

Toulmin, S. E. (1958). *The uses of argument*. Cambridge, England: Cambridge University Press.

Tracy, K. (1991). Introduction: Linking communicator goals with discourse. In K. Tracy (Ed.), *Understanding face-to-face interaction: Issues linking goals and discourse* (pp. 1–17). Hillsdale, NJ: Lawrence Erlbaum Associates.

Trapp, R. (1986). The role of disagreement in interactional argument. *Journal of the American Forensic Association, 23,* 23–41.

Trapp, R. (1990). Arguments in interpersonal relationships. In R. Trapp & J. Schuetz (Eds.), *Perspective on argumentation: Essays in honor of Wayne Brockriede* (pp. 43–54). Prospect Heights, IL: Waveland.

Trapp, R., & Hoff, N. (1985). A model of serial argument in interpersonal relationship. *Journal of the American Forensic Association, 22,* 1–11.

Walton, D. N. (1992). Plausible argument in everyday conversation. Albany, NY: State University of New York Press.

Watzlawik, P., Beavin, J. H., & Jackson, D. D. (1967). *Pragmatics of human communication*. New York: Norton.

Wenzel, J. W. (1985). Toward a normative theory of argumentation: Van Eemeren and Grootendorst's code of conduct for rational discussions. In J. R. Cox, M. O. Sillars, & G. B. Walker (Eds.), *Argument and social practice* (pp. 139–155). Annandale, VA: Speech Communication Association.

Willbrand, M. L., & Rieke, R. D. (1991). Strategies of reasoning in spontaneous discourse. In J. A. Anderson (Ed.), *Communication yearbook* (Vol. 14, pp. 414–440). Beverly Hills, CA: Sage.

Witteman, H. (1992). Analyzing interpersonal conflict: Nature of awareness, type of initiating event, and management styles. *Western Journal of Communication, 56,* 248–280.

Zietlow, P. H., & Sillars, A. L. (1988). Life stage differences in communication during marital conflicts. *Journal of Social and Personal Relationships, 5,* 223–245.

9 A Competence-Based Approach to the Study of Interpersonal Conflict

Brian H. Spitzberg
San Diego State University

Daniel J. Canary
Ohio University

William R. Cupach
Illinois State University

Although conflict is ubiquitous, it is almost unanimously disliked. Conflict encounters seem capable of lowering people to their most base instincts, and, yet, out of conflict we often derive our most productive achievements. But how people transform the tensions of conflict into productive messages and outcomes evades simplistic thinking or prescriptions. Such are the paradoxes of interpersonal conflict. The purpose of this chapter is to show that competent management of interpersonal conflict requires an awareness of various factors that affect people's impressions of each other and of their conflict messages. To accomplish this objective, we present a rationale for examining conflict from a competence-based approach. We then discuss what precisely is meant by competence, and how it functions in conflict management. Next, we explore the assertiveness literature for clues about competence in conflict management behaviors. We then review the research that has direct implications for the study of conflict and competence. We conclude this chapter by presenting avenues for future research.

Why a Competence-Based Approach?

There are several reasons to utilize a competence-based approach to investigate conflict management behaviors. First, focusing on issues of competence unburdens us from making generalizations about the use of skills. Sillars and Weisberg (1987) demonstrated how ambiguities and structural complexities during conflict resist generalizations about what constitutes "effective" conflict management skills. For example, some texts advise people to use "I-statements" (e.g., "I feel you make fun of me when you talk in that tone of voice."). Although the use of I-statements can inhibit the use of escalating messages, such is not always the case. Indeed, using I-statements can be just as inflammatory as not using them (e.g., "I think you're a horse's ass"). Prescribing such skills does not adequately represent competence in managing interpersonal conflict. Instead, a competence-based approach relies on the parties' assessments of what they consider competent in given contexts. Accordingly, we describe quality communication from the participants' point of view in lieu of generalizations about skillful conflict behaviors.

Second, and related to this, we can examine conflict in terms of the criteria that participants judge as important. Researchers have examined several components of communication competence, including adaptability (Duran, 1992), conversational involvement (Cegala, 1981), and empathy (Redmond, 1985). Spitzberg and Cupach (1984) identified two relatively inclusive criteria, appropriateness and effectiveness. Appropriateness concerns upholding the relational and situational expectations, and effectiveness refers to the ability of the communicator to achieve his or her goals in the conversation.

Third, in conflict situations, the focus on perceptions of behaviors reveals the values people attach to those behaviors. In other words, people interpret behavior and allow or disallow such behaviors to affect them. At the relational level, perceptions of competence filter the effects of behavior on relational characteristics. There is not a mechanistic causal link from behavior to outcome; instead, people evaluate those behaviors in their assessments of competence.

The concept of competence offers a heuristic approach to conceptualizing conflict processes. However, the construct of competence itself is highly complex, and requires clarification.

A Conceptualization of Competence

Competence in interaction has been conceptualized in a multitude of ways (Spitzberg & Cupach, 1984). Competence, broadly speaking, is a synonym for either quality or ability. That these are not exact synonyms for each other reflects a fundamental definitional problem. Competence is a coin with two sides: skill and impression. On the one side, researchers and teachers have traditionally been interested in the objective behavioral traits, skills, or abilities that comprise competence. In this vein, competence consists of identifiable capacities a person possesses that enable him or her to perform to a specified level of observable proficiency to obtain a goal. On the other side, competence has more recently been redefined as a subjective evaluation of the quality with which someone performs (Spitzberg & Cupach, 1984). The reason for this change was that all human interaction is contextual, and, therefore, a given behavior may be evaluated as competent in one context, but incompetent in another. It is not the behavior itself that is competent, but its evaluation in a particular context that constitutes the location of the construct.

This definitional debate has been active for some time (e.g., McCroskey, 1982; McFall, 1982; Rubin, 1990; Spitzberg, 1983; Wiemann & Bradac, 1985). However, most theorists have settled on appropriateness and effectiveness as inclusive, valid, and useful criteria. Appropriate interaction avoids the violation of valued rules, norms, or expectancies in a given context or contexts. This does not presume that an interactant is merely being polite or conforming, since rules can be broken in the process of negotiating new rules. Effective interaction obtains valued outcomes, objectives, or goals. This does not presume that a person is entirely conscious of the ends being sought, because the opportunities of any given interaction are often evolutionary, and, at other times, relatively mindless or inaccessible to conscious articulation. The combination of these two criteria provides for a very useful conceptualization of optimal, or competent, interaction.

If appropriateness and effectiveness are crossed as dimensions, then they create a grid with four cells. A person who is inappropriate and ineffective violates rules and fails to obtain desired outcomes. Such a person's interaction is minimizing in orientation (e.g., to block out the sound of a neighbor's loud music, you turn up your own stereo). A person who is appropriate but not effective does nothing wrong, per se, but also attains no valued objectives through interaction. This person is merely sufficing (e.g., you try to ignore the neighbor's loud music and hope it will soon cease). A person who maximizes is effective but inappropriate; this person achieves valued outcomes, but at the cost of violating standards of decorum, consensus, or relational preference (e.g., you confront your neighbor with, "Who the hell do you think you are? Turn down the stereo or I'll have you evicted!"). In contrast, a person who is both appropriate and effective is optimal by achieving valued ends while maintaining the integrity of the relational context (e.g., you tell your neighbor that the loud music prevents you from working, and you ask that it be turned down). Of course, these examples are prototypical representations.

THE FUNCTIONAL ROLE OF COMPETENCE IN CONFLICT

The relevance of this grid to conflict should be immediately apparent when it is overlaid on the ubiquitous two-dimensional model of conflict orientation (Blake & Mouton, 1964; see Fig. 9.1). Competing, or distributive,

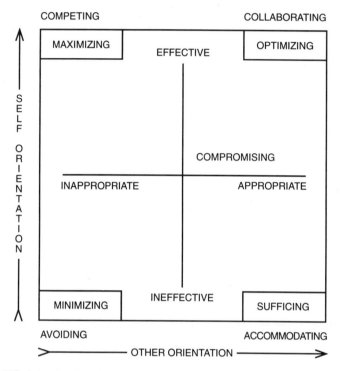

FIG. 9.1.   Overlay of competence dimensions onto conflict dimensions.

behavior is very similar to a maximizing orientation, in which the finite interpersonal resources are sought regardless of the consequences to others. Avoiding would often be characteristic of an interactant who can neither fulfill expectations for behavior nor obtain valued ends. A person overly concerned with appropriateness to the exclusion of self-interests is likely to accommodate to others. A person who seeks a middle ground between self and other interests, in turn, is likely to compromise between the two, thereby being somewhat effective and somewhat appropriate. However, the now traditional ideal of "win-win" conflict management is very similar to the notion of appropriate and effective interaction. Appropriateness en-sures that care is shown to the other parties' interests and expectations, while effectiveness represents a pursuit of the self's interests.

The integration of these two grids also emphasizes the perspective that competence places on conflict. Conflict is not problematic simply because it is unpleasant, although it is also often unpleasant. It is problematic because conflict management is difficult to conduct competently. Specifically, parties in conflict may believe that the other person is pursuing a goal that frustrates their own. This simultaneously violates expectations regarding the interaction and reduces the likelihood of both parties achieving their valued personal objectives. Unless the parties understand that conflict episodes handicap the attainment of both appropriateness and effectiveness, then they may become perplexed in their experiences of conflict. But if one takes into account that being competent involves negotiating in such a way as to optimize both parties' appropriate and effective responses (which conflict makes difficult), then understanding of conflict messages and productive outcomes may increase. Knowing how conflict and competence interrelate should also enable more productive management of conflict interactions.

Competence may function in a variety of ways in interpersonal conflict situations. Its role depends, in part, on whether competence is conceptualized as an ability or as an evaluative impression. As an ability, competence facilitates the enactment of behavior that is likely to produce positive conflict outcomes. As an impression, competence can serve as a cognitive process. Each of these is briefly considered next.

Competence as Antecedent to Conflict Management

When competence is viewed as an ability, it operates as an antecedent condition to conflict interaction that affects the process and outcomes of conflict. The competent communicator is characterized by several traits that enhance effective communication, including behavioral flexibility (Duran, 1992), assertiveness (Galassi, Galassi, & Vedder, 1981), and confidence (Conger, Wallander, Mariotto, & Ward, 1980). These traits, in turn, tend to be positively associated with productive conflict outcomes. Similarly, traits such as high need for achievement, low need for dependence (Utley, Richardson, & Pilkington, 1989), and an internal locus of control (Canary, Cunningham, & Cody, 1988) appear to facilitate cooperative strategy use.

Individuals who view themselves as competent communicators also possess positive self-efficacy beliefs (e.g., Rubin, Martin, Bruning, & Powers, 1993). That is, competent communicators tend to believe that they are capable of performing behaviors that are effective in producing desired outcomes. Thus, a self-fulfilling prophecy occurs (Sternberg & Kolligian, 1990): A belief in the likelihood of success, based on a history of success in conflict situations, is likely to breed further success.

Competence as Outcome of Conflict Management

It is also useful to conceptualize competence as an interpersonal impression (Spitzberg & Cupach, 1984). In this vein, competence in conflict is consistent with the cognitive-exchange focus described by Cahn (1992). Viewed as an evaluative impression, competence can obviously be conceptualized as a communicative outcome in its own right (Jones, 1989). As a judgment of the quality of the communicative process, competence is an indicator of the relatively constructive or destructive nature of conflict behavior. It serves as a proxy for the affective reaction to the conflict communication; that is, perceived competence of a partner's communication is an indication of one's own communication satisfaction (Spitzberg & Hecht, 1984). For example, Cupach (1982) studied the relationship between self-reported conflict tactics and one's own communication satisfaction, as well as the partner's communication satisfaction. For both self and partner, satisfaction was more positively associated with cooperative conflict tactics than with either competitive or avoidant tactics.

Competence as Intervening Variable in Conflict Management

Intervening factors may either mediate or moderate the effects of the independent variables on the dependent variables. As a mediating variable, competence functions as an interpretive screen between conflict behaviors and outcome variables. As a moderating variable, competence interacts with the conflict behaviors to affect outcome variables.

Research reveals that competence functions as a mediator between conflict behavior and episodic and relational outcomes (Canary & Cupach, 1988; Canary & Spitzberg, 1989). As a mediating influence, positive outcomes in conflict are brought about because a partner's behaviors are interpreted as relatively competent. Negative outcomes occur because behaviors are seen as relatively incompetent. In this light, conflict behaviors produce constructive or destructive outcomes only indirectly, through the perceptual frame of competence assessments (of those same conflict behaviors).

To illustrate how competence operates as a mediating variable, consider an example of two friends: Bill and Sandra. During a conflict episode between the two, Bill perceives Sandra handling the conflict. Bill makes a judgment about Sandra's communication. If he thinks she is appropriate and effective, he will likely judge her conflict communication to be competent. To the extent that Sandra is judged to be competent, Bill derives positive outcomes. He feels relatively good about Sandra. In the longer term, the perception of competence likely translates into positive thoughts and feelings about the relationship, such as trust and relational satisfaction.

Competence also functions as a moderator variable, stressing how biases and distortions in perception can modify the impact of behaviors on outcomes. Thus, if Sandra is "objectively" collaborative and integrative in her conflict behaviors, but Bill has a negative opinion of Sandra because of a previous episode, he may perceive her behavior in the present episode to be relatively incompetent, or at least as less competent than it otherwise might have been. As a consequence of the negative perception regarding Sandra's competence, some outcomes are likely to be less positive than they might otherwise be, in spite of Sandra's best "constructive" behavioral efforts. Sandra's behavior, by itself, is not sufficient to predict Bill's outcomes (and in an extended model, Sandra's outcomes). Rather, Sandra's behavior, in conjunction with Bill's perception of Sandra's episodic competence, will jointly affect the conflict outcome.

Competence, therefore, can play any of three basic roles in conflict episodes: antecedent, consequent, and intervening. Which role is stressed obviously depends on one's conceptualization of competence and the types of questions being asked. To examine some of the questions that have been asked of competence in the conflict literature, the two most relevant domains of research (i.e., assertiveness and interpersonal conflict) are reviewed.

RESEARCH ON ASSERTIVENESS AND COMPETENCE

Assertiveness has been actively researched since the 1960s. Although it has been defined and conceptualized in a number of ways, assertion is generally viewed as an interactional orientation that involves a defense of basic human rights, honest emotional expression, and functionally reinforcing communication in problematic situations (e.g., Galassi, Galassi, & Vedder, 1981; Rakos, 1991). As a strategy, assertive behavior has fairly consistently been differentiated from the two alternative interactional orientations of passive and aggressive behavior. The strategy of assertiveness involves the skilled expression of one's desires, feelings, and/or rights without violation of those of the other parties involved. Aggression, in contrast, is some form of expression without regard for the rights of others. Passivity is typically a form of withdrawal from the interaction, or a failure to express one's own interests. This tripartite scheme has been consistently supported in the research (Bakker, Bakker-Rabdau, & Breit, 1978; Hedlund & Lindquist, 1984).

That assertiveness is closely related to interpersonal conflict is obvious, and yet the conflict literature has largely ignored its relevance. There are two reasons why the two literatures deserve integration. First, the distinctions among assertive, aggressive, and passive behavior are virtually identical to the common division of conflict behavior into integrative, distributive, and avoidant strategies, respectively (Sillars, Coletti, Perry, & Rogers, 1982). Second, assertion can be often viewed as a form of incipient conflict, or "conflict waiting or about to happen." Assertion is most relevant to situations in which people must resolve a problematic interpersonal situation in which personal preferences are weighed against those of the other parties.

Assertiveness is also closely intertwined with notions of competence. First, the structure of assertion is the accomplishment of personal objectives in a manner that accounts for the interests of other involved parties. This is almost identical to the notion of interaction that is effective and yet appropriate. Indeed, some time ago, Galassi, Galassi, and Vedder (1981) strongly recommended scrapping the construct of assertiveness in favor of the construct of social skills and social competence. Second, numerous studies of assertiveness utilize designs in which behaviors are manipulated or coded and then related to impression outcomes such as appropriateness (e.g., Lewis & Gallois, 1984) or competence (Crawford, 1988; Kelly et al., 1982; Kern, Cavell, & Beck, 1985; Zollo, Heimberg, & Becker, 1985). Although competence in these studies is often labeled a factor concerning task expertise, it is also usually analyzed along with a factor of social attractiveness.

Assuming that most assertion is a form of incipient conflict, the assertiveness literature yields three basic conclusions in relation to competence. First, when viewed by uninvolved third parties, assertive behavior is generally viewed as more competent than passive behavior, which, in turn, is viewed as more competent than aggressive behavior. However, second, for conversational partners, assertive behavior is often seen as more productive but less likable and satisfying than passive behavior, and both are viewed as more competent than aggressive behavior (Delamater & McNamara, 1991; Kelly et al., 1982; Lowe & Storm, 1986; Sereno, Welch, & Braaten, 1987; Zollo, Heimberg, & Becker, 1985; for reviews, see Delamater & McNamara, 1986; Gervasio & Crawford, 1989). It appears from this research that assertion is seen as normatively competent, but is not optimally competent in the relationship. We think this is because most assertion places priority on effectiveness rather than appropriateness of interaction.

Third, there is a fair amount of evidence, though somewhat mixed, that the findings noted previously are moderated by sex, relational context, and form of assertive message. Specifically, both men and women appear to be more forgiving of men being assertive than of women being assertive (Crawford, 1988; Lowe & Storm, 1986; Wilson & Gallois, 1985; cf. Levin & Gross, 1984). People also appear to be more forgiving of an assertive friend than an assertive stranger (Gormally, 1982; Lewis & Gallois, 1984). In addition, when empathic or consideration clauses are added to the assertive message, in which the other party's interests are overtly acknowledged, the negative impact of assertion is often reduced (Kern, Cavell, & Beck, 1985; Sereno, Welch, & Braaten, 1987; Wildman & Clementz, 1986; cf. Levin & Gross, 1984, 1987). Other factors, such as nonverbal behaviors used with the assertive message (Rose & Tryon, 1979), may also moderate the link between assertive behavior and perceived competence.

In summary, the research indicates that assertion and passivity are both functionally mixed tactics in response to problematic interpersonal encounters. Assertion appears to be effective, but often at the cost of interpersonal attraction, and, perhaps, harmony. Passivity is often attractive, but obviously not very effective in terms of short-term goals of the interactant. However, the literature is very consistent in displaying that aggressive behavior is judged as incompetent by virtually everyone.

RESEARCH ON CONFLICT AND COMPETENCE

Communication Strategies and Outcomes

People choose to work with the other, work against the other, or work away from the other (e.g., Davitz, 1969), and they adopt communication strategies reflecting these choices. Strategies refer to the general approach people use to achieve an interaction goal, whereas tactics reference the particular behaviors that institute the strategy (Newton & Burgoon, 1990). Hence, in our view, conflict behaviors are manifested in three strategies: integrative (working with the partner), distributive (working against the partner), and avoidant (working away from the partner). Similar three-factor schemes have been identified in other studies as well (e.g., Putnam & Wilson, 1982; Rands, Levinger, & Mellinger, 1981; Sillars, 1980; Spitzberg & Marshall, 1990). Integrative behaviors are manifested in such actions as seeking areas of commonality, exchanging information, attempting to understand the other, and compromising. Distributive behaviors are displayed in competitive actions such as threats, intimidation, criticism, and counterproposals. Avoidant behaviors attempt to detract attention from the conflict, and they range from direct denials to topic evasions. These strategies are enacted both verbally and nonverbally (Newton & Burgoon, 1990).

Research suggests that people are more satisfied with integrative tactics and less satisfied with distributive and avoidant tactics (e.g., Belk & Snell, 1988; Fitzpatrick, Fallis, & Vance, 1982; Sillars, 1980). In addition, integrative tactic use has been positively linked to relational satisfaction and stability, while distributive behaviors have been found to reflect relational dissatisfaction. For example, Ting-Toomey (1983) found that people in satisfied marriages engage in supportive and confirming sequences and avoid the complain-defend and confront-defend sequences that dissatisfied couples enact. Similarly, Margolin and Wampold (1981) found that nondistressed couples, relative to distressed couples, engaged in higher rates of "problem-solving," neutral, and positive verbal and nonverbal behaviors. There is also strong evidence that satisfied couples not only share more positive and less negative communication (e.g., Gottman & Krokoff, 1989; Gottman & Levenson, 1992; Huston & Vangelisti, 1991; Markman, 1981), but also display lower rates of negative reciprocity (e.g., Billings, 1979; Filsinger & Thoma, 1988; Gottman, 1979; Ting-Toomey, 1983).

If relational satisfaction, relational stability, and marital adjustment are considered desired outcomes of competent communication, then the literature varies greatly in its picture of competent conflict behaviors. Filsinger and Thoma (1988) found that relationships with high levels of female interruption at time one had lower stability and satisfaction five years later. This can be interpreted as a competence issue, given that interruptions are normatively considered as incompetent (Wiemann, 1977). Gottman and Levenson (1992) observed that long-term stability in marriages is sustained by a "balancing" of positive and negative interaction, in which the ratio of positive behaviors to negative behaviors is consistently higher than in unstable relationships. And although adaptability is often viewed as competent, Nicotera (1991) found that people who use single tactics, rather than those who use multiple tactics, are more satisfied. It may be that competent interactants either know what works best and stay with that tactic, or they tend to change tactics only when they are dissatisfied. However, Koren, Carlton, and Shaw's (1980) study of nondistressed couples showed that they were more likely than distressed couples to use responsive communication, indicating some occurrence of adaptation. In a paradoxical result, Roloff and Cloven (1990) found that both the number of expressed conflicts as well as the number of unexpressed (or latent) conflicts are negatively related to relational satisfaction. Collectively, it appears that distributive behavior is commonly associated with relational maladjustment, but beyond this finding, the existing research offers little consistency in the picture of what constitutes competence in conflict.

Perhaps the most extreme form of distributive conflict behavior is physical violence, yet the research on the effect of violence on relational satisfaction is surprisingly mixed. In their review of violence studies, Sugarman and Hotaling (1989) found that "in roughly six of every ten relationships that did not terminate, the violence is reported to have had no effect on, or to have actually improved the relationship" (p. 14). Across three separate studies of relational violence, a third of relationships reported that the relationship improved after the occurrence of violence (Cate, Henton, Koval, Christopher, & Lloyd, 1982; Henton, Cate, Koval, Lloyd, & Christopher, 1983; Makepeace, 1981). In light of such findings, it is understandable when Holtzworth-Munroe et al. (1992) reviewed several data sets and found that "Across the studies, up to one third of the nondistressed husbands had been violent toward their wives during the course of their relationship and approximately 10%–20% had been violent in the past year" (p. 86). The point worth noting is that people do not necessarily view violence as incompetent or unidirectionally related to relational outcomes.

How violence affects relational outcomes is likely to depend largely on the standards for competence and the manner in which violence occurs. For example, Margolin, John, and Gleberman (1988) found that physically aggressive couples could be differentiated from verbally aggressive, withdrawing, and nondistressed/nonaggressive couples in terms of husbands' higher rates of negativity and wives' escalation and then deescalation of negative behaviors (perhaps a demand-withdraw pattern). Additionally, Holtzworth-Munroe and Anglin (1991) found that violent men did not differ from nonviolent men in the competence of their responses to a number of relationally problematic situations, but they did produce less competent responses to particular situations involving rejection from their wives, jealousy, and challenges from their wives. It appears that subtle expectations and particular patterns of communication frame the enactment of violence, and that the competence of such activity cannot be determined a priori. This implies that competence involves judgments that do not inhere in the behavior itself.

This possibility has been addressed in a series of studies (Canary & Cupach, 1988; Canary & Spitzberg, 1987, 1989, 1990; Cupach, Canary, & Serpe, in progress). In these studies, integrative tactics have been consistently associated with competence. More specifically, integrative tactics have been associated with perceptions of partners' appropriateness, effectiveness, global competence, and communication satisfaction. On the other hand, distributive behaviors have been negatively linked to appropriateness, effectiveness, global competence, and communication satisfaction. Avoidance also has correlated negatively with competence and desirable relational outcomes, but the correlations have typically been fairly small (see also Smolen, Spiegel, Bakker-Rabdau, Bakker, & Martin, 1985).

Which strategy do people refer to when making assessments of the communicator's competence? The answer to this question varies according to the competence criterion under question. For example, Canary and Spitzberg (1990) found that judgments of specific appropriateness (i.e., the appropriateness judgments of particular segments or behaviors of the interaction) were more strongly associated with distributive behaviors, whereas judgments of general appropriateness (i.e., the appropriateness judgments of the entire episode) and effectiveness were more strongly linked to integrative tactics. In an experimental study, Canary and Spitzberg (1987) likewise found that distributive behaviors were seen as specifically inappropriate, and integrative behaviors were viewed as generally appropriate and effective. These findings suggest that people judge isolated competitive messages apart from the overall manner in which the communicator behaved.

Avoidance tactics vary in their perceived competence, according to several factors. One factor is whether people value autonomy or confrontation (Sillars & Weisberg, 1987). Those who value autonomy likely perceive avoidance as highly functional, whereas those who value confrontation likely see avoidance as dysfunctional (Fitzpatrick, 1988; Fitzpatrick, Fallis, & Vance, 1982; Sillars, Pike, Jones, & Redmon, 1983). A second factor is who reports the avoidance. If the communicator assesses the merits of his or her own avoidance, it is probably evaluated more favorably than if the partner judges the communicator's avoidance (Canary & Cupach, 1988; Canary & Spitzberg, 1989). Belk and Snell (1988) found that couples' use of bilateral avoidance was more associated with liking and loving and self-disclosure than when the avoidance tactic was unilaterally enforced (cf. Christensen & Shenk, 1991).

A Competence-Based Model of Conflict

A competence-based model of interpersonal conflict assumes that conflict messages are assessed according to competence criteria, and then these interpretations affect relational outcomes (Canary & Cupach, 1988; Canary & Spitzberg, 1989). One important set of outcomes is relational quality. Although most equate relational quality with satisfaction, we conceptualize quality as comprised of the feature characteristics of relationships; specifically, control mutuality, trust, and intimacy, in addition to satisfaction (for a similar typology, see Millar & Rogers, 1976). Control mutuality refers to sharing agreement on who makes the decisions in the relationship (Morton, Alexander, & Altman, 1976). Trust refers to risking oneself to the partner because the partner is believed to be honest and beneficent (Larzelere & Huston, 1980). Intimacy refers to knowledge about the partner and liking what one knows (Altman & Taylor, 1973).

Do assessments of competence mediate the effects of conflict tactics on relational outcomes? The initial evidence suggests they do: Three studies utilizing structural equation modeling have shown that integrative and distributive conflict tactics affect relational outcomes primarily through competence evaluations (Canary & Cupach, 1988; Canary & Spitzberg, 1989; Cupach, Canary, & Serpe, in preparation). Avoidance, which is relatively ambiguous as an appropriate or effective response, has a small negative effect on perceptions of competence when the partner's perceptions of avoidance are utilized, but not when the actor's self-reported conflict behaviors are used. Table 9.1 presents the general competence model represented in the three studies summarized here.

Three specific findings regarding this summary model merit comment.

TABLE 9.1
Model of Conflict Tactics and Relational Outcomes, with Competence as an
Intervening Variable

Conflict Message Behaviors →	Competence Assessments →	Relational Outcomes
Integrative tactics (+)	Appropriateness	Trust
Distributive tactics (−)	Effectiveness	Control mutuality
Avoidant tactics (+ / −)		Intimacy
		Satisfaction

Note: A positive sign indicates that integrative tactics are positively associated with competence assessments of appropriateness and effectiveness; a negative sign indicates that distributive tactics are inversely associated with competence assessments. Avoidant tactics may be positively or inversely linked to competence perceptions in ways indicated in the text.

First, conflict behaviors, competence evaluations, and relational outcomes represent empirically as well as conceptually distinct phenomena (Canary & Spitzberg, 1989). Second, in one longitudinal study (Cupach, Canary, & Serpe, in preparation), conflict behaviors at time 1 predicted conflict behaviors approximately a month later, but conflict behaviors at time 1 did not predict relational features apart from the competence evaluations. Nor did the relational outcomes at time 1 predict subsequent conflict behaviors, contrary to our own speculation. This suggests that conflict patterns are stable. Finally, the standardized coefficients for the path between competence evaluations and relational outcomes have been moderate to large. The estimates have been .145 to .250 for single indicators in Canary and Cupach (1988), .662 for multiple indicators in Canary and Spitzberg (1989), and .451 for multiple indicators in Cupach, Canary, and Serpe (in progress). These findings reveal that competence judgments of conflict behaviors substantially affect relational characteristics. However, we should also be quick to point out qualifications to these findings.

Qualifying the General Findings

The positive tie between integrative behaviors and positive relational outcomes is qualified by several factors. Enacting integrative behaviors may not necessarily indicate harmony in the home. Gottman (1979), for example, reported that satisfied and dissatisfied couples alike reciprocate integrative behaviors. Gottman reported that lack of reciprocating negative behaviors is more discriminating of satisfaction than the reciprocation of positive behaviors. Moreover, Gottman and Krokoff (1989) found that husbands' negative interaction behaviors (e.g., expression of anger) were inversely associated with satisfaction when measured at the same time, but negative behaviors were positively associated with increases in relational satisfaction measured three years later. In other words, although expressions of anger may be seen as incompetent at the time of their use, in the long run anger may be seen as beneficial to the relationship.

Moreover, couple type affects how conflict behaviors are assessed. For example, Sillars Pike, Jones, and Redmon (1983) found that egalitarian (i.e., independent) couples' relational satisfaction was positively associated with negative emotional displays during conflict, but their satisfaction was inversely associated with neutral emotions. Independent couples appear to prefer any emotional exchange over neutrality. But, as mentioned, autonomous couples (i.e., separates) prefer blatant forms of avoidance, such as explicit denials of conflict ("No, nothing is wrong, I promise"; Sillars, Pike, Jones, & Redmon, 1983). Conflict behaviors thus appear to be valued differently in different kinds of marriages: Some couples value direct confrontation over most issues (i.e., independents), some value confrontation over important issues only (i.e., traditionals), and some couples value avoidance (i.e., separates).

The link between integrative behaviors and assessments of competence must also be qualified. Canary and Spitzberg (1990) found that partners agreed the least on whether one of them had used integrative messages during a conflict; correlations between actor and partner perceptions of actors' strategy use were strongest for distributive behavior, then avoidant, and then integrative tactics. It is likely that people expect others to treat them in a cooperative manner, and integrative behaviors are thus often perceived, though not necessarily enacted. Distributive or avoidant behaviors are more salient because their use is generally negative and unexpected (Canary & Spitzberg, 1990; Sillars, Pike, Jones, & Murphy, 1984).

Another important qualification is that, because of the dyadic nature of conflict management, the partner probably projects his or her conflict behavior and experience onto the actor. Perhaps the most robust empirical generalization in the conflict literature is that people tend to reciprocate conflict behaviors (e.g., Burggraf & Sillars, 1987; Sillars, 1980). Moreover, satisfied couples tend to reciprocate positive behaviors, whereas dissatisfied couples tend to reciprocate negative conflict and for longer periods of time (Sillars, Wilmot, & Hocker, 1993; Ting-Toomey, 1983). This reciprocation of behavior makes it difficult to determine how to assess one person's communication competence apart from the other's. In addition, during such exchanges one person likely reads into the partner's behavior his or her own feelings and attitudes (Wilmot, 1987). And because one's field of experience more readily focuses on the partner's communication behavior (Storms, 1973), one likely overestimates the partner's responsibility for the conflict due to the partner's negative actions. In other words, actors cannot see their own faces distort in anger or winces, or hear the disconfirmation in their own conflict tactics, but they can clearly see their partners' negative nonverbal affect displays and distributive verbal cues. Hence, the partner's negative behaviors are more salient than their own and are judged more keenly. But when the partner acts as expected, with cooperation, then the actor more readily accepts responsibility for the conflict and assesses the partner's behaviors as competent (Sillars, 1980).

CONCLUSIONS

The primary purpose of this chapter has been to show that competent management of interpersonal conflict requires an awareness of many factors and findings (often counterintuitive) that affect people's assessments of each other and their conflict messages. In light of the research issues and findings, we offer three avenues for future research.

First, we are interested in exploring the microstructures of conflict. Sillars, Wilmot, and Hocker (1993) reviewed five structural characteristics of conflict tactics: variety, or number of alternative messages used; continuity, or the number of issues discussed; symmetry, or the extent to which partners mirror each other's behaviors; stationarity, or the phases of conflict couples enact; and spontaneity, or the degree to which individuals monitor and censor their own actions. The Sillars Wilmot, and Hocker review suggested that the most competent management of conflict would involve a moderate level of each of these factors. That is, competence is likely to associated with (a) a wide repertoire of conflict behaviors that focus discussion on the issues at hand; (b) extensive but not exhaustive discussion of important problematic issues; (c) matching of the partner's integrative actions, but not distributive actions; (d) phases that do not ensnare the relational partners; and (e) a balance between self-monitoring and free use of conflict tactics. These predictions are warranted for two reasons. First, there is a dearth of research linking perceptions of communicator competence to observations of microlevel conflict behaviors. Second, we could demarcate the precise forms of conflict behavior that most influence competence evaluations. For example, in two studies, specific appropriateness has been most affected by distributive tactics. At issue is what particular conflict behaviors are referenced when assessing specific appropriateness, and what did the communicator do to adapt, to recover, or to fail in transforming the specific inappropriate interaction into a more general appropriate interaction.

A second issue for future research stems from attributional processes during conflict. Specifically, partners quickly make attributions, including competence evaluations, given the actor's conflict behavior. Again, one reason for this is that people's field of experience is outwardly focused. It is possible to turn the communicator's field of experience inward by having the communicator view a video recording of his or her behavior in conflict (e.g., Knudson, Sommers, & Golding, 1980). One could compare those who view themselves on video with those who do not, using competence ratings of self and partner. Communicators who become more internally focused with the use of the video recording should offer harsher evaluations about self and kinder evaluations about the actor, versus those who remain externally focused.

A final consideration concerns the prospect of intervention. On the one hand, a competence approach typically suggests the possibilities of skills training and improvement of conflict processes (e.g., Patterson, Hops, & Weiss, 1975). However, such moves are conceptually (Sillars & Weisberg, 1987) and empirically (Jacobson, Follette, & Elwood, 1984) problematic. As a sobering indication of the need for better understanding the notion of conflict intervention, Jaffe, Sudermann, Reitzel, and Killip (1992) found that after an educational workshop with high school students, males experienced as many undesirable attitude changes as desirable ones; that is, in several respects, males appeared to become more violent and prone to sexual aggression after undergoing an intervention program designed specifically to reduce this likelihood. Clearly, continued investigation of the role of competence in relational conflict is warranted.

REFERENCES

Altman, I., & Taylor, D. A. (1973). *Social penetration: The development of interpersonal relationships*. New York: Holt, Rinehart and Winston.

Bakker, C. B., Bakker-Rabdau, M. K., & Breit, S. (1978). The measurement of assertiveness and aggressiveness. *Journal of Personality Assessment, 42*, 277–284.

Belk, S. S., & Snell, W. E., Jr. (1988). Avoidance strategy use in intimate relationships. *Journal of Social and Clinical Psychology, 7*, 80–96.

Billings, A. (1979). Conflict resolution in distressed and nondistressed married couples. *Journal of Consulting and Clinical Psychology, 47*, 368–376.

Blake, R. R., & Mouton, J. S. (1964). *The managerial grid*. Houston, TX: Gulf.

Burggraf, C. S., & Sillars, A. L. (1987). A critical examination of sex differences in marital communication. *Communication Monographs, 54*, 276–294.

Cahn, D. D. (1992). *Conflict in intimate relationships*. New York: Guilford.

Canary, D. J., Cunningham, E. M., & Cody, M. J. (1988). Goal types, gender, and locus of control in managing interpersonal conflict. *Communication Research, 15*, 424–446.

Canary, D. J., & Cupach, W. R. (1988). Relational and episodic characteristics associated with conflict tactics. *Journal of Social and Personal Relationships, 5*, 305–325.

Canary, D. J., & Spitzberg, B. H. (1987). Appropriateness and effectiveness perceptions of conflict strategies. *Human Communication Research, 14*, 93–118.

Canary, D. J., & Spitzberg, B. H. (1989). A model of perceived competence of conflict strategies. *Human Communication Research, 15*, 630–649.

Canary, D. J., & Spitzberg, B. H. (1990). Attribution biases and associations between conflict strategies and competence outcomes. *Communication Monographs, 57*, 139–151.

Cate, R. M., Henton, J. M., Koval, J., Christopher, F. S., & Lloyd, S. (1982). Premarital abuse: A social psychological perspective. *Journal of Family Issues, 3*, 79–90.

Cegala, D. J. (1981). Interaction involvement: A cognitive dimension of communicative competence. *Communication Education, 30*, 109–121.

Christensen, A., & Shenk, J. L. (1991). Communication, conflict, and psychological distance in nondistressed, clinic, and divorcing couples. *Journal of Consulting and Clinical Psychology, 59*, 458–463.

Conger, A. J., Wallander, J. L., Mariotto, M. J., & Ward, D. (1980). Peer judgments of heterosexual-social anxiety and skills: What do they pay attention to anyhow? *Behavioral Assessment, 2*, 243–260.

Crawford, M. (1988). Gender, age, and the social evaluation of assertion. *Behavior Modification, 12*, 549–564.

Cupach, W. R. (1982, May). *Communication satisfaction and interpersonal solidarity as outcomes of conflict message strategy use.* Paper presented at the International Communication Association Conference, Boston.

Cupach, W. R., Canary, D. J., & Serpe, R. T. (in preparation). *Relational and episodic influences on the use of conflict strategies: A longitudinal replication and extension.* Unpublished report under preparation, Illinois State University, Normal, IL.

Davitz, J. R. (1969). *The language of emotions.* New York: Academic.

Delamater, R. J., & McNamara, J. R. (1986). The social impact of assertiveness: Research findings and clinical implications. *Behavior Modification, 10*, 139–158.

Delamater, R. J., & McNamara, J. R. (1991). Perceptions of assertiveness by women involved in a conflict situation. *Behavior Modification, 15*, 173–193.

Duran, R. L. (1992). Communicative adaptability: A review of conceptualization and measurement. *Communication Quarterly, 40*, 253–268.

Filsinger, E. E., & Thoma, S. J. (1988). Behavioral antecedents of relationship stability and adjustment: A five-year longitudinal study. *Journal of Marriage and the Family, 50*, 785–795.

Fitzpatrick, M. A. (1988). *Between husbands and wives: Communication in marriage.* Newbury Park, CA: Sage.

Fitzpatrick, M. A., Fallis, S., & Vance, L. (1982). Multifunctional coding of conflict resolution strategies in marital dyads. *Family Relations, 31*, 61–70.

Galassi, J. P., Galassi, M., & Vedder, M. J. (1981). Perspectives on assertion as a social skills model. In J. D. Wine & M. D. Smye (Eds.), *Social competence* (pp. 287–345). New York: Guilford.

Gervasio, A. H., & Crawford, M. (1989). Social evaluations of assertiveness: A critique and speech act reformulation. *Psychology of Women Quarterly, 13*, 1–25.

Gormally, J. (1982). Evaluation of assertiveness: Effects of gender, rater involvement, and level of assertiveness. *Behavior Therapy, 13*, 219–225.

Gottman, J. M. (1979). *Marital interaction: Experimental investigations.* New York: Academic.

Gottman, J. M., & Krokoff, L. J. (1989). Marital interaction and satisfaction: A longitudinal view. *Journal of Consulting and Clinical Psychology, 57*, 47–52.

Gottman, J. M., & Levenson, R. W. (1992). Marital processes predictive of later dissolution: Behavior, physiology, and health. *Journal of Personality and Social Psychology, 63*, 221–233.

Hedlund, B. L., & Lindquist, C. U. (1984). The development of an inventory for distinguishing among passive, aggressive, and assertive behavior. *Behavioral Assessment, 6*, 379–390.

Henton, J., Cate, R., Koval, J., Lloyd, S., & Christopher, S. (1983). Romance and violence in dating relationships. *Journal of Family Issues, 4*, 467–482.

Holtzworth-Munroe, A., & Anglin, K. (1991). The competency of responses given by maritally violent versus nonviolent men to problematic marital situations. *Violence and Victims, 6*, 257–269.

Holtzworth-Munroe, A., Waltz, J., Jacobson, N. S., Monaco, V., Fehrenbach, P. A., & Gottman, J. M. (1992). Recruiting nonviolent men as control subjects for research on marital violence: How easily can it be done? *Violence and Victims, 7,* 79–88.

Huston, T. L., & Vangelisti, A. L. (1991). Socioemotional behavior and satisfaction in marital relationships: A longitudinal study. *Journal of Personality and Social Psychology, 61,* 721–733.

Jacobson, N. S., Follette, W. C., & Elwood, R. W. (1984). Outcome research on behavioral marital therapy: A methodological and conceptual reappraisal. In K. Hahlweg & N. S. Jacobson (Eds.), *Marital interaction: Analysis and modification* (pp. 113–129). New York: Guilford.

Jaffe, P. G., Sudermann, M., Reitzel, D., & Killip, S. M. (1992). An evaluation of a secondary school primary prevention program on violence in intimate relationships. *Violence and Victims, 7,* 129–146.

Jones, E. E. (1989). The framing of competence. *Personality and Social Psychology Bulletin, 15,* 477–492.

Kelly, J. A., St. Lawrence, J. S., Bradlyn, A. S., Himadi, W. G., Graves, K. A., & Keane, T. M. (1982). Interpersonal reactions to assertive and unassertive styles when handling social conflict situations. *Journal of Behavioral Therapy and Experimental Psychiatry, 13,* 33–40.

Kern, J. M., Cavell, T. A., & Beck, B. (1985). Predicting differential reactions to males' versus females' assertions, empathic-assertions, and nonassertions. *Behavior Therapy, 16,* 63–75.

Knudson, R. M., Sommers, A. A., & Golding, S. L. (1980). Interpersonal perception and mode of resolution in marital conflict. *Journal of Personality and Social Psychology, 38,* 751–763.

Koren, P., Carlton, K., & Shaw, D. (1980). Marital conflict: Relations among behaviors, outcomes, and distress. *Journal of Consulting and Clinical Psychology, 48,* 460–468.

Larzelere, R. E., & Huston, T. L. (1980). The dyadic trust scale: Toward understanding interpersonal trust in close relationships. *Journal of Marriage and the Family, 42,* 595–604.

Levin, R. B., & Gross, A. M. (1984). Reactions to assertive versus nonassertive behavior: Females in commendatory and refusal situations. *Behavior Modification, 8,* 581–592.

Levin, R. B., & Gross, A. M. (1987). Assertiveness style: Effects on perceptions of assertive behavior. *Behavior Modification, 11,* 229–240.

Lewis, P. N., & Gallois, C. (1984). Disagreements, refusals, or negative feelings: Perception of negatively assertive messages from friends and strangers. *Behavior Therapy, 15,* 353–368.

Lowe, M. R., & Storm, M. A. (1986). Being assertive or being liked: A genuine dilemma? *Behavior Modification, 10,* 371–390.

Makepeace, J. M. (1981). Courtship violence among college students. *Family Relations, 30,* 97–102.

Margolin, G., John, R. S., & Gleberman, L. (1988). Affective responses to conflictual discussions in violent and nonviolent couples. *Journal of Consulting and Clinical Psychology, 56,* 24–33.

Margolin, G., & Wampold, B. E. (1981). Sequential analysis of conflict and accord in distressed and nondistressed marital partners. *Journal of Consulting and Clinical Psychology, 49,* 554–567.

Markman, H. J. (1981). Prediction of marital distress: A 5-year follow-up. *Journal of Consulting and Clinical Psychology, 49,* 760–762.

McCroskey, J. C. (1982). Communication competence and performance: A research and pedagogical perspective. *Communication Education, 31,* 1–8.

McFall, R. M. (1982). A review and reformulation of the concept of social skills. *Behavioral Assessment, 4,* 1–33.

Millar, F. E., & Rogers, L. E. (1976). A relational approach to interpersonal communication. In G. R. Miller (Ed.), *Explorations in interpersonal communication* (pp. 87–104). Beverly Hills, CA: Sage.

Morton, T. L., Alexander, J. F., & Altman, I. (1976). Communication and relationship definition. In G. R. Miller (Ed.), *Explorations in interpersonal communication* (pp. 105–126). Beverly Hills, CA: Sage.

Newton, D. A., & Burgoon, J. K. (1990). Nonverbal conflict behaviors: Functions, strategies, and tactics. In D. D. Cahn (Ed.), *Intimates in conflict: A communication perspective* (pp. 77–104). Hillsdale, NJ: Lawrence Erlbaum Associates.

Nicotera, A. M. (1991, November). *The use of multiple conflict handling tactics: A multi-method study of communication satisfaction, goal-attainment effectiveness, and strategy.* Paper presented at the Speech Communication Association Conference, Atlanta, GA.

Patterson, G. R., Hops, H., & Weiss, R. L. (1975). Interpersonal skills training for couples in early stages of conflict. *Journal of Marriage and the Family, 37,* 295–303.

Putnam, L., & Wilson, C. E. (1982). Communicative strategies in organizational conflict: Reliability and validity of a measurement scale. In M. Burgoon (Ed.), *Communication yearbook* (Vol. 6, pp. 629–652). Newbury Park, CA: Sage.

Rakos, R. F. (1991). *Assertive behavior: Theory, research, and training.* London: Routledge.

Rands, M., Levinger, G., & Mellinger, G. D. (1981). Patterns of conflict resolution and marital satisfaction. *Journal of Family Issues, 2,* 297–321.

Redmond, M. V. (1985). The relationship between perceived communication competence and perceived empathy. *Communication Monographs, 52,* 377–382.

Roloff, M. E., & Cloven, D. H. (1990). The chilling effect in interpersonal relationships: The reluctance to speak one's mind. In D. D. Cahn (Ed.), *Intimates in conflict: A communication perspective* (pp. 49–76). Hillsdale, NJ: Lawrence Erlbaum Associates.

Rose, Y. J., & Tryon, W. W. (1979). Judgments of assertive behavior as a function of speech loudness, latency, content, gestures, inflection, and sex. *Behavior Modification, 3,* 112–123.

Rubin, R. B. (1990). Communication competence. In G. M. Phillips & J. T. Wood (Eds.), *Speech Communication: Essays to commemorate the 75th anniversary of the Speech Communication Association* (pp. 94–129). Carbondale, IL: Southern Illinois University.

Rubin, R. B., Martin, M. M., Bruning, S. S., & Powers, D. E. (1993). Test of a self-efficacy model of interpersonal communication competence. *Communication Quarterly, 41,* 210–220.

Sereno, K. K., Welch, M., & Braaten, D. (1987). Interpersonal conflict: Effects of variations in manner of expressing anger and justification for anger upon perceptions of appropriateness, competence, and satisfaction. *Journal of Applied Communication Research, 15,* 128–143.

Sillars, A. L. (1980). The sequential and distributional structure of conflict interactions as a function of attributions concerning the locus of responsibility and stability of conflicts. In D. Nimmo (Ed.), *Communication yearbook* (Vol. 4, pp. 217–235). New Brunswick, NJ: Transaction.

Sillars, A. L., Coletti, S. F., Perry, D., & Rogers, M. A. (1982). Coding verbal conflicts: Nonverbal and perceptual correlates of the "avoidance-distributive-integrative" distinction. *Human Communication Research, 9,* 83–95.

Sillars, A. L., Pike, G. R., Jones, T. S., & Murphy, M. A. (1984). Communication and understanding in marriage. *Human Communication Research, 10,* 317–350.

Sillars, A. L., Pike, G. R., Jones, T. S., & Redmon, K. (1983). Communication and conflict in marriage. In R. Bostrom (Ed.), *Communication yearbook* vol. 7, (pp. 414–422). Beverly Hills, CA: Sage.

Sillars, A. L., & Weisberg, J. (1987). Conflict as a social skill. In M. E. Roloff & G. R. Miller (Eds.), *Interpersonal processes: New directions in communication research* (pp. 140–171). Newbury Park: Sage.

Sillars, A. L., Wilmot, W. W., & Hocker, J. C. (1993). Communicating strategically in conflict and mediation. In J. Wiemann & J. Daly (Eds.), *Communicating strategically: strategies in interpersonal communication.* Hillsdale, NJ: Lawrence Erlbaum Associates.

Smolen, R. C., Spiegel, D. A., Bakker-Rabdau, M. K., Bakker, C. B., & Martin, C. (1985). A situational analysis of the relationship between spouse-specific assertiveness and marital adjustment. *Journal of Psychopathology and Behavioral Assessment, 7,* 397-410.

Spitzberg, B. H. (1983). Communication competence as knowledge, skill, and impression. *Communication Education, 32,* 323-328.

Spitzberg, B. H., & Cupach, W. R. (1984). *Interpersonal communication competence.* Beverly Hills, CA: Sage.

Spitzberg, B. H., & Hecht, M. L. (1984). A component model of relational competence. *Human Communication Research, 10,* 575-599.

Spitzberg, B. H., & Marshall, L. L. (1990, July). *The topography of relational violence and abuse.* Paper presented at the International Society for the study of Personal Relationships Conference, Oxford, England.

Sternberg, R. J., & Kolligian, J., Jr. (Eds.). (1990). *Competence considered.* New Haven, CT: Yale University.

Storms, M. D. (1973). Videotape and the attribution process: Reversing actors' and observers' points of view. *Journal of Personality and Social Psychology, 27,* 165-175.

Sugarman, D. B., & Hotaling, G. T. (1989). Dating violence: Prevalence, context, and risk markers. In M. A. Pirog-Good & J. E. Stets (Eds.), *Violence in dating relationships* (pp. 3-32). New York: Praeger.

Ting-Toomey, S. (1983). An analysis of verbal communication patterns in high and low marital adjustment groups. *Human Communication Research, 9,* 306-319.

Utley, M. E., Richardson, D. R., & Pilkington, C. J. (1989). Personality and interpersonal conflict management. *Personality and Individual Differences 10,* 287-293.

Wiemann, J. M. (1977). Explication and test of a model of communicative competence. *Human Communication Research, 3,* 195-213.

Wiemann, J. M., & Bradac, J. J. (1985). The many guises of communicative competence. *Journal of Language and Social Psychology, 4,* 131-138.

Wildman, B. G., & Clementz, B. (1986). Assertive, empathic assertive, and conversational behavior. *Behavior Modification, 10,* 315-331.

Wilmot, W. W. (1987). *Dyadic communication* (3rd ed.). New York: Random House.

Wilson, L. K., & Gallois, C. (1985). Perceptions of assertive behavior: Sex combination, role appropriateness, and message type. *Sex Roles, 12,* 125-141.

Zollo, L. J., Heimberg, R. G., & Becker, R. E. (1985). Evaluations and consequences of assertive behavior. *Journal of Behavioral Therapy and Experimental Psychiatry, 16,* 295-301.

10 A Holistic Approach to Dispute Resolution at a Community Mediation Center

Clare Danielsson
Ulster-Sullivan Mediation, Inc., Highland, NY

In the local mediation office, the phone is ringing again. "Hello, is this the Mediation Center?" It's an angry voice, full of tension and belligerence.

"Yes, it is—how may I help you?" The intake coordinator is warm and friendly.

"It's that blasted dog next door. It's been barking all night for weeks! I've had barely 10 minutes of sleep since they got the dog! I finally said enough is enough, you know, and I called the police. They said they wouldn't do anything about it until I tried calling you people. What are you going to do about it? And whatever it is, it better be fast, because I can't take much more of this," says the exasperated caller.

"Have you tried calling your neighbor to talk this over?" the coordinator asks quietly.

"Are you crazy? He's not going to listen to me! I want this aggravation stopped!"

"You see," says the coordinator, "we're going to be calling your neighbor, and asking if he will meet with you to work out a solution. I need to know whether you've already spoken with him. It makes a difference in how we will approach him."

"Oh." The man's voice is quieter now, more thoughtful.

This is the way in which mediation intervenes in the conflict process. Mediation is a process that helps people resolve a conflict using a neutral third person. Mediation agencies are asked to intervene, just as the police are asked to intervene, in situations where there is doubt that the parties to a conflict can or will talk things through and reach a peaceful solution on their own.

In the next few minutes, the intake coordinator at a mediation center will ask the caller questions to find out as much as possible about the situation: Have you ever spoken to this neighbor before? What happened then? What's the nature of the relationship? Then the intake coordinator will conduct a discussion of how to begin a relationship under these difficult circumstances. Is it simply a matter of overcoming exhaustion, staying calm, and working it out — or does this unknown neighbor give the irate resident reason to be afraid? Has the caller witnessed his neighbor displaying a hot temper, or shooting tin cans in the backyard with a handgun? The mediation coordinator needs to know this, to determine whether or not it is a suitable case for mediation or if the caller should get help elsewhere.

THE MEDIATION CENTER

Ulster-Sullivan Mediation, Inc., which handles situations like the one just described, is a private, not-for-profit organization that operates in two counties in New York State. The organization's Mission Statement says it is dedicated to improving the problem-solving abilities of all individuals, so that differences may be appreciated instead of being a source of strife.

This article describes Ulster-Sullivan Mediation's work, focusing on the training and outreach programs needed to fulfill the Mission Statement. The aim of this chapter is to give an in-depth picture of one mediation center's efforts to serve its two counties.

ORIGINS

Chapter 847 of New York State's Laws of 1981 made community dispute resolution centers possible. Free mediation services became available to Ulster County residents in 1983, and to Sullivan County residents in 1984.

The center is called by people seeking assistance with a dispute. The center's coordinator arranges for trained volunteer mediators to sit down with the disputants and help resolve the issues. (Paid staff do not usually do the actual mediating.) The coordinator sorts out the issues over the phone, reviews the list of available volunteers, schedules two of them as co-mediators, and arranges for all to meet at a neutral place at a convenient time. Centers are funded through a contract with the Office of Court Administration's Community Dispute Resolution Centers Program (OCA CDRCP),[1] ensuring mediation's availability as an alternative for criminal,

---

[1]Director, Office of Court Administration, P.O. Box 7039, Alfred E. Smith State Office Building, Albany, NY 12225.

civil, small-claims, and family cases. Cases often involve landlord–tenant disputes, interpersonal disputes, harrassment, and assorted other problems. In the last five years, mediation centers have expanded their programs to add specialized services for youths, schools, the adult working community, and community organizations. The services provided are determined by the needs and requests of the community and, in some cases, by statewide initiative (e.g., mobile home owner–park owner mediation or family–school district disputes related to special education, real estate contract disputes, etc.).[2]

OUR REGION

Ulster County is a largely rural area midway between New York City and Albany, on the western shore of the Hudson River. It encompasses great diversity: apple farms, an IBM headquarters in the historic county seat of Kingston, the Schawangunk Mountains, and a State University of New York college at New Paltz. Its population in 1990 was 165,000. Sullivan County, directly west of Ulster, is even more rural. Once the vacation capital of the Catskills, many of its former resort hotels are now community residences for developmentally disabled adults, or Eastern meditation ashrams. Its population numbers 70,000. Each county has a community college. Overall, the region contains six state prisons and two youth detention centers.

Ulster County had approximately 55 active volunteer mediators in 1992, whereas Sullivan County had 32. Since 1983, 200 volunteer mediators have been trained. The average volunteer mediator in New York State is 46 years old, with 4 or more years of college and 3½ years in the dispute resolution field (Christian, 1987). Five hundred seventy-five cases were handled in 1992, of which 26% were generated by the Ulster County Family Court (e.g., custody, visitation, and child support matters), 23% were school conflicts between youths (resolved by peer mediators), and 21% were community call-ins, individuals who had heard of the program through media or word of mouth. Sixteen percent were referred by public agencies, such as consumer fraud or social services, and 12.5% were referred by town or village courts. Statistically, then, each mediator could co-mediate every month, but the realities of people's schedules tend to mean that some are available and able to mediate much more often than others. A total of

---

[2]The New York State Association of Community Dispute Resolution Centers (NYSACDR) contracts with other state agencies such as the Division of Housing and Community Renewal, and with independent associations such as the New York State Association of Realtors. NYSACDR's address is 244 Hudson Ave., Albany, NY 12210.

3,240 mediations have taken place in the past decade, serving approximately 8,000 disputants (two or three at a time) (Danielsson, 1978, 1992).

To introduce conflict resolution skills to a wider range of community members, including schools and youths, the center began offering 2- and 3-day training sessions in 1987. As of 1993, 1,000 persons, from fourth graders through retirees, have participated. Ten out of the 20 school districts in the area have active peer mediation programs in at least one building, and 3 have in-school trainers (Ulster-Sullivan Mediation, 1992).

CONFLICT RESOLUTION: GENERAL PRINCIPLES AND HISTORY

The roots of conflict resolution are as old as recorded history. All major religions and cultures discourage violence and have established peaceful means of dispute resolution, especially within face-to-face communities. The brilliance of indigenous peoples in inventing ways of resolving conflict has been documented by anthropologists working on many continents.

Extended families, religious groups, and associations that function as face-to-face communities have ways of establishing standards of behavior and resolving differences without resorting to formal court procedures. Traditionally, only serious criminal cases and matters related to warfare were considered to require the intervention of courts and governments.

Interpersonal issues and minor disputes were once addressed by the different reconciliation processes of these smaller affinity groups. Today, the bonding ability of families, churches, and community organizations is not enough to hold people together and perform this function. Courthouses have had to take up the slack. Some members of the legal profession, not feeling comfortable in this role, have begun to seek alternative processes that can respond to the need for assistance with conflict resolution. Any courtroom decision creates a winner and a loser, between whom friendship and goodwill are often destroyed. In cases involving neighbors, co-workers, or other members of face-to-face communities, living in close proximity becomes extremely difficult if one has been judged right and the other wrong. "Sure, we won the court case, and now our driveway is three feet over," said a fourth grader. "But you know what? The neighbors don't come to visit anymore. They used to bring cookies."

Mediation's perspective is future oriented: Yes, today we have a problem, and it needs to be discussed. Apologies and restitution, while they may be in order, relate to the past and are not enough. More important, what can be done differently to prevent a recurrence?

In the United States, the community dispute resolution movement began in the 1970s, a result of discussion concerning the overload of minor disputes that were clogging the legal system. In 1969, the Ford Foundation funded the Institute for Mediation and Conflict Resolution to train residents of New York City in the handling of community disputes. In 1976, the U.S. Justice Department, under President Carter, established Neighborhood Justice Centers as pilot programs in three cities: Los Angeles, Atlanta, and Kansas City. These provided a forum for the resolution of minor disputes as an alternative to arrest and formal court action. These programs served as models for later programs (Bell, 1992).[3] The term *alternative dispute resolution* (ADR) is widely used to describe these processes. The American Bar Association publishes a directory of the more than 400 centers that have come into existence in the last 15 years.[4]

Mediation itself has been a familiar idea in the Western world. By the 1970s, mediation and arbitration had become the dispute resolution methods of choice in labor–management disputes, as an alternative to the industrial warfare of strikes and lockouts. The American Arbitration Association, established in 1926, has had an elaborate network of mediation, fact finding, arbitration, and mini-trials in place for many years. The application of alternative dispute resolution techniques to personal disputes built on this long history of union–management conflict resolution procedures. The establishment of the federal Neighborhood Justice Center pilot programs was an attempt to begin applying these methods in the broader community.

Federal funding of Neighborhood Justice Centers was short lived, but people became excited by the concept. It took root as a response to the need of communities to find ways of reconciling various disputes.

Dispute Resolution Centers found many and varied sponsors. The 1980s were a decade of practical experimentation in communities and schools. Mediators were excited by the opportunity to teach lifelong dispute resolution skills. In 1973, educators in Rochester, New York, attempting to respond to racial difficulties in their schools, opened a Community Justice Center. It was a cooperative venture, involving the City of Rochester and the American Arbitration Association. Community activists opened the San Francisco Community Boards Program in 1976, which later expanded to do pioneering work with youths and schools. Quakers, Mennonites, and other religious societies began work in the difficult field of prison reform and victim–offender reconciliation.

---

[3]For free copies of the NIDR *Forum,* write to NIDR, 1901 L Street, NW, Suite 600, Washington, DC 20036.

[4]ABA Special Committee on Dispute Resolution, 1800 M. Street, NW, Suite 600, Washington, DC 20036.

ADR TERMS DEFINED

Mediation is a process that helps people resolve a conflict using a neutral third person (Simmel, 1950). This third person mediates; that is, he or she facilitates discussion between the others. All mediators are *facilitators*, but all facilitators are not mediators. The term *facilitator* (facilitate: to make easier) can be applied to anyone who uses diplomatic language, new ideas, and good communication and problem-solving skills to make a group's process easier (or at least less difficult). Whereas a mediator has a specific goal — the resolution of a conflict (preferably with a written agreement as a result) — a facilitator may simply use his or her skills to allow a smooth, productive meeting to take place.

An *ombudsperson* (originally a Swedish term) is a neutral third party who intervenes specifically in disputes between individuals and government agencies. State nursing homes, for example, have ombudspersons, who may suggest changes but have no power to command them. An ombudsperson's tools are persuasion, integrity, and character (see Zagoria, 1988).

In labor–management ADR there are *fact finders*, third parties in a less neutral role, whose job it is to investigate the facts of a situation and issue a (usually nonbinding) recommendation. Fact finders have no parallel in interpersonal mediation.

Moving further along the continuum from neutrality, we come to the *arbitrator*, a third party authorized by the disputants to resolve the dispute. The parties to an arbitrated dispute have agreed in advance to abide by the arbitrator's decision, which is, in this situation, more binding than that of a judge. A judge's decision can be appealed to a higher court, while an arbitrator's cannot. Most people have probably heard of arbitration through the publicity surrounding the Lemon Law, under which an arbitrator determines whether or not a seller must replace a buyer's car because it is a "lemon."

Some mediation programs utilize a med/arb model for community and interpersonal disputes. In med/arb, mediation is attempted first. If no resolution is forthcoming, arbitration is suggested. The parties sign an agreement to abide by the third party's decision, and decide whether they want the previous mediator or someone else to decide the matter. Ulster-Sullivan Mediation's board of directors decided against a med/arb model, and only interpersonal mediation is practiced in these counties' Mediation center.

The mediator, as a neutral third party, must help disputants to stop fighting and begin negotiating. In the negotiation process, both parties state what happened, how they feel, what they want changed, etc. When both parties work together toward a solution, the process is called *collaborative negotiation*, and it is this process that a mediator facilitates. Sometimes all the mediator needs do is set the tone, create a setting where both parties feel safe and respected, and keep silent. His or her very presence can be enough to remind both parties that they are in this together, and that their common good is as important as each one's personal gain.

The only third party intervention familiar to most people is that of an authority with the power to impose a decision: a police officer, parent, teacher, boss, or judge. This authority may or may not have any skills or knowledge of various ways to help people resolve differences and regulate their own behavior. After a bad conflict experience, negative behavior may stop, but this does not mean that those involved have learned anything about problem solving. Often, people will simply try to avoid all conflict and responsibility in the future; the price of making mistakes is just too high.

COMMUNITY CONFLICT TODAY – AND TOMORROW

The 1990s will probably remain a time of turbulence and rapid change, a continuation of the information revolution already occurring. Madeline Crohn (1992), president of the National Institute for Dispute Resolution, called attention to the following trends:

> The United States will be more fragmented along the lines of race, culture, nationality of origin, wealth, age, and interest – so that the "melting pot" concept will be replaced by one of the "mosaic society." . . .

> Poverty will persist and grow, and the middle class will continue to thin and create new poverty; poverty will be borne increasingly and disproportionately by female-headed, African American, and Hispanic families.

> . . . [R]esearch tells us that women and men deal with disputes differently in the workplace, because women identify disputes as personal ones, are then labeled as troublemakers and, as a result, may be bypassed in terms of promotions. Research shows also that racial stereotyping and anger has increased over the past ten years – due to economic competition, increased immigration, and higher visibility of racist organizations – and that these disputes are fueled by increasing prejudice and violence. (p. 4)

One of the basic premises of dispute resolution is that each conflict contains within it the seeds of its resolution. It's a question of how the matter is reframed.

We are living on a small planet. The plus side to the crises created by modern technology is better communication: We are rapidly becoming a global village. The mosaic of fragmentation and individuation also has its positive aspect: The unique potential of each individual can be realized; no one need remain an undifferentiated member of a category, a race, or a gender.

The challenge is coping with this diversity. Moreno (1972), defined the significant encounter between two individuals: "eye to eye, face to face . . ." as the essence of the personal and social healing process (see also Danielsson, 1972). (Interestingly, the application of this principle to victim–offender mediations within the legal system is becoming more and more accepted as its socializing potential is realized. It reintroduces the relationship of persons to people who have been dehumanized and seen as villains or objects.)

Each of us is different, every single individual. To meet face to face, encounter one another in a safe setting, try to hear each other's view of reality, and "walk a mile in each other's shoes" make up the basic creative interaction from which all else follows. This principle is as important for groups as it is for individuals. The dispute resolution movement is the beginning of a public acceptance of responsibility for the creation of a safe environment in which such encounters can take place—a safe common ground.

DISPUTE RESOLUTION EDUCATION AND SYSTEM DESIGN

The need for professionally trained persons, skilled in intervening in disputes, is being increasingly acknowledged by academia. The major curriculum at George Mason University in Virginia is conflict resolution. Other programs include Harvard Law School's School of Negotiation, a summer program at Syracuse University, master's program at Antioch, and a program at New York City's John Jay College of Criminal Justice. Ten years ago, only 25 law schools included dispute resolution in their programs; today, 150 offer these courses (Crohn, 1992).

The New York State law that established the dispute resolution centers also required them to "provide neutral mediators with at least 25 hours of training in conflict resolution techniques." The New York State Unified Court System's Community Dispute Resolution Centers Program outlines the core content of the training curriculum. It must include history of dispute resolution, relevant New York State law, center intake procedures, and all elements of the actual dispute resolution process. It also specifies that an apprenticeship period must follow training. No statewide certification of mediators exists; each volunteer is certified by a county program director for that program only. Programs must use trainers who are on the

CDRCP's State Certified List. Most program directors are certified trainers, as each program needs a steady source of skilled community volunteers.

Becoming skilled in conflict resolution absolutely requires hands-on experience. It cannot be mastered through reading and study; a person must become fully involved.

Graduate programs in medicine, law, or education must build internship or fieldwork components into their requirements. At lower educational levels, hands-on application of theory is considered part of a progressive or alternative education for youths, or apprenticeship if job related. Practicing life-survival skills, which is an apt definition of dispute resolution, does not quite fit into any of these categories. It is a new social innovation, born of necessity, nurtured by the court system, and useful everywhere. Community volunteers are trained to increase the "glue" holding societies and families together in a time of violence and fragmentation, and to give children the necessary social skills that earlier generations learned at home in order to transcend the impact of technology and social change.

At Ulster-Sullivan Mediation, mediation is taught to a class of no more than 24, by means of mini-lectures, discussions, a variety of group activities, role playing, and simulation. Reading materials are minimal. Training sessions are deliberately intensive: 4 hours for fourth graders, full days for adults. As people tire and relax, old habits and resistances break down and the path is cleared for new learning to take place. Sometimes a conflict will surface during a training, and is addressed on the spot. More often, what surfaces is spontaneity. The presentation of new skills in a safe environment, where it is possible to make mistakes, is the best training formula known. As John Dewey (1938) argued, "Education, in order to accomplish its ends for both the individual and society, must be based upon experience—which is always the actual life experience of some individual" (p. 89).

Some skill can be obtained through simulations in the classroom, but there is no substitute for the experience of doing neutral problem solving with genuinely angry or upset individuals. All training programs are followed by an apprenticeship, typically at least five actual mediations. At the first, the new mediator will simply observe. In the second and third, he or she assists an experienced mediator, and by the fifth session, the apprentice may be contributing as a full and equal co-mediator. During internship, new mediators learn to imbue the process with common sense, spontaniety, and intuitive wisdom. We have found that mediators of any age who complete the training and then do not have the opportunity to conduct at least a fair amount of mediation tend to forget the process, as experience is needed to assimilate and integrate this new approach to disputes.

CURRENT ULSTER-SULLIVAN MEDIATION TRAINING PROCEDURES

The procedures and content involved in mediation training are very similar, whether training a group of school peer mediators or adult community volunteers. The following describes the training of adults; youth training is discussed further in a later section. The similarities between the two are more important than the differences.

Adult training time totals 28 hours, and usually involves one full weekend and supplementary evening sessions. Mediators role play at least three complete mediations in training, in order to build confidence and competence. All role plays are followed by discussion and brainstorming focused on how they might have been improved and affirmation for hard work well done. Experienced mediators attend the final session, to assist in supervising the novices' last role plays. Disputes covered in role plays may include the classic barking dog, harassment, minor assault, breach of contract, landlord–tenant (the return of security deposits being another classic), consumer–merchant, small claims, bad checks, noise, trespassing, employer–employee disputes at worksites, and a variety of interpersonal issues. The topics are based on the types of cases that we are frequently asked to handle.

Student trainings for fourth through twelfth graders are shorter (16 hours, in 4- or 6-hour sessions) because the types of cases handled by student mediators tend to be less diverse. Gossip and rumors, misunderstandings, friendship, ex-boyfriend–ex-girlfriend disputes, and similar interpersonal issues form the basis of role plays for this group, as these will constitute the bulk of their caseload.

The trainer and county coordinator will begin assigning cases to new mediators when it is felt that they are ready, and will register code numbers for them at the New York State Unified Court System's CDRCP office (because all case records are kept anonymous).

After a case, a mediator will be debriefed by phone on the following day. In this way the coordinator is kept abreast of the situation in case another call should come in about it, and the mediator receives the needed support of sharing the experience without violating confidentiality. (In Grades 4–12, this is done in person.)

THE MEDIATION PROCESS

The process begins with discussion and setup of the environment in which the actual encounter will take place. Considerable attention is given to the layout of the room, who may or may not be present, how the parties will be greeted, and the handling of unexpected situations (e.g., a disputant who arrives intoxicated). The premise here is that a correctly set up mediation will succeed. If there is no chance of success, this is usually obvious within the first five minutes. Sometimes mediators need to end sessions immediately, reschedule, or switch strategies — for example, begin with individual caucuses, in which the mediator confers privately with each disputant. Violence or threats of violence that could result in false contracts or coerced solutions must be brought to light, as such matters cannot be mediated.

The basic mediation session includes the following sections, whether it is a situation involving children or adults: the mediator's opening statement, uninterrupted time, exchange, building the agreement, writing and signing the agreement, and the mediator's closing statement.

The Mediator's Opening Statement

The explanation of the mediator's role is given, and the rules of the process are explained. The disputants then must agree to try to resolve the matters that brought them there. Adults are asked to sign a consent form, indicating their sincerity of purpose, their understanding of the mediator's neutrality and the confidential nature of the process, and the fact that neither the mediators nor the center itself are liable. No court can subpoena mediation records, and mediators, by law, cannot testify in court for either party.

This opening statement, ceremonial in tone, sets the scene for all that follows. Often, both parties are anxious and uncertain. Their perception of the mediator's respect for them and control of the situation can encourage them to try for new solutions to old problems — to take risks. The experience can then become educational, and disputants become more competent in coping with life's difficulties. Conversely, if the disputatants doubt the reliability or reputation of the third party, his or her actual skills or credentials matter very little. Neutrality and the ability to listen may be honed in training, but if these qualities are not part of an individual's value system, all the training in the world cannot make that person an effective mediator. The mediator must be able to inspire in the disputants the trust and confidence crucial to beginning the process. Without this trust, disputants are not likely to feel that it is worthwhile even to begin.

Uninterrupted Time

This is when each disputant, in turn, gets the chance to explain the situation without questions or interruptions. The other party can make notes, but must not speak up until the party whose turn it is for uninterrupted time has finished.

Exchange

Now each disputant can reply to the other's remarks. The mediator says very little, simply making sure that the parties don't interrupt each other, which is often a challenge in itself. The presence of a third party, a silent representative of the larger community, is the ingredient that makes this dialogue different. The dispute is no longer private, but is taken seriously by the "public," as represented by the mediator. As a result, disputants speak and listen differently than they might when encountering each other alone. Some mediations, when the dispute has been a matter of misunderstanding and misinterpretation, are resolved at this stage, without very much mediator assistance. In a safe space, with a structured process supporting them, issues can be resolved quickly. The mediator simply provides the proper atmosphere, rather like a strategically placed potted plant.

Building the Agreement

This is when the mediator's skilled intervention really begins, with the use of listening and communication skills and "mediator language." Elementary school mediators commonly reframe or restate each statement made. Adults use this technique only when necessary. An emotionally loaded remark may need to be translated into neutral language, giving perspective and distance. "I statements," which are presented as personal opinion rather than blame, judgment, and recrimination, can be modeled and elicited by the mediator. Open-ended questions, which invite people to respond thoughtfully and bring up underlying concerns, are another tool. Working toward an agreement is always the most complex part of the session. It means moving away from what has existed and opening new, clear lines of communication so that a plan for a better future can emerge. The basic rules and the structured process promote this outcome. However, the mediator's skill must be applied in a way that allows the disputants to let go of negative behavior, brainstorming the issues to create a better future for themselves.

Writing and Signing the Agreement

If a formal agreement is reached in an adult case mediated through the center, the agreement is written down and signed by both parties, with the mediator signing as witness. This agreement has the legally binding force of a contract. If a partial agreement or none at all is reached, what will happen next must be clarified, for this too has its consequences.

Mediator's Closing Statement

The disputants are thanked for coming to the session, regardless of whether or not an agreement has been reached. It took courage to try, and the relationship will have been altered in some way by the simple fact of the two parties' sitting down and listening to one another.

The closing is ceremonial but important. Disputants often have mixed feelings: grateful for the process, yet embarrassed by their need of it. As one disputant said to a mediator, "Thank you very much! I hope I never have to see you again." They need the mediator to be neutral, anonymous, and respectful. The Chinese, who have practiced mediation for 1, 000 years, say that just as a tree has bark, a person has a face. The process must allow both persons to save face. Thus, they may look with dignity into the eyes of someone with whom they have had a serious disagreement and with whom they must continue to co-exist. The physical or emotional distance may have altered, but the co-existence is an inescapable fact.

SCHOOL PEER MEDIATION PROGRAMS

The spread of mediation into the educational community was a response to a great need: the need to reduce the truancy and dropout rates, the incidence of violence, and related social unrest that jeopardize the learning process for youths.

The more than 2, 000 conflict resolution programs that exist in U.S. schools today can be grouped into four main models. The oldest is the Quaker-originated Children's Creative Response to Conflict (CCRC).[5] The Quakers developed a program for elementary school students, stressing communication, cooperation, and affirmation as the setting for conflict resolution. This holistic approach, further developed by the Educators for Social Responsibility, has been adapted to adult programs as well, such as the Alternatives to Violence Program (AVP) for prison inmates. AVP, in turn, is being adapted for use in secondary schools.

Other programs stress intense, specialized training for a small group of students, who are then available to their peers as mediators. Disputes are referred through the school discipline system, and mediation becomes a voluntary alternative to seeing the assistant principal, the usual disciplinarian. Two well-accepted models used in many schools today are those of the Community Boards Program[6] and the School Mediators' Alternative Resolution Team (SMART), a program begun in 1983 under the auspices of the New York City Victims Services Agency.[7]

---

[5]CCRC publishes textbooks and songbooks for classroom use and provides training in CCRC methods. Write to CCRC, Box 271, 523 N. Broadway, Nyack, NY 10960.

[6]Community Boards publishes a complete, highly adaptable curriculum and offers a five-day training program for school personnel on startup, training, implementation, and follow up of programs at all levels. Their address is 149 9th St., San Francisco, CA 94103.

[7]Training materials used in the SMART program are not widely distributed outside of programs funded by the Victim Services Agency. Their address is 50 Court Street, Room 910, Brooklyn, NY 11201.

A fourth approach involves educating all students in conflict resolution at one grade level, as a supplement to a peer mediation program.[8] This introduces problem solving to everyone, and encourages students to try it themselves.

Ulster-Sullivan Mediation began introducing peer mediation programs to the school systems in its two counties in 1987, using the SMART model for junior and senior high schools and the Community Boards model for elementary schools. We now include CCRC concepts in training as well.[9]

Peer mediation is a highly visible way to introduce the concepts of problem solving and nonviolent conflict resolution to both faculty and students. A small group of specially trained students, who are able to produce agreement between disputing peers referred by the discipline system, has a positive impact on school climate and especially on the behavior of those directly involved. Skeptical adults notice that properly trained students can become excellent problem solvers.

However, the peer mediation model has its limitations. In some schools, the climate is so favorable that many more students want the training than are realistically needed as mediators. In one school, this excess of mediators was responded to by a skilled coordinator who opened the mediation table to students who wished to negotiate their own solutions. They had learned the necessary conflict resolution skills, and simply needed a quiet, safe setting in which to apply them. This skilled coordinator, a key figure in the program's success, is now leaving. It remains to be seen how the program will weather her departure, not an unusual difficulty for a program of this type to face. In another school, an initially successful program could not break through the strong community taboo against admitting to the existence of any problem whatsoever. Conflicts were denied, making for a lack of referrals, and the anger that was pushed underground resurfaced in scapegoating incidents — a group problem, requiring a group solution. The success of any individual program depends on skilled coordination, continuity of leadership, funding for training or the development of an in-house trainer, and the school's overall culture.

Peer mediation training begins with the first phone call from the school district. This is a "top-down" program; if the administration and faculty do not support it, it stops there. Once the peer mediation program has administrative and faculty support, an adult coordinator, and a mediation room, the education of the student population begins. There may be a series

---

[8] A 6-week conflict resolution curriculum for ninth graders by Dr. Vivian Einstein-Gordon is available from West Publishing Company, 164 W. Hillcrest Drive, #200, Thousand Oaks, CA 91360.

[9] USMI publishes School and Youth Newsletter, which details its programs, and an instructional comic book, Teenage Mediators in Space, for grades 7–12. Write USMI, 150 Kisor Rd., Highland, NY 12528.

of presentations to classes, often including a role play of an actual session, or a general assembly explaining the procedure. (One Ulster County high school has produced its own videotape, which is shown to all incoming ninth graders). The voluntary nature of the procedure is stressed, and students are told whom to see in order to begin the process on their own initiative. Following the presentation, ballots are passed out, and students are asked to nominate potential mediators. They may nominate themselves or others. The faculty coordinator and trainer then reviews the nominations, often interviewing the nominees to determine whether or not they are interested, willing to take the training, and can commit time and energy to the program. The faculty coordinator then makes the final selections. Ideally, the entire school community has a hand in creating its peer mediation program, making it one of total involvement.

Training

Peer mediation training for seventh through twelfth graders begins with a general introduction to different styles of conflict resolution: problem solving, denial, and confrontation. The training moves on, delving into a deeper understanding of what mediation is and what it is not. The students learn a brief introductory statement, an explanation of the process, and the enunciation of the four basic rules: (a) Disputants must agree to solve the problem, (b) there is to be no name calling or bad language, (c) disputants must not interrupt each other, and (d) disputants must be as honest as they can. These excellent principles are useful in direct negotiation and general living, as well as in mediation.

Written agreements are standard practice for high school mediators. Elementary school students record verbal agreements in a simple report for their coordinator.

It is important to remember that traditional disciplinary procedures still rule the mainstream in most school systems. Expulsion, suspension, time-out rooms, and other punishments teach students to depend on authority figures to control or resolve conflicts, and good behavior is seen as resulting from external control. The peer mediation movement has demonstrated that many young people can learn internal control and problem-solving skills, and self-regulate their own and their peers' behavior. A significant innovation can be found in Iowa, where conflict resolution is now a mandatory subject for all education students in the state university system.[10] New Mexico also has a statewide conflict resolution approach in

---

[10]Contact Director of Education and Research, Iowa Peace Institute, PO Box 480, Grinnell, IA 50112.

place for schools and youths,[11] and other new developments are occurring rapidly.

Most peer mediation programs, however, continue to depend on dedicated, committed individual educators who are willing to take on the struggle and sacrifice necessary to change established ways of thinking. They typically carry a full load of other work, receive no extra compensation, and often face logistical hurdles (no space for sessions, no time to supervise) on their own. Yet NAME[12] reports a constant nationwide flow of requests for start-up assistance. The need for these skills, the educational value of the positive approach to conflict, and the reality that conflicted students can learn "correct" behavior are beginning to be recognized by administrators. Integrating a new way of learning into an established discipline or justice system is challenging for all concerned.

COMMUNITY OUTREACH PROGRAMS

New applications of mediation continue to be found, as people realize its potential as a response to ongoing societal stress and strain. Ulster-Sullivan Mediation's offerings of services and training continue to respond to these needs. Through public speaking engagements and press releases, we attempt to call to the public's attention the options and services we offer.

The Worksite Conflict Resolution Course originated with requests for assistance in improving worksite communications. Employees and union representatives informed us of a growing reluctance to using existing grievance procedures, which is seen as legalistic, unfriendly, and win or lose. Both employers and employees knew that the mediation process offered a sense of genuine opportunity to work out improvements in the workplace. Ironically, in today's world of instantaneous high-technology communications, many still need help in communicating with their own colleagues.

This course is now part of our expanded training package. Power imbalances inherent in the employer–employee relationship are mitigated by the fact that today's organizations understand the importance of employee involvement. Businesses are changing, moving in the direction of more flexible, less centralized management policies. It has been estimated that within the next 10 years, 75% of the American work force will need retraining, because higher levels of communication, problem solving, and organizational skills are needed in all levels of the workplace hierarchy. This trend has implications for school programs as well, because these skills are becoming increasingly recognized as essential in the workplace.

---

[11]New Mexico Center for Dispute Resolution, 510 2nd St., NW, Albuquerque, NM 87102.
[12]National Association of Mediators in Education, 425 Amity St., Amherst, MA 01002.

A new Ulster-Sullivan Mediation training program, the Basic Course in Conflict Resolution, is offered to all area residents. It allows individuals to explore the basics in a 21-hour program, and continue on to become community mediators, if they are interested. It provides basic conflict resolution skills that individuals can bring to their organizations, schools, or workplaces, generating interest among others who have never experienced this approach. Monthly evening workshops are offered as a follow-up for graduates of the Basic Course, as 21 hours of training are only a beginning.

Another response to community needs is the 2-hour weekly problem-solving class taught by our staff as part of the Ulster County Community Corrections Program, which serves first-time felons with a history of drug and alcohol abuse. We also publicize and support the Alternatives to Violence Project. Originally designed for the prison population, AVP requires teams of civilian and inmate facilitators for each 3-day weekend. The entire program — Beginning, Advanced, and Training for Trainers — takes 9 days, and provides excellent community-building experiences for all participants as well as a superb training program in group facilitation and conflict management. AVP also offers community workshops for civilians, as issues of violence and alienation are hardly unique to the inmate population. We encourage trained mediators (or anyone else!) to experience AVP, both for an excellent lesson in group dynamics and structure, which can then be applied to multiparty disputes, and for a structured, surprisingly safe, and educational encounter with a population many people would prefer to ignore or forget. AVP charges no fee, simply requesting donations and requiring that persons seeking an AVP Facilitator's Certificate lead at least two trainings subsequent to completing the program.[13]

Advanced training for mediators wishing to expand their skills is available as well. One major specialty is family mediation. Parent–child mediation training, consisting of one extra day, has been available since 1986, and Sullivan County has recently been handling many such cases, which are intensive in terms of intake time, mediator time, and required funding (Shaw, 1984). A few community mediator take advanced training to become divorce mediators, a speciality requiring in-depth knowledge of family law and family economics. Staff members often join the Society of Professionals in Dispute Resolution (SPIDR).[14]

Our intense involvement in Ulster County Family Court is generating new kinds of collaborative efforts in response to the unique challenges it presents. Family Court mediators receive additional training on visitation,

---

[13]AVP, New York Yearly Meeting, Religious Society of Friends, 15 Rutherford Place, New York, NY 10003. Volunteers are always welcome.

[14]SPIDR, 815 15th St., NW, Suite 530, Washington, DC 20005.

custody, and child support issues as well as on some aspects of family law, such as the New York State Child Support Standards Act. With the Ulster County Task Force for the Prevention of Child Abuse, we have developed a parenting class for divorcing couples. Husbands and wives attend separately, and are educated about the financial and emotional effects of divorce on their children and themselves, with a strong emphasis on problem solving. The use of mediation within the Family Court building generates issues we must handle, such as the lack of neutrality implicit in the setting, the lack of private space, the time constraints imposed by busy court calendars, and disputants' state of mind. The handful of highly experienced mediators available in family court on weekday mornings are welcomed and often utilized.

The region has its collective disputes, and Ulster-Sullivan Mediation is being increasingly asked to facilitate multiparty dispute resolution between groups concerned with school budgets, community–organizational board issues, and environmental/land use issues of all kinds. Concern for community well-being is thus taken to yet another level, as expressed in the agency's Mission Statement. Other areas in which community mediation centers handle multiparty disputes include Rochester, Oneonta, Dutchess County, Chemung County, and Washington Heights in New York City. Other New York State counties offer various services and programs according to regional needs and the talents of their staff.

CONCLUSION

Historically, any third party intervention is seen by independent-minded American disputants as a threat, reducing the autonomy of the disputants in reaching their own solutions. The genius of the Neighborhood Justice Center movement lies in the introduction of the mediator, a third party with a specific social status, who intervenes in a positive fashion and takes away none of the disputants' power to decide for themselves. This is a much-needed new dimension in American justice. The frontier ethos no longer serves us. Vast open space is a thing of the past. We can no longer move as soon as we see our neighbor's chimney smoke, and a duel at high noon today is likely to maim some 10-year-old bystander. In contemporary society, neither fight nor flight is the best way to achieve results.

But the American love of confrontation has healthy roots: the belief that each person is entitled to a day in court, that citizenship and belonging confer to all the ability to encounter the different other as an equal.

For centuries, the monarchs of England clashed with feudal lords in a frustrating series of lose–lose interactions. The creation of the House of Commons, a third party, in the 14th century is considered the beginning of modern British history.

The transforming power of third party intervention, coupled with the American love of confrontation, is creating a new force that may become a worldwide hope. Most cultures consider face-to-face encounters over differences to be bad manners, preferring instead shuttle diplomacy. The structured encounter of the mediation session may be one of America's finest contributions to a world struggling to function as a single, global entity.

REFERENCES

Bell, G. (1992, Winter). Improving The Administration of Justice. NIDR *Forum*, 5–9.

Christian, T. F. (1987). *The community dispute resolution centers program annual report.* Albany, NY: Unified Court System.

Crohn, M. (1992, Winter). Statement before the U.S. House of Representatives Subcommittee on Intellectual Property and Judicial Administration. NIDR *Forum*, 2–6.

Danielsson, C. (1972). Redemptive encounter: Its use in psychodrama, ancestral sociodrama, and community building. *Group Psychotherapy and Psychodrama, 25* (4), 170–181.

Danielsson, C. (1978, November). Friends, neighbors, and disagreements. *Fellowship Magazine, 44* (11), 10–13.

Danielsson, C. (1992). *Ulster-Sullivan mediation: A five year overview.* Highland, NY: USMI.

Dewey, J. (1938). *Experience and education.* New York: Collier.

Moreno, J. L. (1972). *Psychodrama* (Vol. 2). Beacon, NY: Beacon House.

Shaw, M. (1984). Parent–child mediation: An alternative that works. *Arbitration Journal, 39* (2), 25–29.

Simmel, G. (1950). *The sociology of Georg Simmel* (K. Wolf, Trans.). New York: Free Press. (Original work published 1908)

Ulster-Sullivan Mediation. (1992, November). *School and Youth News, 2,* 1–8.

Zagoria, S. (1988). *The ombudsman: How good governments handle citizens' grievances.* Cabin John, MD: Seven Locks.

Author Index

223

Subject Index